BETSY ANN PLANK

BETSY ANN PLANK

The Making of a Public Relations Icon

KARLA K. GOWER

UNIVERSITY OF MISSOURI PRESS

Columbia

Library of Congress Cataloging-in-Publication Data

Names: Gower, Karla K., author.
Title: Betsy Ann Plank : the making of a public relations icon / Karla K.
    Gower.
Description: Columbia, Missouri : University of Missouri Press, [2022] |
    Includes bibliographical references and index.
Identifiers: LCCN 2021048477 (print) | LCCN 2021048478 (ebook) | ISBN
    9780826222596 (hardcover) | ISBN 9780826274731 (ebook)
Subjects: LCSH: Plank, Betsy Ann. | Businesswomen--Biography. | Leadership
    in women.
Classification: LCC HD6053 .G68 2022 (print) | LCC HD6053 (ebook) | DDC
    650.1092 [B]--dc23/eng/20220105
LC record available at https://lccn.loc.gov/2021048477
LC ebook record available at https://lccn.loc.gov/2021048478

™ This paper meets the requirements of the
American National Standard for Permanence of Paper
for Printed Library Materials, Z39.48, 1984.

Typefaces: Garamond and Aktiv Grotesque

To all the strong women I am blessed to have had,
and continue to have, in my life.

CONTENTS

ILLUSTRATIONS

PREFACE

IN THE SPRING of 2000, Betsy Ann Plank was invited to visit the College of Communication and Information Sciences at the University of Alabama as the Elmo I. Ellis Visiting Professional-In-Residence. Betsy was a 1944 alumna of the University but had not been back to her alma mater since her graduation. She was also well known as the "First Lady" of public relations, having numerous "firsts" to her credit. She was, in a word, famous, at least in public relations circles. And to this then-fledgling assistant professor, intimidating.

I knew Betsy had requested bios and resumes in advance from all the public relations faculty, and that was the problem. My background was law, not public relations. I was convinced she would not be happy with my hire. Regardless, I agreed to meet with her the afternoon of the day of her arrival. Once I got into my office that morning, I decided to check my mail. As I turned the corner to go down the long hallway to the mail office, I saw the College's development officer in the distance walking with a short, older lady. I knew immediately it was Betsy. My first reaction was to turn around and flee, hoping they hadn't seen me. But I steeled myself and continued. I was going to meet her eventually anyway. May as well get it over with, I thought. As I approached them, I put out my hand and said, "Betsy, I'm Karla Gower." She took my hand in both of hers and said, "Of course, you are, my dear." She immediately put me at ease and that was the essence of Betsy.

I refer to her here as "Betsy," although I use Plank in the book, because that's what everyone called her, executives and students alike. She had this innate ability to make you feel like you were the only one who mattered at the moment. Although the number of people who knew or met her are dwindling, her memory continues to live on in students. She resonates with them. Perhaps, it is because she is just "Betsy," which makes her approachable. Or because her words of wisdom remain relatable: Be an eternal student; say yes to every opportunity; and importantly for a woman even today, if you are going to marry, marry a saint.

I had the good fortune to work with Betsy in my position as director of the Plank Center for Leadership in Public Relations at The University of Alabama from 2007 until her death in 2010. She taught me a great deal about public relations but also about managing people and relationships. If you were lucky enough to be questioned by her about a topic she was interested in, she would designate you a co-conspirator. For example, in her last year, she was particularly concerned about the low numbers of male students who were going into public relations. She wanted to know what I thought. Why were they picking business over public relations? What could we (as co-conspirators) do to solve the problem? Betsy read broadly and thought deeply about her chosen profession, always seeking to make the practice better.

Betsy has much to teach us all about how to live our lives. She was passionate about her work and lived her life with love and laughter. She listened to people and treated everyone with respect and dignity, expressing empathy and giving hope to all. Betsy was not perfect by any means. None of us are. She and I had moments when we clashed. Fortunately, neither of us took those moments personally. She had strong opinions about things and high expectations that could lead to angry outbursts. But she respected people who stood their ground.

The Plank Center with its focus on leadership and mentorship is her tangible legacy to public relations. But Betsy's gift to us all goes beyond that. Her story, including her contributions to public relations, needs to be told. When she died in 2010, she left her estate, including her papers and personal artifacts, to the University for the Center. Those materials form the basis of this biography. Thankfully, Betsy's mother, Bettye, passed a love of history on to her daughter. Bettye saved letters, photos, and other documents that were passed down to Betsy, who in turn kept up the practice, keeping not just what her mother saved but adding her own papers, letters, and speeches to the collection. Woven together, the various pieces in the collection provide rich details of Betsy's life.

Newspaper and journal articles supplemented Betsy's files, as did materials in other archives. Yevgeniya Gribov, archivist for the Girl Scout National Historic Preservation Center in New York, graciously searched the archives for references to Betsy and sent me copies of what she found.

The librarians at the Chicago History Museum kindly gave me access to their Welfare Public Relations Forum collection. Not all the details from those documents made their way into this biography, but they enriched my understanding of her.

I, of course, have many people to thank for their support and help during the writing of this biography. My advertising and public relations "family" have been there for me for more than twenty years. They are why I've stayed at the University. I want to especially thank Dr. Bruce Berger, who was hired at Alabama the same year I was and who was the first director of the Plank Center. He has mentored and supported me throughout my career at Alabama and offered wise counsel when I needed it. He graciously read the manuscript for this book more than once. Jessika White, the first Communication Specialist hired by the Plank Center and a good friend, never knew Betsy but came to feel as though she did through her position with the Center. She too read an early version of this book and provided feedback. The members of the Plank Center Board have always supported and encouraged me, and for that I will always be grateful. Not all of them knew Betsy, but they all embody her spirit and passion for leadership and the profession.

I also want to thank Mary Conley, associate acquisitions editor, and Andrew Davidson, editor in chief of the University of Missouri Press, for believing in the project from the beginning. Mary, who was a joy to work with, read each version with the detailed eye of an editor, always giving constructive feedback, as did the two anonymous reviewers. Dr. Susan Curtis, professor emerita of history and American studies at Purdue University, deserves a special thank you for her insights and suggestions and her tremendous copyediting skills. It was a pleasure working with her. The final product is better by far for all their efforts.

Writing the history of a person's life is not an easy task, especially when that person still lives in the recent memory of many. Those who knew Betsy have their own opinion of what she was like, including her beliefs and values. This book may or may not line up with their memory of her, but I did my best to be true to what the documents reveal, knowing that we are all multifaceted beings. We show different sides of our personalities to different people at different times. Rarely are we our true selves, even when we are alone. Betsy was no different than the rest of us in that regard. But I confirmed details where I could and indicated when I couldn't.

At the end of the day, the analysis, interpretation, and conclusions drawn are mine alone, as are any errors or omissions. My only hope is that it lives up to Betsy's expectations for how the story of her life might be told. Thank you for that opportunity, Betsy, and Godspeed!

BETSY ANN PLANK

INTRODUCTION

The real power of a leader is in the number of minds he can reach, hearts he can touch, souls he can move, and lives he can change.

—Matshona Dhliwayo

IN THE BALLROOM of Detroit's Sheraton-Cadillac Hotel on a chilly November day in 1972, a petite redhead, standing barely five-feet tall, stepped confidently to the podium and into the spotlight. Betsy Ann Plank was about to address the attendees of the national conference of the Public Relations Society of America (PRSA) for the first time as their new chair elect. It was an occasion, she told those present, that allowed for "no hidden agendas. We have no time for that." Public relations was facing a crisis of identity. The activism of the sixties had convinced businesses that positive public relations had an impact on the bottom line, which meant practitioners were being increasingly called on to solve problems and anticipate trends. It was time, she said, "to rethink our role, our responsibilities, and our capabilities."[1] It was time to grow up.

After throwing down the gauntlet and challenging practitioners "to become professional in fact as well as in title," Plank concluded on a hopeful note. She was confident in her ability to lead the organization at this critical juncture. Referencing British philosopher Alfred North Whitehead's line that "the panic of errors is the death of progress," she assured the assembled that during her tenure "there will always be errors. But no panic. Above all, there will be progress."[2]

The speech was pure Plank. It was brutally honest about the state of the profession, but it pointed no fingers. They were all to blame. At the same time, it was forward thinking and motivational; it was inspiring and aspirational. It also made no mention of the fact that the forty-eight-year-old Plank had just become the first woman to hold the chair's position in

3

PRSA's twenty-five-year history.[3] The omission was by design. She believed gender had nothing to do with her ability to practice her craft well, so she chose not to draw attention to it, a strategy that contributed to her success in the field. In fact, being the first woman chair of PRSA was not her first time being a "first." Through the span of her sixty-three-year public relations career, she broke new ground on numerous occasions.

Ten years before she assumed the highest office in PRSA, Plank became the first woman president of the Publicity Club of Chicago. Five years later, she was elected president of the Chicago Chapter of PRSA, the first woman to hold that office. In fact, she was the only person to serve as president of four different Chicago communications organizations.[4]

Her career spanned both agency and corporate practice. At the time she assumed the PRSA presidency in 1973, she was the executive vice president and treasurer of the Daniel J. Edelman agency (now Edelman). That same year she joined AT&T and the Bell System. At Illinois Bell, she became the first woman to head a department, directing urban, community, and educational affairs, as well as dealing with issues management and economic development. After her retirement in 1990, she continued to counsel and serve public relations organizations, becoming the first woman for whom a center for public relations is named. She served as chair of the board of advisors of that center, The Plank Center for Leadership in Public Relations, housed at the University of Alabama, until her death in 2010.[5]

In addition to the formal leadership roles she held, Plank worked tirelessly and selflessly to promote and strengthen public relations education generally (it was one of the areas she mentioned as a focus in her inaugural address as chair elect of PRSA) and the Public Relations Student Society of America specifically. For her efforts, Plank received numerous accolades. She is the only person to have received PRSA's three highest honors: the Gold Anvil as outstanding U.S. professional, the Paul Lund Award for exemplary civic and community service, and the Patrick Jackson Award for distinguished service to PRSA. In 1979, she was the first woman elected by readers of the trade publication, *Public Relations News*, as its Professional of the Year, and, in 1984, the publication named her one of the World's 40 Outstanding Public Relations Leaders.

Despite Plank's success in public relations and her impact on PRSA and PRSSA, as well as other associations, she has not been the subject of any scholarly studies. Of course, she was not the only active and influential woman in public relations during the 1960s and 1970s. But it was Plank who rose to the highest level of the field's national association at a time when its leadership and membership were predominantly male. How was a diminutive woman from a small town in Alabama able to excel as a leader in that milieu? I explore that question and consider the factors that contributed to her success and shaped her identity as a public relations leader.

While "great person" histories can be problematic in that they put too much emphasis on individuals' ability to shape and impact their surroundings, ignoring the social conditions in which they operated, biographies can and do serve a significant purpose. Margaret Wilkerson's comments about the importance of biographies of African American women are equally applicable to public relations practitioners: "Excavating our history is crucial if we are to understand who we are . . . ." and where we came from.[6]

This work contributes to the historical literature on women in public relations by examining Plank's life and career within the larger context of public relations professionalization at a time of social change. Plank started her career in 1947 when public relations was seeing significant and rapid growth. She practiced through the social turmoil of the 1960s and 1970s and the changes those decades brought to her field and to women practitioners.

When Plank accepted her first job in public relations in the late 1940s, she became part of a select group. Of the 733 new active members of PRSA admitted between 1949 and 1952, fewer than thirty were women. That number increased over the years, but women were still the minority at just twenty-six percent when Plank took the helm of PRSA two decades later, making her exceptional for her time.[7] Yet, despite those successes, her story can still be instructive to new generations of women entering the profession. Today, women account for almost three-quarters of the field, but men continue to dominate at the highest levels of the practice. While Plank faced more outright gender discrimination than may exist now, how she negotiated the masculine business environment to become a leader offers lessons for young women entering public relations.

One defining feature in Plank's success is that she worked within the system rather than from outside it. Plank opted to work hard, do a good job, and earn her way in a man's world, rather than become a women's rights activist to force change. As she garnered the trust of male public relations practitioners and developed working relationships with them, they, in turn, put her into positions of leadership. Each time she became the first woman to head a professional association or a corporate department, it was because a man sponsored her candidacy for that position. It could be argued that she was simply the beneficiary of men who were enlightened enough to recognize that a woman could do the job, and that she was therefore aided by the feminists who were raising people's consciousness to gender discrimination at the time. In other words, she happened to be in the right place at the right historical time. There is some truth to that, but that also ignores the fact that she had been developing her leadership skills over many years and was ready for the roles she was put into, and that she assumed some of those roles before there was widespread awareness of gender discrimination.

As evidenced by descriptions of her, Plank possessed many of the traits of a leader.[8] She was known for adding "luster" to the profession through her personal qualities of understanding, compassion, integrity, good judgment, perceptiveness, and humor, among others. Additionally, she was described as having "a special charisma, supported by intelligence and hard work." That special charisma included the uncanny ability to cajole people into doing what she wanted done but could not do on her own. As Ron Culp, one of the founding board members and former chair of The Plank Center, noted, "She knew her personal capabilities and how to engage others to help her achieve her goals."[9]

Plank described her approach to leadership as rolling up her sleeves, figuring out the right thing to do, and going to work. How exactly did one arrive at "the right thing"? Dr. Bruce Berger, the first director of The Plank Center, recollected that her answer to that question was always ethics. "Leaders need ethics and a strong will and a strong sense of 'right,' which they get to when they hear from all sides, when everyone shares their insights," he remembered her saying. Once a decision was made, it must be attacked "with all we have."[10]

For Plank, leadership in public relations was especially crucial because of the nature of the profession, a profession that communicates on behalf of organizations and groups of people. As Bruce Berger recalled it, she said, "Communication affects our understanding, our emotions, our beliefs. . . . Public relations leaders help organizations do the right things and communicate honestly and ethically. Then show it with behaviors."[11]

Plank's leadership traits, such as her tenacity, competitiveness, and empathy, along with her collaborative and networking skills, were honed from the time she was a child. Encouraged to do what she wanted to and pushed to be the best at it by the adults in her life, Plank began the process of becoming a leader early on, setting the stage for the development of dimensions of leadership that are particularly important for excellence in public relations: vision and self-reflection, team collaboration, ethical orientation, relationship building, strategic decision-making capability, and communication knowledge management. Keith Burton, former Plank Center chair and emeritus board member, perhaps summed her up best when asked why she was a strong leader: "She was bigger on the inside than on the outside. That's what real character and integrity are—being bigger on the inside. She had heart and a boldness that other people will never know."[12]

In terms of leadership style, I argue that Plank was a servant leader. As the name suggests, servant leadership involves leading and serving. It was Plank's need to serve, stemming from her Presbyterian faith, that motivated her to lead. The "serving" component in this leadership model is accomplished "through listening, healing, stewardship, fostering personal growth, and building community." "Leading" as a servant leader is not about domination but rather "role modeling, conscious initiative, and creating an environment of opportunity for followers to grow and thrive." Although similar to other leadership models, the focus of servant leadership is what distinguishes it from the others. Servant leaders believe in "the intrinsic value of each individual." Thus, instead of inspiring followers to higher performance for the sake of the organization, as is the case with transformational leadership for example, servant leaders are concerned with "what is best for the follower and trust followers will do what is necessary for the organization." It is this emphasis on the individual for the individual's sake that can be seen in Plank's leadership. She took seriously a quote on a pen set that sat on her desk: "Treat people as if they were what they ought to be, and you help them to become what they are capable of being."[13]

On the other side of that pen set was another quote: "There is no limit to what can be accomplished if it doesn't matter who gets the credit." She said it was a daily reminder to her to be humble, a characteristic of servant leaders, along with authenticity and empathy. Another characteristic of a servant leader is the ability to provide direction such that others know what is expected of them. Culp described Plank as being "gracious but firm in requests to her team; they knew exactly what was expected. No gray areas so she gained early alignment on most projects." Importantly, in terms of

Plank, servant leaders serve "multiple stakeholders including their communities and society as a whole." Plank believed public relations practitioners were especially driven to solve community problems, always answering the call for help. Plank's own commitment to public service was legendary in Chicago.[14]

It should be noted that being a servant leader does not imply weakness or servility despite the word "servant." Certainly, Plank held her own in any setting. Instead, servant leadership, like the philosopher Kant's perspective, "emphasizes the responsibility of the leader to increase the autonomy and responsibility of followers, to encourage them to think for themselves." Ultimately, the goal of servanthood is "to help others become servants themselves so that society benefit[s] as well."[15]

Plank's servant leadership style was a product of her upbringing and a factor in her success. The style also fit with her understanding of public relations and its role in society. That understanding can be seen in how she conceptualized the field:

I. PUBLIC RELATIONS IS ROOTED IN DEMOCRACY

Plank believed that public relations is "rooted in a democratic society where people have freedom to debate and to make decisions—in the community, the marketplace, the home, the workplace and the voting booth." Public relations provides organizations with a voice with which to participate in the public discourse. She saw the role of public relations in organizations, then, as building and maintaining "good relations with groups and individuals whose opinions, decisions and actions affect the vitality and survival of those organizations."[16]

At the heart of a democracy is the belief that individuals are rational beings who are capable of self-governance; that is, they can settle their political disputes through dialogue and compromise. For Plank, public relations was essential to ensure that individuals debated with access to all of the many points of view on a subject. The duty of a public relations practitioner was to treat everyone with dignity and respect by being open and honest, a Kantian approach closely tied to her faith and to servant leadership.

2. RELIGIOUS FAITH AND PUBLIC RELATIONS ARE CONNECTED

Plank was raised Presbyterian and many of the church's tenets can be found in her attitudes and actions. For Presbyterians, everything happens according to God's plan, including who gets into heaven and who does not. Work is a calling from God, regardless of the type or nature of the work, and thus infused with spiritual consequences, "a powerful motivator to perform [it] with excellence."[17] While the emphasis on one's work is distinctly individual, it was believed that God worked through the community. The acceptance of God meant an increase in the love for one's neighbors.

Plank's family and church instilled in her from a young age the importance of "hard work, duty, thrift, self-discipline, and responsibility." Her strong work ethic and desire to excel were important factors in her ability to lead others as was her belief that she had a duty to be involved in the community because "every person owes his or her best in time and talents to the human community and paying that debt adds unique value to one's life." She saw public relations as more than simply a job. It was her calling. She had been called to protect, nurture, and strengthen the profession of public relations.[18]

3. PUBLIC RELATIONS IS A PROFESSION

The theme of the professionalization of public relations emerges in the second half of Plank's life. She believed that public relations was a proud and noble profession along the lines of law and medicine. But she knew it was not seen that way by those outside the field. She saw her role as the defender and promoter of its image. Because professions operate in the public interest and require a specialized education, she worked to strengthen public relations education and to have it recognized as a crucial preparer of the next generation of practitioners.

4. PUBLIC RELATIONS IS GENDER NEUTRAL

In Plank's ideal world, public relations would be gender neutral; it would be neither a man's nor a woman's profession. She became an adult in the post-World War II era of the "feminine mystique" and was an established practitioner during the second wave of feminism. She faced discrimination because of her gender, but she was still successful in a man's world. She would not have described herself as a feminist; instead, she thought of herself as one of the "good ole boys," and she carefully managed that image. She belonged to very few women-only organizations, opting instead for professional associations, and rarely gave speeches on the topic of women in public relations. As her consciousness was raised in the late 1960s and early

1970s, however, she came to recognize the subtle and sometimes overt sexism she faced, but she never really resolved the tension between her success as a woman and the extent to which she benefited from feminism.

To gain insight into Plank as a public relations and servant leader and trace how she developed into that role, it is necessary to explore the entirety of her life. Therefore, the book begins with a look at Plank's Southern roots because, although she spent her adult life in Chicago, she was a product of the deep South. That heritage impacted the woman Plank became, as did the fact that she was an only child. The first chapter also captures Plank's growing maturity as a college student at Bethany College in West Virginia. As is the case with many students when they enter college, it was Plank's first time living away from home. She grew from the varied academic and social experiences. She also faced heartache for the first time and a loss of innocence, an episode that revealed her inner strength and left her with great empathy for others dealing with trying circumstances.

Rallying from difficult times, Plank fell in love and married. Although the marriage itself was ill-fated, the relationship led her to Chicago and ultimately to public relations. Thus, the second chapter examines her initiation into the field in the 1950s. The third chapter marks her emergence as a public relations leader. Working for Edelman, Plank came into her own, becoming president of the Publicity Club of Chicago, the president of the Chicago chapter of PRSA, and eventually the national PRSA chair.

Chapter four focuses on her PRSA chairmanship and its trials and tribulations. As she was completing her term as chair, she was recruited to AT&T in New York. But after just a few months, she returned to Chicago and joined Illinois Bell. Chapter five examines this period of her life until her retirement from active practice in 1990.

The final chapter begins after the death of her second husband, who was the love of her life, and the impact of that loss. To sustain herself, Plank turned her energy to public relations education and professionalism. That focus led her back home to the South and to the establishment of The Plank Center for Leadership in Public Relations, her tangible legacy. The chapter ends with her death in May 2010.

The story of Plank's life is not just a public relations story; it is also a woman's story. Certainly, Plank practiced public relations through a period of growth and change in the profession and helped usher in an era of greater focus on education and professionalism. But it was also a time that saw great societal change for women, change on which Plank was reluctant to comment. Plank made mistakes in her personal life but ultimately found her passion professionally and personally. It is a story of how a petite Southern woman became a leader in public relations.

CHAPTER 1

An Uncommon Heritage

The uncommon heritage of the University and the family whose panache and style it shaped and nurtured walks with me every day.

—Betsy Ann Plank

BETSY ANN PLANK was born on April 3, 1924, in the shadow of The University of Alabama. She would be the only child born to Richard (Dick) and Bettye Hood Plank.[1] She would also be the only grandchild on either side of the family, solidifying her position as the center of everyone's attention. Her family instilled in her a belief in the importance of education and the Protestant work ethic. She also benefited from a heritage of strong Southern women who were crucial to her development.

THE FAMILIES

Looking back on her childhood in Tuscaloosa and her connection with The University of Alabama, Plank described it as "an uncommon heritage." UA's presence was threaded throughout her young life. There was its physical proximity, of course—she lived most of her first six years just blocks from the campus—but there was more. Both her parents attended UA, as had her mother's older sister, Adelyne, and her father's younger brother, Stacey, although none of them graduated. In 1927, Stacey was killed in a car accident returning to Tuscaloosa after attending a UA football game at Georgia State.[2] The others left school early for various reasons.

Prominent individuals from the university and town were regular visitors in Plank's maternal grandmother's home. Some of the notables included Hudson Strode, a UA creative writing professor and prolific author; "Uncle" Tom Garner, Tuscaloosa's most successful choral director, choir leader, and music critic; Dr. Richard "Dick" Foster, who would later become university president; and Agnes Ellen Harris, dean of the school of home economics.[3]

But the "uncommon heritage" of which Plank spoke involved more than her family's connection to the university. Plank's family itself was uncommon for the time.

Her grandmother, Annie Hood, a classical pianist, insisted that all her children learn how to play a musical instrument because she believed being able to play music was akin to mastering the social graces. Her children, on the other hand, thought it was only so she would have someone to accompany her in concerts, and there may have been some truth to that. Regardless, she did instill a love of music in at least her two oldest children, Adelyne and Billy. Billy, whom Plank described years later as "impetuous," moved to Chicago, joined a jazz band, and became a professional musician. But it was Adelyne, who bore the burden of Annie's own musical dreams and desires, and whose musical talents along with her charisma led to the family's greatest success.[4]

Adelyne was a talented musician, but more importantly, she was a performer, a trait Betsy inherited. In 1919, at the age of twenty-two, Adelyne accepted an offer from the Edison Phonograph Company to accompany a singer by the name of Vernon Dalhart on tour. Dalhart was already an established recording artist at thirty-five and married with two children at the time. Together Dalhart and Adelyne recorded several duets and performed around the country to packed venues. When her contract ended, she formed the Pantheon Singers. The group of three women, including Adelyne, and two men toured the Midwest and Canada in the early 1920s. Later, she would once again join Dalhart.

Adelyne was at her best when she took on the characters in her songs, such as Calamity Jane. "I'm Calamity Jane," she would boast in song, "I've blazed the trail and rode the plain, I'm fast on the draw, don't care for the law, I'm the famous Calamity Jane!" In the 1930s, strong resourceful female characters who matched wits with men and beat them at their own game dominated Adelyne's recordings. Her looks and size belied the strength and range of her voice. Even as an adult, she had trouble reaching the piano pedals, and her small hands had to stretch for the keys.

Adelyne may have inherited Annie's musical talent, but it was Plank's mother, Bettye, who was most like Annie, at least according to Plank. Bettye had Annie's "stature and steel, common sense and honest-to-God auburn hair," a description that would apply equally to the adult Plank. Standing just four feet ten and never weighing more than ninety-five pounds, Bettye was a force to be reckoned with. Outgoing and lively, Bettye was seventeen—"looking twelve and going on thirty"—when she met Dick Plank.[5]

Dick was originally from Birmingham about fifty miles northeast of Tuscaloosa. His parents, Charles and Mary, had moved to the city from Georgia in 1911 for Charles's work with the Tennessee Coal, Iron and Railroad Company. Charles was active in the community as a member of both the Elks and Masons. He was also a musician, playing saxophone and directing the Shriners' Zamora Temple band. Mary was a bookkeeper and an aspiring artist. The couple worked hard and saved their money to ensure their children, Dick and Stacey, could attend The University of Alabama. Plank later wrote that the brothers were blond and attractive, with the charismatic Stacey being "our very own F. Scott Fitzgerald."[6]

Dick majored in civil engineering at UA. But it was not always easy. He hustled to make ends meet, waiting tables at Alpha Tau Omega, the fraternity to which he belonged, and working weekends as a soda fountain jerk in downtown Tuscaloosa.[7] Although Dick was certainly marriage material with his strong work ethic and "straight arrow" character when they met, Bettye was not quite ready to settle down. Not long after their courtship began, Bettye, whom Dick called "Little Girl," left him and Tuscaloosa for a big-city experience in Chicago, where her sister Adelyne was performing with the Pantheon Singers.[8] Dick begged her to come home, and after several months, she finally did. The two were married on December 10, 1922.[9]

The *Tuscaloosa News* described the bride as "one of the loveliest girls who was ever reared in this city." Taking after her mother, Bettye was involved "cheerfully and willingly in every cause" in the community, "deeming it a privilege to lend a helping hand." For his part, Dick was described as "esteemed and admired by a wide circle of friends."[10] Immediately following the ceremony, the newlyweds left for Birmingham where Dick was now working for Alabama Power. The couple planned to live for the time being with his parents.

PLANK'S EARLY CHILDHOOD

But two years later, a pregnant Bettye moved back to Tuscaloosa to be with her mother, Annie. She continued to live in the Hoods' two-story, red-brick house on 8th St. after Betsy's birth in April. Plank spent much of her first six years in that house with Bettye, her Uncle "Ish," and Mama, as she called her grandmother.[11] No mention is made of Dick living with them although doing so would not have been feasible at the time. Birmingham and his job were at least an hour away by train, and the couple could not afford their own car. Taking the train daily between the two cities would have been time-consuming and expensive for a young couple on a budget. More likely, he continued living with his parents in Birmingham during the week and traveled to Tuscaloosa to see his wife and daughter on weekends.

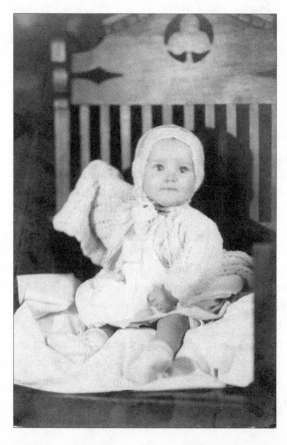

Fig. 1: Betsy Ann Plank at six months old, 1924, taken at her Grandmother Annie's house in Tuscaloosa, Alabama. All photographs courtesy of the Betsy Ann Plank Papers, the Plank Center for Leadership in Public Relations at The University of Alabama

Dick's stay in Birmingham ended up being a short one. The Depression came early to the South, and Dick was forced to go where he could find a job to support his family. By the time of the couple's fifth wedding anniversary, he was working in Augusta, Georgia, and living in a hotel. With Dick working so far away and unable to make trips home often, it was a trying time for them. Whether it was living at home with her mother, the separation from her husband, or simply wanderlust, Bettye was not content sitting still. In May 1929, when Betsy was five, Bettye set sail for England with two other Tuscaloosa women to study sign language.[12] Betsy appeared to deal well with her mother's four-month absence, crying only occasionally. Annie and Plank's nineteen-year-old uncle Ish, whom she adored, helped ease her pain.[13]

The following year, Bettye headed back to New York City for an extended visit with Adelyne, and Plank was once again left behind in Tuscaloosa. When her mother departed, the six-year-old Betsy lay on her bed and cried. As Annie described it in a letter to Bettye, Annie lay down beside

Fig. 2: Betsy at four years old, 1928, taken at her Grandmother Annie's house in Tuscaloosa, Alabama. Courtesy of the Plank Papers

Fig. 3: Annie Hood surrounded by three of her four children. Adelyne is standing on the left, Betsy's mother, Bettye, is sitting on the arm of the chair, and Betsy's Uncle "Ish" is standing behind Bettye. Ca. 1934. Courtesy of the Plank Papers

her granddaughter while the two talked. Plank soon forgot she had said goodbye to her mother and shifted her focus to something she could control. "Well, Mama, let's go downstairs and dress me and I'll help you clean up the house." Plank chatted with Adele and Sam Beale, Annie's African American servants, as she worked. Annie overheard her say: "Sam, did you know my mother went to NY [sic] this morning and I cried when she told me good-bye. Sam said: What you do dat for? Betsy said: Well, I don't know what made me do it. Wasn't that a foolish thing to do?"[14]

Shortly after, life for the Planks grew more traditional, and for the first time since Betsy's birth, the three lived together on a full-time basis. Dick was now working in Roswell, Georgia, a small city in the northwest corner of the state. Betsy attended her first elementary school there, but it would not be her last. She went to eight schools in all before entering high school: two in Alabama and one each in Georgia, Kentucky, Louisiana, Mississippi, Pennsylvania, and Virginia.[15]

Although the *Tuscaloosa News* described a seven-year-old Betsy as "the personification of all that is winsome and fascinating" and a "universal

Fig. 4: Betsy sits on her father's lap, while Bettye looks on. Ca. 1934. Courtesy of the Plank Papers

favorite in the juvenile set because of her personal charm and ready wit," Plank was lonely as a child. It is a sentiment shared by many only children, but the family's constant moving made the loneliness worse. She was never in one place long enough to develop those close childhood friendships that last a lifetime. On the other hand, being thrust into so many new schools taught her how to be flexible and adapt to new environments. She was "always the 'new kid on the block,'" which meant she learned early about coping on her own. She gained the skill to read people and size them up quickly to fit in. Plank credited this early training in relationship building to her later ability to handle meetings in which she was the only woman.[16] While the chaos of constantly relocating was undoubtedly emotionally and socially taxing on young Betsy, her adaptability in new surroundings showed hints of the leader she would become.

Of all the towns, Winchester, Kentucky, nestled in the mountains and eighteen miles from Lexington, came to feel the most like home for her. Dick had found a position in the aerial photographic department of the U.S. Forest Service, making maps, charts, and blueprints from aerial photos of the forests near Winchester. The family stayed in the town with a population of 8,200 long enough to move into an apartment with a bedroom for Betsy. The prospect of having her own room was an exciting one for the nine-year-old. "MY OWN ROOM," she wrote in a 1933 diary entry about the move. The other entries are typical of a pre-teenage girl, describing boy crushes and girlfriend squabbles. The writing style suggests, however, a maturity beyond her years. Only children, because of their early adult interaction, tend to be more mature than their peers in intelligence, achievement, motivation, and self-esteem while in elementary school. That certainly held true for Plank at this stage in her life.[17]

She was, no doubt, as active in Winchester as she appears to have been in Wellsboro, Pennsylvania, where the family moved next. The local newspaper described the ten-year-old Betsy as "a talented actress and pianist" who "is charming in appearance." She appeared in several vaudeville programs and recitals, and her name was even used to promote future events. In encouraging people to attend an upcoming benefit for the Parent-Teachers Association, the *Wellsboro Gazette* noted that "Betsy Ann Plank, that little star who made such a hit in the Christmas pageant," would be singing several numbers.[18]

Two years later, the family finally settled in Mt. Lebanon, Pennsylvania, after Dick took a position as a civil engineer with the Peoples Natural Gas Company in Pittsburgh. Plank entered Mt. Lebanon High at the age of twelve, having skipped two grades, and quickly became active in the school and the community. Her senior yearbook indicates she was chair of the Ways and Means Committee, and a member of the Banquet Committee, a National Honor Society, and the merit parade. Betsy had always loved to write, spending kindergarten recesses "crayon-writing 'books' on folded leaves of paper raided from the Girls' Room." So, it is no surprise that she wrote a column for the school newspaper and became editor-in-chief of the yearbook when the opportunity presented itself. The Mt. Lebanon newspaper described her as "a little package of energy and personality" who had been selected as "'most likely to succeed' among her classmates."[19] Her yearbook photo shows a pleasant-looking teenager with a shy smile and chin-length hair worn straight with tight curls at the ends in the style of the day.

HIGH SCHOOL DAYS

It was in high school that Plank first came across an adult who did not immediately adore her. Intelligent and a good communicator, Plank had been liked and treated as special by every grown-up she had met, probably because she pandered to them. But in her 1937 diary, she wrote about her science teacher, a man she described as a "mechanical robot" who "never looks at you other than to ask you or answer a question." Because of his aloofness, she found him intriguing and sought to make him like her. "I'll find out his type and he'll like me. Oh yes, he will when I get through with him," she wrote. After careful observation, she decided that the "robot" probably actually possessed a "dynamic" personality. She concluded that, "He's kind and thoughtful. He acts humorless, insinuating, insulting, inhuman and mocking *only* to cover an inferior complex."[20]

The teacher's indifference to her charms bothered Plank to the extent that she even dreamed about him. Confident that she could win him over if she were to meet with him individually, she approached him after class and asked if he could go over an assignment with her. She was surprised when he said yes and thought she had made progress. But then, she later wrote in her diary, "he reprimanded me for talking in class when he was. Fool!" She may not have liked him for that, but their interaction taught her an important lesson. Sometimes charisma exists "only in the eyes of the beholder." Not everyone was going to find her captivating and willing to do her bidding. Regardless of how the teacher really felt about Plank or what kind of personality he had, she earned an "A," not only in his class, but in all five of her subjects that year.[21] Her determination to be successful and earn high grades continued through her senior year.

It was not simply a matter of doing her best; Betsy wanted to be the best, and she was competitive about her grades. She complained in her diary when a girl beat her by one point in Latin, and when she figured another girl would get the lead in the school play, which would put her ahead of Plank in national honor and activity points. Betsy wrote, "God, for the first time in my life I voice a plea to please, God, don't let her win." Other times, she exhibited a maturity beyond her fifteen years. Regarding the school play that year, she noted that the selection of "Our Town" would be "an excellent draw for the community, but doubtful for Junior audience."[22]

EARLY INFLUENCES

In addition to school activities, she also had an interest in national and international politics. She noted the 1940 passing of William Edgar Borah, a prominent Republican U.S. senator from Idaho. About his death, she wrote, "I am very sorry and yet I cannot but feel he is another supporter of the 'old guard' . . . . 'individualism for sake of itself' has gone, perhaps for the best." She also wrote that while she found the news that Lord Sinha of Raipur, a Hindu peer, would soon sit in the British House of Lords exciting, she did not know enough about the matter to have an opinion on it.[23] She was clearly intrigued by current events and exhibited an intellectual curiosity about the world. Her family fostered that interest. Politics were discussed nightly over the dinner table, and Betsy was encouraged to contribute to the conversation. Her family made it clear they valued her opinions.

Years later, looking back on her childhood, Plank recalled being spoiled by her family but at the same time being held to high standards, all born out in her diary entries. In one, she stated she hoped she would get an "A" in arithmetic because otherwise she would "get heck." Her favorite toys were dolls, puzzles, and electric trains, the latter being a Christmas gift from her father when she was five because that was what she wanted even though it was considered a "boy's" toy at the time.[24] Plank described both sides of her family as remarkable and loving. They provided her with a sense of trust and security. "No one in my family ever told me there was anything I couldn't achieve," she wrote. At age ten, she announced she wanted to be the first American "presidrix," an adaptation of aviatrix, the term used to describe Amelia Earhart. According to Plank, no one laughed at her ambition or her use of "presidrix."[25]

In addition to Earhart, those who made the teenage Plank's short list of role models were inspiring women who had achieved high levels of success in their respective fields: journalist Dorothy Thompson, U.S. Secretary of Labor Frances Perkins, and tennis star Helen Wills Moody.[26] A few other prominent and newsworthy women in the 1930s could have served equally well as role models, most notably Eleanor Roosevelt. But the women she identified had qualities that spoke to her. Thompson was a journalist, who wrote a monthly column for *Ladies Home Journal* from 1937 to 1961, and a radio commentator. *Time* magazine in 1939 called her the second most influential woman next to Eleanor Roosevelt. Some even refer to Thompson as "The First Lady of American Journalism." Plank loved to write and naturally would have looked up to Thompson and what she was able to accomplish through her journalism. Coincidentally, Plank is sometimes referred to as "The First Lady of Public Relations."[27]

Perkins broke through barriers to become the first woman appointed to a Cabinet position, serving as Secretary of Labor from 1933 to 1945, which coincided with the period during which Betsy developed an interest in policy making and world affairs. Very different from Perkins and Thompson was Moody. She was "the first American-born woman to achieve international celebrity as an athlete." She won thirty-one Grand Slam tennis titles, including nineteen singles titles.[28] Plank had no aspirations to become a professional athlete, although she did take up tennis in her teens, but she possessed a competitive fire and the same grit and determination Moody demonstrated on the court. As for Earhart, she captured the imagination of many a young girl even before her ill-fated last trip. When Earhart's plane disappeared in 1937, like other girls, the thirteen-year-old Betsy would have been deeply affected by it.

Such high-profile women were rare and therefore extremely important exemplars for young girls of that time, but Plank's most influential role model was her Aunt Adelyne. Betsy and Adelyne had a special bond although, given Adelyne's recording and performing schedule, it is doubtful they spent much time together when she was young. For her part, Adelyne must have seemed larger than life to the young Plank who loved to play dress up in her aunt's cast-off stage gowns, which she later described as "grace-notes to the central message: it was 'all right' for a 'niceSoutherngirl' (sic) . . . to be educated for a genuine career."[29] Adelyne not only had a career; she was a single woman, traveling the country unchaperoned with a married man, performing in packed music halls, and singing songs about resourceful, barrier-breaking women. She sent a powerful message indeed.

Although Plank's mother, Bettye, never worked outside the home, her youthful wanderlust was also nontraditional for a woman in the 1920s and 1930s. Plank recalled Bettye giving her life advice such as, "Don't bother being in the kitchen; anybody can be in the kitchen. Go practice the piano."[30] Of course, both Adelyne and Bettye had inherited their mother's fire and zest for life. Annie was a housewife as well but came from a wealthy Southern family who believed in the importance of education for women and had the money to provide it for their daughters. Born in 1872, Annie had role models from among the upper-class women of the New South, women who had weathered the Civil War and Reconstruction comparatively unscathed relative to lower-class women and women of color and had emerged all the stronger for it. Annie allowed Adelyne to leave home on her own at an early age to pursue a musical career at a time when performing on stage was considered rather unsavory, and never voiced an objection to

Fig. 5: A publicity still of Plank's Aunt Adelyne, taken by a professional photographer (unknown) in the 1920s. At the time, Adelyne was performing with the Pantheon Singers, which toured parts of the United States and Canada from 1921 to 1926. Ca. 1921. Courtesy of the Plank Papers

Bettye's decision to leave her husband and young daughter to tour Europe for four months, two bold positions for a woman of the 1920s.

Plank's heritage was indeed uncommon. She came from a "long line of steely Southern women," and she had inherited their strength and competitive fire.[31] Although her childhood had been a lonely one, being an only child meant she was doted on by the adults in her life. They built her confidence by encouraging her to express herself and treating her opinions with respect. At the same time, being an only child came with high expectations. She was encouraged and rewarded to be the best at whatever she pursued. The support and encouragement she received early on became essential once she started school.

With each move and new school, she was forced to find ways to fit in and adapt to new circumstances, developing personal skills and learning how to interact with other children. Joining the Girl Scouts and Girl Reserves, as well as being involved in school activities, helped speed up her ability to make friends. Her teachers and parents, recognizing her potential, encouraged her to develop leadership abilities. The process continued in high school where Plank was active in clubs and student government, serving as editor-in-chief of the yearbook and chair of the Ways and Means Committee. By the time Plank graduated from high school in the spring of 1940, a competitive fire within her had been lit. She knew a college degree and then work would be in her future.[32]

LEAVING HOME

Plank was just sixteen when she enrolled at Bethany College, a liberal arts institution thirty-nine miles from her home in Mt. Lebanon and nestled in the foothills of the Allegheny Mountains. The first private college in West Virginia, Bethany had been founded in 1840 by Alexander Campbell, one of the principals of the Christian Church (Disciples of Christ), which grew in western Pennsylvania and Kentucky as a nineteenth-century protest movement against denominational exclusiveness.[33]

Campbell's mission for the school was "the instruction of youth in the various branches of science and literature, the useful arts and the learned and foreign languages." He believed in the importance of a close interaction between faculty and students in the educational process, something the faculty continues to endorse. The College valued high moral standards as well as intellectual rigor, diversity of thought, personal growth, and responsible engagement with public issues, all of which the young Plank found compelling. The campus, with its ivy-covered buildings, also fit with her mental image of what an institution of higher learning should look like.[34]

By 1940, the pain of the Great Depression was beginning to ease. Increased wages and spending fueled a feel-good attitude. Hollywood translated the mood into movies such as "Gone with the Wind" and "The Great Dictator." Jazz from Benny Goodman and Count Basie, among others, filled the airwaves. At the same time, war clouds loomed on the horizon. Germany invaded France that May and, along with Italy, controlled most of Western Europe with the exception of England. Some in the United States called for President Roosevelt to send troops to the aid of Great Britain, which Germany was bombing on an ongoing basis. By September, the United States instituted its first peacetime draft, requiring men between the ages of twenty-one and thirty-six to register for a lottery. If selected, the men would have to serve a twelve-month term in the military, although as tensions rose in Europe the length of the term increased.[35]

When Plank arrived at Bethany College that fall, she was one of just 410 students on campus. The majority came from Ohio, Pennsylvania, or West Virginia although a growing number were from New York and New Jersey. Having a college education was still a rather elite prospect. Only five percent of the population held a bachelor's degree; the percentage of women holding degrees was even smaller, although that was changing. Nationally women made up forty percent of college students in 1940. Still, the career path for most women was not a choice but an expectation: marriage and then children. According to the 1940 census, almost twelve percent of women between the ages of fifteen and nineteen were married with that percentage shooting up to sixty-eight percent for twenty- to thirty-four-year-old women.[36] Plank took it on faith that she too would marry and have children. But the girl who once declared she wanted to be "Presidrix" was also serious about a career, and Bethany College was the first milestone on that path.

As with many college freshmen, Plank's adjustment to her new surroundings was not an easy one. She had moved around as a child and knew well how it felt to walk into a new school not knowing anyone, but this was different. She was, for the first time, away from home, and she missed the security of her family's constant presence. That first fall, she was very

Fig. 6: Plank in her late teens studying in her dorm room at Bethany College. Ca. 1940–1943. Courtesy of the Plank Papers

homesick. Her parents offered to visit her on weekends, but she said no. While she would have loved to see them, she feared watching them leave would make it all the harder.[37]

To cope with her loneliness, Plank busied herself. In her first semester, she was granted a special privilege to take eighteen hours of coursework instead of the usual fifteen. She enrolled in American history, government, biology, Spanish, and a sophomore English literature course, which she tested into. The sixth class was on the Old Testament, taken at her counselor's urging, but one she soon dropped because it was at eight o'clock in the morning and that was too early for a night owl like Plank. All students attended Bethany Chapel services on Tuesdays and Thursdays at 10 a.m. The fifty-minute services alternated between a devotional one day and a lecture, musical presentation, or drama the next.[38] Living in a dormitory helped with the loneliness. With her roommates, she tried out for choir and investigated sororities.

Betsy found kinship in the Zeta Tau Alpha sorority. The sorority's purpose was "to intensify friendship, promote happiness among its members, and in every way to create such sentiments; to perform such deeds, and to mould [sic] such opinions as will conduce to the building up of a nobler and purer womanhood in the world."[39] In 1935, the Zetas ranked fourth in terms of grade point average among the nine sororities and fraternities on campus, suggesting the girls were not all serious and enjoyed their time in college. The Beta Theta Pi fraternity with whom the Zetas tended to socialize fared even worse in terms of grade point average, ranking last.[40] It was through her interactions with the Betas that Plank grew close to Ray Rappaport, or "Rap" as she called him.

RAY "RAP" RAPPAPORT

Like most of their freshman class of 177, Rap was eighteen, two years older than Betsy who had skipped two years of high school. Despite being younger, Betsy was more mature than many of her peers, especially in self-esteem. At the same time, she lagged behind in other areas.[41] She had, for example, little to no experience with members of the opposite sex. Although she had had high school crushes, she had not dated prior to college. One of the things she found attractive about Rap was that he seemed genuine and more mature than his fraternity brothers. He was intellectual, sensitive, and aspired to be a doctor.

Betsy and Rap met in class their first semester, both freshmen and new to the school, but their first official date was not until the end-of-year dance in May 1941. Anticipating the night, she asked her mother for a formal dress. She wanted "No stripes, no ruffles, no sailor collars, but pique might be cute." She instructed her mother to "Make it smooth, not too sophisticated. He's not the type."[42] And he was not. Rap enjoyed the outdoors; much of their time together was spent hiking in the woods around Bethany, discussing the weighty issues of the day and collecting specimens for his science classes. He reminded Plank of her father. Both men were reserved and felt deeply, characteristics that balanced the impulsiveness Plank shared with her mother. Having to separate at the end of the spring semester seemed a cruel fate for the budding romance, but Betsy and Rap wrote to each other over the summer as they had promised, he from North Bergen, New Jersey, she from Mt. Lebanon.

Rap's letters that first summer were full of his adventures working in a factory that made tin cans, a job that first required a medical examination. Rap wrote, "The doc stared in my eyes, brushed his hand over my pulse, pointed a stethoscope at me and then spent five minutes telling me that for my size I had one of the thickest necks he had ever seen. Wasn't he a flatterer?"[43] Plank analyzed every word of his letters, often reading too much into them, a problem that plagued their relationship for its duration. Rap was her first boyfriend, and she was never quite sure she trusted his feelings or hers.

FINDING A DIRECTION

Nonetheless, the romance survived the summer and continued when they got back to school that fall. By then, they were no longer wide-eyed freshmen, but sophomores who knew the routine and had settled into campus life. Rap was pre-med and worked as an assistant in the biology lab. For her part, Betsy was still undecided on what direction to take with her life. She announced to her parents at one point that she was going to major in biology. A professor had convinced her she should because she was one of the top students in his class.[44] That foray was short lived. She might have opted for public relations had she known about it, but Bethany did not offer any courses in it at the time. In the early 1940s, few universities did. The first U.S. university public relations course, "Publicity Techniques," was taught at the University of Illinois in 1920. Edward Bernays, the self-proclaimed father of public relations, taught the first U.S. course actually called "Public Relations" three years later at New York University. But other universities would not follow suit until 1945 and the end of World War II.[45]

Despite her indecision regarding a major, Plank always seemed to gravitate toward history, English, and political science. Dr. Florence Hoagland, the head of the English department, thought Plank "had plenty of brains but no common sense." Her seeming inability to focus on the future and her diffidence toward it contributed to Hoagland's assessment, no doubt. But it was also true that Betsy was never one to turn down an opportunity for adventure. And while she was competitive about grades, she did not have the sense of urgency or the weight of expectations on her that Hoagland would have had attending college a generation earlier.[46]

Plank was a hard worker, but she also enjoyed herself. She did not have to justify her presence in college to anyone. She had the benefit of not being the first person in her family to attend college. For that matter, she was not even the first woman in her family to do so. Her grandmother Annie graduated from the Tuscaloosa Female College in 1890, two years before The University of Alabama began admitting women, and her mother and Aunt Adelyne both attended the University although neither graduated. The result was that Plank appeared to have a nonchalant attitude that perplexed Hoagland. She was worried about Betsy and thought the girl needed something to "work for," to focus her, even recommending an exchange fellowship to Peru, a suggestion Plank thought unrealistic given her family's finances and her own interests.[47]

For a brief time, Plank did consider journalism as a major after she learned Bethany had an excellent program.[48] Although she did not pursue it as a major, journalism made more sense for her than biology did; Betsy loved to write and had enjoyed working on her high school yearbook. At Bethany, she was a contributing writer for the *Bethanian*, a magazine for current students, staff, and alumni that the Student Board of Publications published monthly from October to May.

Plank started contributing articles to the *Bethanian* in the spring of her freshman year. The next fall, she was asked to join the editorial staff, and a month later was made Literary Editor, which, she told her parents, "means a hell of a lot of work, no pay, little honor, and even little writing of my own, but jeepers, I like it." And she was good at it, so good that her name came up for consideration to be the next year's editor of the whole magazine. The current editor, who would be graduating at the end of the year, told her he had to submit two names for the position and hers would be one. As she wrote her parents, "the board will naturally favor a male, but the honor and mere suggestion of that $200 scholarship [that came with the position] and extracurricular work is wonderful."[49] It was the first time she acknowledged the possibility of a gender barrier, but it was more a recognition of reality than a complaint. Her goal was not to be the first woman editor; she just wanted the position.

Plank got the opportunity to show she could handle the editorial responsibilities later that spring when the editor left for military training. In his absence, Plank became the temporary editor of the *Bethanian*, and the February issue was all hers. She wasted no time in putting her stamp on it. As she warned her mother, "since [the issue] slams the administration frequently and with cause, there will be some repercussions." In a note on the copy she sent home to her parents, she told them to read the issue because "it's potent and a bit revolutionary to quote the faculty." The faculty were being more than a bit reactionary with that assessment. Plank did not criticize the administration so much as blame the student body for its apathy. She acknowledged in her editorial the "many unfair, high-handed actions of the administration," but scolded the students, telling them outright, "we have absolutely no right to voice dissension until we are rational and courageous enough to act." In fact, "This lethargy we personify is the most disgusting loathsome attitude possible for students."[50]

Plank's irritation with the students' failure to get involved or even to care was palpable. From childhood, she had been instilled with a firm belief in the power of democracy, and the ability of people to reason, to govern themselves. Those beliefs sustained her, her whole life. And yet the students around her, who had a democratically elected body in the Student Board of Governors (SBOG) to represent them, opted not to participate in the process. Students themselves had rendered the SBOG impotent, and that irked her. The administration had no reason to explain its actions because students failed to demand explanations. But they could and should make their voices heard, collectively through the SBOG, because "Bethany is what we—you—make it, and the incidence for any fault that exists in the management of our affairs lies with us until we have made an effort to correct it."[51] Plank apparently had no trouble taking on the student body or the administration over issues that affected the College, but she did not challenge gender issues even if they impacted her directly. Ironically, it was a trait that would later serve her well as a woman in public relations.

Regardless of the "revolutionary" February issue and her gender, Plank was chosen to be the editor of the *Bethanian* the following fall. But it was a short-lived and difficult tenure. In her view, the *Bethanian* had gotten too stuffy. So, she decided to shake things up and make the magazine more interesting to students, a decision that led to a clash with the business manager. In January 1943, she resigned "forcibly." As she wrote her parents, "It was a question of the business manager or me—of whether he ran the whole magazine or me." It didn't, she assured them, involve her temper or a hasty decision. It had been festering like an open wound for too long. "I've been considering a resignation since November, and I should have done it then because I've worked and worried and cried and taken too much in hanging on," she wrote. The business manager "didn't care what was in the magazine and [thought] that a magazine could be written in one weekend and [said] that he knew as much about editing as any printer or engraver or me. Oh well, to hell with it." And yet there was remorse; "I'll miss it though." It could have been that the business manager did not like working for a woman, or that Plank was difficult to work with. She certainly could be argumentative. She also may have tried to control every aspect of the publication, taking on the responsibility of ensuring the end product was perfect, which was a trait she carried with her until the end.[52] Or perhaps it was simply that he did not like her ideas for change. Regardless they clashed, she left, and he won.

Plank's father understood her pain and told her they were proud of her work on the magazine. He reminded her to learn from the experience, however unpleasant, and that it would benefit her in the future. "I know you will have the grace however not to let personalities enter into the situation or your mind to the extent of letting them overshadow the principles involved. If there has been any clashing of personalities—temper your own with reason and consideration, then forget the other fellow's. Be willing and helpful if your help is asked and needed." To which Betsy retorted, the "*Bethanian* affair was entirely one of personalities." That, in fact, was why she gave in and did not stay to fight. "I'm no good," she declared, "at anything but logic and principles."[53]

Although Plank knew she would miss working on the *Bethanian*, she also regretted, for her parents' sake, the loss of the $200 scholarship she would have received as editor. Even though her father's position with the Peoples Natural Gas Company in Pittsburgh was secure, her parents were careful with their money, the Great Depression still fresh in their minds. Fortunately, Betsy had received a $600 tuition scholarship payable over four years to attend Bethany, which certainly helped, but that still left a $100 tuition shortfall. Plus, the additional costs of attending the school, including room and board, were about $430 annually. Plank's parents made up the $530 difference, but not without first receiving an itemized accounting from her for all expenses. She often apologized for the cost of her textbooks and other necessities, and her parents encouraged her to get a part-time job on campus to help defray the expenses. Eventually, she found a position in the library, to which she took a great liking. The work even led her to consider becoming a librarian. The first step in that process, she told her parents, would be getting a master's degree in history. Two of her professors had suggested that "graduate schools might be hard up enough to even give [her] a scholarship."[54]

It was true that with a shortage of male students because of the war, graduate programs needed applicants, which improved the odds of women being accepted. But her professors' comments also reflected Plank's reality at the time. She had always been an excellent student and at the top of her class in elementary and high school, even being highly competitive about grades. On the scholarship examination she had taken to get into Bethany, she had scored the fifth highest among her female counterparts. And in the annual Exceptionally Able Youths Rating sponsored by the Civic Club of Allegheny County, Betsy had tied for twenty-sixth among some 725 high school students who took the test.[55]

But at college, although she worked hard, grades did not come as easily. They were still important to her but no longer defined her. As she wrote to her parents in her second semester at Bethany, "May I pave the way for my grades? The mid-semesters I took were bad and the results should show and I ain't kiddin' as you will consequentially see." Part of the problem was that she had other things going on in her life now. She was active in her sorority, planning dances and rush activities, as well as serving as the Woman's Social Chair for the College and mentoring younger students.[56] In addition, she was a member of the International Relations Club, and her editorial work on the *Bethanian* took up a great deal of time. And of course, there was Rap.

A TEST OF CHARACTER

When Rap asked her to go steady in the fall of 1941, she initially said yes, but broke it off a short time later because she thought perhaps the relationship had developed too fast. As she explained to her mother, "For the first time, I realize just how young seventeen is."[57] To Rap, the idea that they should date other people to see if they really did love each other made no sense, but he obliged. Then the war intervened.

The draft had been expanding since it was first instituted the previous fall; it now included men between the ages of eighteen and forty-five. Rap's fraternity brothers were being called up one by one. Waiting on his own number to be called weighed heavily on him. In the safe confines of Bethany College, he told Betsy he was not afraid of war or death. He would willingly die to save another individual, but the idea of dying on foreign shores for an abstract notion such as patriotism was not compelling. And then, on December 7, Japan attacked Pearl Harbor. Rap wrote to Betsy that evening, knowing immediately the effect the attack would have on the country. And indeed, the following day the United States entered the war. The result was a flood of men volunteering to protect the country. Between 1940 and 1946, about ten million men were selected via the draft, while thirty-five million volunteered.[58]

Just as patriotism was an abstract concept for Rap, so was the war itself for Plank, and for most Americans, until Japan attacked Pearl Harbor. Even after, she expressed little empathy for the young men called up in the draft. She knew they were leaving and where they were going and certainly felt badly for them, but "there's so little use in admitting it," as she told her mother. During the College's first air-raid practice in September 1942, Plank described the campus as "bedlam, but the scenery was beautiful. They should turn out the lights more often." Even after her father was tapped to head a government survey of the natural gas supply lines in the United States, the gravity of the situation was difficult for her to grasp.[59] It was not that she took the war lightly, but she viewed it through a rational and detached lens, often coolly debating the war's merits over dinner with her parents. She had removed herself emotionally from the war, which allowed her to maintain a psychological distance. It was a coping mechanism carefully honed through numerous moves and new schools as a child.

Rap did not possess that capability. He had already decided he was not ready to die for his country but knew it was only a matter of time before he would be called upon to do so. Despite their different views on war, Betsy recognized Rap's pain and sought to console him. They resumed their relationship, and she accepted his fraternity pin, even though the pin was inscribed with someone else's name on the back of it because Rap did not yet have one of his own.[60] Still Betsy remained guarded, promising herself she would not give in and tell him she loved him.

Plank described their relationship as "natural" and easy. Rap said she was "the most intelligent person" he had ever spoken to, as well as "the most forgiving and wonderful person" he had ever known. But she could also try his patience. She was constantly analyzing people, trying to understand what motivated them and how they thought, just as she had with her teacher in high school. For Rap, how a person's mind worked did not seem to be worth very much. And it bothered him that she was always testing their relationship, putting them through "crises," which, he wrote, "you weren't able to figure out and by which you admitted you didn't learn anything—but yet you claimed were necessary."[61] Still, Rap admitted he enjoyed their arguments and missed them when they were apart. For Plank, arguing was a form of mental exercise. Her parents had encouraged her to debate, to voice her opinions, and to defend them over dinner from the time she was a young child. In many ways, the Rap/Plank correspondence during this time mimics that of her parents before their marriage. In both cases, the men's letters are rather dark and contemplative, providing glimpses into their souls, while Betsy and her mother tease and cajole in theirs, giving little away about their own feelings.

Much as her mother and father did, Betsy and Rap complemented each other. He was a pessimist who "didn't expect to finish college or even live to a decent age," while Plank was an eternal optimist. Despite their differences, the relationship deepened, and sex became an issue. Plank was reluctant to take such a step. It was, after all, a risky activity for women at the time. The first birth control pill in the United States would not be approved for sale for another seventeen years. Plank risked pregnancy and the "life-changing options" that would come with it: "an illegal abortion of doubtful safety, a shotgun wedding, forced adoption, or single motherhood." Of course, they both faced expulsion from Bethany should anyone find out. For his part, Rap was not convinced that pregnancy was the threat people made it out to be or at least, he tried to persuade Betsy of that. The existing methods of protection were more efficient than young people were led to believe, he argued. Otherwise, "the population would not be so static."[62]

Although it had clearly been a topic of conversation between them for some time, they were both taken by surprise the night the act actually occurred. In her typically detached and logical way, Betsy analyzed the situation. She was neither "a moralist nor an immoralist," she told Rap. The affair had caught her in a search for principles she did not yet possess, although she hoped to find the right ones eventually. She knew that he, on the other hand, had a moral code regarding physical relationships: He had planned on remaining celibate until marriage. Thus, she said, it had been his responsibility to be the stronger of the two at that moment. He had broken his code and that had caught her off guard.[63]

Rap may have told her he intended to save himself for marriage, but his letters certainly suggest that that thought was already out the window when it came to Betsy. Still, she set out the facts: 1) they were both conscious at the time; 2) both enjoyed it, or they would have stopped; and 3) they were more puzzled at themselves in light of their moral codes than they were ashamed. Ever the pragmatist, Plank simply noted that what was done was done. At the same time, she could not let it go, figuring the only action open to them was to analyze and reanalyze the event until they understood why it had happened.[64]

After weighing the consequences, Betsy decided it best to end their relationship rather than continue the intimacy. Not surprisingly, Rap was unhappy with that arrangement. He told her he loved her even if she didn't believe it. It was not force of habit that made him want to be with her, he wrote, because he did not "get them [sic] quite that strong."[65] He may have been a pessimist, but he was also persistent. Eventually he won her over, and she agreed to go home with him that summer to meet his parents.

Plank found the Rappaports to be very nice, "sort of on the matter-of-fact Pennsylvania Dutch side." Although she liked Rap's father and sister well enough, she thought his mother was "a blight on the entire family." Unfortunately for Plank, she was the first girl Rap had ever brought home, and the obvious closeness of their relationship threatened his mother's dream of Rap becoming a doctor, making her resentful of Betsy's presence. Rap had often complained to Betsy that his family was not warm and affectionate, but she thought he was exaggerating, until she met them. As she explained to her parents, "They lack so much affection, or maybe we have too much, but as [Uncle] Billy said Saturday, we're a hell of a family, but we have a hell of a lot of fun."[66]

Plank spent two weeks with the Rappaports and would have stayed even longer had she not clashed with Mrs. Rappaport one night while Rap was out with friends from high school. Although it was late, Plank had had enough and left, taking a bus, train, and cab to her Uncle Billy's place in New York City, arriving unannounced at three in the morning. Plank was hurt and disappointed by Rap's failure to defend her, which came through clearly in her letter to him. She described him as still tied to his parents with "so many tiny cords of dependence." She loved him but had lost respect for him. He had always said there was just her and biology. "If you can't defend me, can't stand by me, the least important of the two, are you going to be able to stand beside your work?" she wrote. For her part, she was going to forget "the whole ill-bred, narrow-minded indecency that were your home and parents." Her letter took the fight out of Rap, and she knew it. She wrote a second one, not to apologize for what she had said but to temper its sharpness. Her point was, she told him, that unless he began "to establish that work and determination and character in the outside world, [he would] never be able to."[67]

Betsy and Rap were able to forgive and forget apparently, because they continued their relationship after that summer. After "due consideration and deliberation," Plank had decided she loved Rap just the way he was. Both were "a bit priggish" and "possessive as hell." He could be petty, she admitted, but then she was "moody and argumentative." Plank even talked to her parents about her long-term plans, which included marrying Rap. Her parents liked Rap well enough and were fine with the idea of their marriage provided they both continued their post-graduate education.[68]

But during the fall semester of their junior year in 1942, Plank came to question Rap's commitment. By February 1943, she became convinced Rap had lost interest in her. In a letter to him, she wrote, "I can be pretty smart and clever about most things—but almost everything I've loved or wanted, I've spoiled. I'm awkward with it. I crush it to death. And that sounds silly, but damn if it isn't true."[69] It is unclear what Plank was referring to here. As a young child, she had lost both grandfathers, but she does not appear to have been particularly impacted by those losses. She never mentioned either of them in any letters or diary entries. She may have been thinking of childhood friends she had to leave when the family moved but that was hardly her fault. It seems likely that her statement was more emotional hyperbole than reality.

Rap responded that he was tired, "very much so, not only of us but of the world in general." The thought of war was beginning to take its toll on him. He felt the need to break away from those things he loved but no longer had interest in, to possibly enjoy them again in the future. Otherwise, he would ruin them forever, he told her. The breakup was hard on Betsy. She had finally allowed herself to be vulnerable, returning Rap's love, and now it was gone. In a letter to her mother, she wrote, "I'm so very tired of school and upset and tired and run down I wish I could come home. . . . I'm not working and I'm not happy and I don't want to hate it here."[70]

Two weeks later, on the evening of Friday, March 12, Plank was taken to the Wheeling, West Virginia, hospital with a sudden illness. The following day, she was described as still "beyond hope," and it was not clear whether she would pull through. Rap had no idea anything had happened to her until he received a message from Bethany College's president, Dr. Wilbur Cramblet, Sunday evening, telling Rap he wanted to see him first thing in the morning. Cramblet has been described as "a man of humble goodness, unpretentious, self-effacing, compassionate, gentle, and endowed with a sturdy faith and steadiness of purpose." But he also believed that the "genius of the small college lies in its ability to deal aggressively with the personal problems of the student." And he wasted no time getting to the point with Rap when they met. Cramblet said Rap was "unsafe" to associate with the opposite sex, and that the only reason he was still in school was to protect Betsy's honor. If Betsy did not survive, Rap would be expelled. If she did, a faculty committee would determine at the end of the semester whether they would be allowed to return to Bethany for their senior year. Regardless, Rap could forget about medical school. All of Rap's dreams were suddenly crushed. He sent Plank a note while she was still in the hospital: "Words won't come even after an hour. Get well please so that you can laugh and smile again."[71]

Later, Rap explained to her that he had thought about killing himself, but as luck would have it all the drugstores were closed by the time he decided to overdose on pills. He even got a C- on a test the next day because he had not studied since he planned on being dead by that time. Rap acknowledged that she was in a more difficult position than he was. He could just leave or enter the army, which he considered. But she had no choice; she had to deal with the situation.[72]

Plank did survive and, when released from the hospital two weeks later, returned home with her parents to Mt. Lebanon. Feeling better, she called her friend, Ruth Rutherford, who had been with her when she went to the hospital. Ruth agreed to keep her informed of what people in school were saying. At the top of one of her letters, Ruth wrote, "I've memorized what you wrote and as per usual destroyed the evidence." In different circumstances, the line would sound like something written by teenage girls who had read too many Nancy Drew books. But in this case, it reflected the seriousness of Plank's situation. Ruth's letter made that clear. A rumor was going around school that a girl in another sorority had been suspended because she was pregnant. Only one girl, wrote Ruth, was "conspicuous by her absence." Of course, it would not have been lost on Plank, that she too was conspicuously absent. And indeed, a friend of theirs told Ruth that she had heard Betsy was "'in trouble' and that the Zetas were trying to keep it quiet." Ruth set the girl straight, giving the College doctor's version, which was that Betsy was suffering from gastrointestinal issues, issues for which he had treated her several times before. Ruth was more worried, however, about one of Rap's fraternity brothers who told his girlfriend that he *knew everything.* If that were the case, then "a real problem presents itself," Ruth wrote.[73]

The situation could have been much worse in terms of rumors, but the war meant the students and staff were preoccupied and distracted by bigger events. Bethany had just announced that the college would be training Navy servicemen beginning July 1. That news and the resulting turmoil on campus stole the show, deflecting attention away from Betsy and Rap, whom Ruth described as a "lost soul with a fruitless future."[74]

While Rap awaited a decision from Bethany on whether he would be allowed to continue his studies in the fall, Plank convalesced at home for the rest of the semester. She would not return to Bethany College. That summer, she and Dot, a friend of hers from Mt. Lebanon, became counselors at an exclusive girls' camp.

A LESSON IN LEADERSHIP

Camp Robin Hood was perched on a mountain outside of Chambersburg, Pennsylvania, about a three-hour drive from Mt. Lebanon. The camp had been co-founded in 1928 by Catherine Ruland and Florence Heald to give "daughters of the wealthy and well connected" an opportunity to spend time outdoors in the summer, engaged in swimming, archery, and horseback riding. The campers and counsellors lived in what were called "tent-a-lows" but were really sections of a lodge. Dot and Plank were assigned to the upper-right tent-a-low of the second lodge. Their ten charges were eleven- and twelve-year-olds, at least one of whom was "spoiled and rottenly clever." Another arrived with twenty-two pairs of shorts and an attitude. In addition to their counselor duties, Dot and Plank worked in the camp store, selling "bobby-pins, hair nets, soap, Kleenex, and other little hoards of scarcities." Plank joked to her mother that if she and Dot worked a little black market they might be able to pay for college.[75]

Initially, Plank and Dot were unimpressed with the other counsellors who "seemed like such a bunch of overgrown glamour snobs." To bolster her application to the camp, one claimed to have gone to Carnegie Tech. "Consequently, she is constantly on guard with the accent and vocabulary. Another is tall, skinny, with straight, wild-red hair, who does her damnedest to be [Katherine] Hepburn with whom she has little in common but admiration. It's kind of funny to watch self-conscious pseudo-sophisticates delicately drop jelly in their laps," Plank reported to her mother.[76]

Ruland ruled the camp with an iron fist, setting in place strict routines, but Plank soon proved her worth and was given the added responsibility of taking care of the camp's finances. The camp's bookkeeper had fallen ill, so Ruland asked Betsy to take over. Accounting had never been Plank's strong suit. To her mother, she wrote, "You should see me struggling over the measly little post office accounts. I fear to think of my health, my mind, and their money," and joked, "Of course, it would be an excellent opportunity for embezzlement."[77]

Although Ruland apparently thought enough of Plank to put her in charge of the books, her attitude toward Betsy and Dot changed with the wind. On one occasion, Ruland gave the two girls permission to leave the camp to go to the general store in town. They returned to find Ruland "up in arms" because they had gone. Plank was insulted and angered by Ruland's response. "That woman is so full of bull she can't even trust herself," she wrote.[78]

Ruland's behavior taught Plank a great deal about leadership and how not to treat others, lessons, she took to heart. She described Ruland as "without a doubt one of the most discourteous, inconsiderate persons" she

had ever met. It was her inconsistency that bothered Plank the most. For
example, after telling Betsy to scrub the store shelves, Ruland walked to her
tent-a-low, demanded to know where Betsy was and began complaining
about her in front of the campers. "There is no excuse for stuff like that,"
Plank complained to her mother, especially when it happened all the time.
Ruland knew their work schedule since she was the one who created it, but
she would often demand they do things just as their shift was up. "Never
a please, never a word of thanks—nothing. We've worked and talked to
those kids about their problems and dammit, helped them too—but after
months, Miss Ruland comes to them, says 'are you having any problems?'
and gets mad at us 'because you never pay any attention to them and I have
to do it all.'" At breakfast one morning, Ruland announced sarcastically in
front of everyone that "it would be nice if [Dot and Betsy] got the office
slips on the bulletin board,"[79] without realizing they were already up.

It was not just Dot and Betsy who were upset with her. Two counsellors
had already gone home with six others about to follow suit. Dot was on the
verge of doing so as well. "Still and all," Plank wrote to her mother, "it's
quite an experience with hypocrisy—one that I never hope to repeat." And
indeed, she didn't. But she learned from the experience and made the best
of it. As she explained to her mother:

> I refuse to bow down to Miss Ruland—particularly when I don't re-
> spect her—however, it is her camp, and my responsibility is to do my
> work well and behave. You realize, of course, that she will give me
> absolutely no credit for this conduct, not unless it were accompanied
> with pretty phrases of adoration . . . . In any case, I am pleased at my
> work and actions. It's been a case of living up to my own standards and
> evaluating them. The constant hypocrisy hurt me at first, cheapened
> a lot of ideals for me. But I'm holding my own now and keeping my
> mouth shut to everyone. In fact, I am actually enjoying myself.[80]

Plank worried that her mother would misconstrue what she had written.
Her letters from camp were a bit out of the ordinary for Plank; she did not
complain often to her mother. But, she explained, defensively, that was because "I've always hesitated before in sharing any of my particularly difficult
situations for fear you miss judge [sic] me. You do that you know. You're
always more than ready to assume that I am wrong or merely exaggerating.
You spoiled me in many things, but never in trust." Plank acknowledged

that her mother had always been sympathetic to what she was experiencing, but "sympathy is far removed from trust and belief in a person."[81]

Plank and her mother had a complicated relationship as mothers and daughters often do. When Plank was young, she and her mother had been close and, to a certain extent, still were, with Plank regaling her with stories of campus antics. Bettye loved hearing them, living vicariously through her daughter. But as Plank grew into womanhood, they often clashed over "silly misunderstandings" because they were so much alike. Both were impulsive and loved adventure. But Bettye also represented a definition of femininity that Plank rejected or at least struggled with during her time at college. Bettye chastised Betsy for behaviors she perceived as risky or unladylike. She kept an eye on her daughter's weight, encouraged her to wear feminine clothes, and taught her the Southern social graces. At the same time, Bettye was also the one with the higher academic expectations for her daughter. She was the one who questioned grades and pushed her to continue her education.

A RETURN TO HER ROOTS

The end of that summer brought new stresses and more uncertainty for Plank. She did not wish to, nor felt she could, return to Bethany College. But neither did she want to stay in Mt. Lebanon. She opted instead to enroll at The University of Alabama for her senior year. The decision made sense. Tuscaloosa was her first home, her grandmother Annie still lived there, and the city held many of her cherished childhood memories. UA offered Plank a fresh start with a clean slate and with it, the opportunity to finish her degree. Once on campus, she quickly became involved with UA's Zeta chapter and by March, found herself assuming the chapter presidency when the then president relinquished the position to get married.[82] To be elected president over girls who had been in the sorority for three or four years indicates that Plank was able to develop strong relationships with her sorority sisters in a relatively short time.

At UA, Plank majored in history and minored in English literature and political science. One of her English professors was Hudson Strode, a well-known poet who also happened to be a family friend. Strode did not believe writing could be taught. One was either born a writer or one was not. But he did think it was a skill that could be developed. Instead of a class, he held a "clinic" on writing for students he believed had real talent. They spent "their entire time writing, revising, polishing, criticizing each other's products, absorbing pungent Strode comments." Plank was already a good writer, but she blossomed under Strode's tutelage. She also joined the Blackfriars Group, an acting troupe on campus, and earned the role of Fluffy Adams in "Junior Miss." With Annie, she went to church each Sunday where she sang in the choir.[83]

In May 1944, a month before Plank's graduation, Annie died at age seventy-two after a brief illness. The loss of "Mama" was hard on her. With Annie's death and her own graduation, Plank's ties to Tuscaloosa were severed, and a chapter closed as she left the state and returned to the North. It also marked the end of her relationship with Rap.

Fig. 7: Plank's 1944 graduation photo taken by a professional photographer (unknown). Courtesy of the Plank Papers

Betsy and Rap had secretly resumed their correspondence over the summer of 1943 with Ruth initially serving as the surreptitious letter carrier. While at Camp Robin Hood, Plank had suddenly called Rap and sent him a birthday gift. They continued to write for the next year, although never with the same intimacy. The Plank/Rappaport committee, as Rap called it, had ruled that Rap could not return to Bethany that fall. With medical school out of the question, he enlisted in the army and was sent to Fort Bliss in Texas. Rap told her stories about the training he endured and the miserable conditions he was experiencing. Because of his science background, he was quickly put to work in the medical corps, soon graduating from giving vaccinations to helping operate on the injured. It was rumored that his detachment might be sent to Louisiana. If so, he hoped to be able to visit Betsy in Tuscaloosa while on furlough, but neither the move nor the furlough materialized.[84]

Rap's postwar plan was to live his life in a "mixture of feverish work and carefree abandon." If there was a woman who would put up with him, "I will do the damnedest to marry her," he wrote. He hinted that he would like for that woman to be Plank, but she didn't take the bait. He had hurt her badly, and she was wary. In the spring of 1944, around the time of Annie's illness, she stopped responding to his letters. After not hearing from her for some months, Rap finally gave up and simply wrote, "So be good. Always, Rap."[85] It was the last time they corresponded.

Their relationship and the events surrounding it affected the course of both of their lives. At one time, they thought they had it all figured out. Rap was going to be a medical doctor; Plank's future was not quite as defined, but she thought she would get an MA in history and become a librarian. Regardless, they would marry and eventually have children. But sometimes life has a way of interfering with the best laid plans. Whatever happened to Plank physically at Bethany ironically sent them on a trajectory that ultimately led them to their true passions—Betsy to public relations, Rap to cell biology.

After the war, Rap finished his undergraduate coursework at Columbia University. He then did a master's degree in zoology at the University of Michigan, where he met his future wife. He received a doctorate from Yale in 1952 and joined the faculty at Union College in Schenectady, New York. Between 1960 and 1993, he published a series of seminal articles on cell division that continue to be recognized in cell biology textbooks. A hallmark of his "legendary" experiments was their simplicity and creativity. In a 2004 retrospective of his work in the *Journal of Experimental Zoology*, it was said that his appeal was based in part on his gift as a storyteller, making his experiments "riveting" reading.[86]

Plank's path to public relations was not as direct. After her graduation from UA, she still was not clear about what she wanted to do. Teaching was a logical career for a woman at that time, but she had avoided education classes in college. She considered learning how to teach to be a waste of time. Thus, she was not eligible for a teaching position. Instead, Plank applied to graduate school and received a fellowship to attend Boston University to study history.

Several weeks after arriving in Boston in the fall of 1944, she walked through the Commons and realized that the world around her was "in the midst of a whole wartime experience and [she] was still studying American Revolutionary History." She felt something was missing in her life. "I had a vision of my becoming a perennial schoolgirl and that was really not the kind of activist life I wanted to lead," she told an interviewer in 1978. She turned around, went to her room, and packed her belongings. Arriving back in Pittsburgh on the bus, the reality of what she had just done hit her. Her mother would be furious. To delay having to face her, Plank rode around Pittsburgh all day on the streetcar trying to find either her father or her Aunt Adelyne, who now lived in the city, for moral support. She found neither. Summoning her courage, she finally went home. As she feared, her mother was not happy with her decision. Looking back on the event, Plank said, "I don't think she ever really understood that at age 20 I had really reached a turning point and had made a decision that I was not going to pursue the academic life, but I wanted to pursue something far more active in business and in the work world."[87]

Plank grew a great deal from her experiences at Bethany College. Her first real leadership opportunity—serving as editor of the *Bethanian*—did not end well. When challenged by the magazine's business manager, she caved to the pressure. Despite claiming that she had resigned over principle, it was in reality about personality, hers versus his. Some of her emotional reaction to the situation may well have been caused by her deteriorating relationship with Rap, because when faced with a true test of character just two months later, she did not give in. She did not succumb to the weight or gravity of the situation, nor would she in the future. Although she chose not to return to Bethany College, Plank resolutely finished her education at The University of Alabama, despite the health scare she faced and the relationship she ended. She was stronger for having gone through everything she did with Rap. It also gave her compassion and empathy for others dealing with difficult times, further developing her maturing emotional intelligence.

But it was Plank's time at Camp Robin Hood that served as an opportunity to begin thinking seriously about leadership. Until then, if she had thought about it at all, she would have said her father was the embodiment of leadership. But Miss Ruland's style forced Plank to think about the concept and what it really meant to be a leader from a follower's perspective. She had found Ruland to be discourteous, inconsiderate, inconsistent, and a hypocrite, and she knew how that made her, and the other camp counselors, feel. Plank realized that an effective leader treated followers with respect and was consistent in messaging and fair in the application of rules. Plank also came to the realization that she had internalized the high standards her parents and teachers had always held her to. She could, and more importantly wanted to, hold herself to those high standards regardless of what others demanded of her.

The inner fire that had been lit in high school was now burning hotter. Plank finally knew what she wanted—a life with meaning. She wanted to have a career that fulfilled her while allowing her to give back to others. Although she was ready to face the world and find her passion, life was just beginning to test her.

CHAPTER 2

Finding Her Passion

I'm not sure my mother was ever convinced that 'public relations' was something any niceSoutherngirl [sic] should be doing.

—Betsy Ann Plank

FACED WITH THE prospect of spending her days cloistered in the hallowed halls of Boston University, Plank came to the realization that graduate work was not for her. She wanted a life of action, not contemplation. It was not easy to tell her parents, especially her mother. She knew they were disappointed with her decision, and to make matters worse she had no idea what she was going to do instead of school. But surely Pittsburgh would provide a door to her future. And it did, but not in the way she anticipated. For the next decade or so of her life, she experienced heartache and loss but also joy, love, and new beginnings.

FIRST JOB AND FIRST MARRIAGE

After a few months of living with her parents while seeking employment, Plank landed a job at a Pittsburgh radio station, KQV, thanks to her Aunt Adelyne's connections. Adelyne had given up life on the stage and moved to Pittsburgh in 1940 to be closer to her sister, Bettye. The music scene had changed since the 1920s, and Adelyne was finding opportunities to perform on the stage harder to come by. But Pittsburgh had been good to her. Shortly after moving to the city, Adelyne landed a contract for what became a highly successful radio show that was essentially a blackface broadcast featuring her as Aunt Caroline, a black mammie who gave out folksy advice and sang Southern folk songs and spirituals.[1] By the time Plank was looking for a job in the fall of 1944, Adelyne was well known in the city's radio circles, which opened the door for her niece to join KQV.

The station had signed on the air as 8ZAE on November 19, 1919, with informal programming, almost a year ahead of the first licensed commercial broadcasting station in the world, KDKA, also based in Pittsburgh. Two years later, KQV, "King of the Quaker Valley," was officially granted its call letters by the U.S. government. Through the years, it was affiliated with several networks, and on occasion operated as an independent station. When Plank was hired in the fall of 1944, it had just come under the ownership of Allegheny Broadcasting, which again changed the network affiliation, this time from the NBC Blue Network to Mutual Broadcasting.[2]

At the time, Mutual was a weak network, which meant its affiliates had to do much of their own programming.[3] The new owners of KQV saw that as an opportunity for growth. It meant they could cater to the community and attract local advertisers, something the station had not been able to do as much of as an NBC affiliate. KQV was a great proving ground for the twenty-year-old Plank who started as a combination switchboard operator, receptionist, and continuity writer for $18 a week on the understanding that as the station grew, she would graduate to writing full time.[4]

Plank did not last long on the switchboard. In no time, she was writing house commercials and documentaries. She loved to write, but her prior formal experience was with high school yearbooks and a college magazine, not radio. Now, for the first time, she had to write for time constraints, usually thirty or sixty seconds, and for the "ear." It was still rare in the late 1940s to be writing words for someone else to read aloud, but she enjoyed learning a new skill. One of KQV's clients for whom she wrote commercials was the B. White Furniture Company. White stipulated that the name of his store be mentioned at least twelve times within a sixty-second commercial. It was a "challenge and a trick" she never forgot. Then, when the new station manager challenged the staff to come up with what had never been attempted—a full-hour, all-Pittsburgh show for Sunday afternoons—Plank showed her initiative, submitting a sample script for a variety show. "Open House" became a venue for new musical talent. She found producing the show to be "great fun."[5]

According to an early resume, Plank also took a major leadership role at KQV in alerting the public to the dangers of burning coal and the importance of smoke control. Pittsburgh residents had long suffered from the effects of being in an area that produced inexpensive, high-volatile bituminous, or soft, coal. Thick smoke, from industries, commercial enterprises, and individual homes, often blocked out the sunlight to such an extent that streetlights remained on all day. Over the years, ordinances were passed to regulate the use of soft coal in industrial and commercial uses, but civic leaders were reluctant to do the same for individual home use, even though experts argued that smoke from domestic furnaces and stoves was "dirtier and more harmful than industrial smoke."[6] Following World War II, David Lawrence became mayor on a campaign promise of a "Pittsburgh Renaissance," which included clean air and a renewed focus on the ordinance.[7]

While Plank may well have been a leader at the station in furthering the mayor's initiatives, she may also have overstated her role on her resume. Scholars give more credit to the earlier efforts of civic leaders to get the ordinance passed in the first place than they do to Lawrence. And local newspapers were more influential in changing attitudes and behaviors on this issue than was radio. Regardless, the station rewarded her for her initiative and work ethic with a promotion to assistant program director.[8]

As her career was taking off at the station, so was her personal life. Shortly after her arrival at KQV, Plank fell in love with her new boss, Ben Kirk, a former KDKA newscaster thirteen years her senior. She described Kirk as having a quiet humor. He was also "very patient, stubborn, [with] very good judgment," the kind of man people who knew her would not think she had the sense to fall in love with. Kirk reminded her in some ways of her father, much as Rap had. And, at least in Plank's eyes, she and Kirk were good for each other. "Our ideas and ideals, ambitions, are much the same. But we complement one another in personality. I'm temperamental and impatient and impulsive, while he's deliberate and level-headed—and what I don't have, he's got—and I have what he needs."[9]

Kirk was married with two small children at the time but had told Plank he was in the process of divorcing his wife. Reared at Mooseheart, an orphanage outside of Chicago, he had worked his way through college and "made a fine success of himself." Because of his marital status, Kirk insisted they keep their love affair secret, and they did for more than a year. Plank was still a little gun shy after Rap and was fine with not telling anyone. She managed to keep it from her parents because she lived at the Salvation Army's Pittsburgh residence for young ladies during the week and only went home to Mt. Lebanon on the weekends. But it was not easy. Child support was pushing Kirk into debt. Standing by her man, Plank learned about "patience and understanding." It took a great deal of faith to hang on to the relationship and "keep [their] love clean and fine as it [had] been."[10] Given that she was staying at the Salvation Army and Kirk presumably was still living at home with his wife, they may not have consummated their relationship at this point, which could explain why she described it as "clean and fine." With sex off the table, for the time being at least, she seems to have idealized their relationship.

At no time did Plank express outwardly any doubt or concern that Kirk's story might not be ringing true, even when they learned Kirk's wife was going to marry his younger brother after knowing him for only three months, and she and Kirk were still married. Instead of seeing red flags, Plank was excited because Kirk would finally be free to ask her to marry him. It would mean, she wrote, "all my life and work and ambitions and love wrapped up in one!" The plan, at least as Plank understood it, was for them to marry in September or October 1946, settle in Pittsburgh, and work together in radio. But as of that June, she still had not told her parents of their relationship or her upcoming engagement again because of Kirk's insistence on keeping the news secret. His desire for privacy was probably because, despite what he had told her, he had not yet filed for divorce and did not, in fact, do so until August; the divorce was finalized that October.[11]

Still, Plank and Kirk waited another six months to marry. When the day finally arrived, Plank wore a "pale blue crepe afternoon dress and a hat of beige net scattered with pink sweet peas. She carried a prayer-book decorated with white orchids," and for the "something old," "a tiny handkerchief of Irish linen and round-thread lace," which her grandmother Annie had carried at her own wedding. Adelyne served as her matron of honor.[12]

MOVING TO CHICAGO

The couple honeymooned in New York City and then returned to Pittsburgh and KQV. They did not, however, set up house as Plank had envisioned. Kirk decided he wanted "to get out of the rut of Pittsburgh radio and strike out for experience in radio or agency sales, in preparation for station management." Four months after the wedding, Kirk moved them to his self-appointed "hometown" of Chicago. It was a city in which she knew no one. He had effectively removed her from her support system and taken her out of her element. Kirk immediately found work in sales at WAAF in Chicago with the possibility of moving into management. Plank was less fortunate.

Fig. 8: Plank at age 23 at the time of her wedding to Ben Kirk in Pittsburgh, Pennsylvania, April 1947. Courtesy of the Plank Papers

With no contacts to help open doors, she struggled to find a job. Being in a strange city with nothing to do was driving her "crazy."[13]

To make matters worse, money was tight, and the living arrangements were less than ideal. Their Near North Side neighborhood was an odd mix of mansions, low-income apartments, and industries in 1947. Despite rent controls, rents still tended to be high as returning soldiers flooded the market at the end of the war. To meet the demand, many landlords subdivided their already small apartments to increase revenue. Plank admitted things were tough. To a friend, she wrote, "I resent terribly the fact that we're not able to exist 'in the style in which, etc.' Nasty little dollar signs keep getting in our way and being lost in a strange city doesn't help at all."[14]

Plank had never experienced such financial difficulties. Even in the darkest times of the Depression, her family always managed to get by. She knew money was tight at the time and did not ask for much, but she also never lacked for anything.[15] Music, the arts, and entertaining friends were always part of her life growing up, and she had taken them somewhat for granted. Now, with Kirk the only breadwinner, such activities were not possible, and she missed them. She desperately wanted a job to pull her own weight, knowing it would give them the discretionary income to enjoy such things. Plus, she was bored at home alone all day. She needed and wanted to be working, to be useful.

But at the time, radio was running scared of television, just as newspapers once feared the advent of radio. Television would not replace radio as the main source of American entertainment and news until the mid-1950s, but the three national networks, ABC, CBS, and NBC, had started regular television broadcasts just after World War II. Chicago only had one experimental television station in 1947, and it had long lines of job seekers.[16] Plank was not looking for a position in television of course, but radio stations were reluctant to hire new people when they were not sure what their economic future might hold. And when they did, they had their choice of candidates, most with more experience than Plank.

Regardless, she stayed active, meeting as many people as she could. She considered accepting a position with the Illinois Association for the Crippled, which ran the Easter Seal campaign. The job involved handling the newspaper and radio promotion for the campaign, which Plank saw as an opportunity to develop contacts in broadcasting. But that position would not come open until December, still a couple of months away.

FINDING A MENTOR

The networking finally paid off, however, when an acquaintance brokered an introduction for her with a woman by the name of Duffy Schwartz. Schwartz was the Midwest Director of the Advertising Council and the wife of Charles Schwartz, a prominent Chicago attorney who had lived in Hull House as a young man and had served as Jane Addams' personal counsel until her death in 1935. Schwartz and her husband were heavily involved in civic and philanthropic associations throughout the city.[17]

Born Lavinia Schulman in 1898, Schwartz moved with her family to Chicago from Cincinnati at the age of twelve after her father opened an electrical contracting business in the city. She attended the University High School, an elite school affiliated with the University of Chicago, where a male teacher encouraged her to attend Vassar, a women's college in Poughkeepsie, New York, and a sister institution to Yale, for an undergraduate degree. The times were tough; it was financially and emotionally challenging for her parents to send their only child away to college. Schwartz's father struggled to keep his company afloat while his daughter was at Vassar. Few Americans were willing to do business with a German-sounding firm during the First World War. And Jews faced discrimination in many educational institutions. But her parents need not have worried about their daughter. Schwartz loved Vassar, which had a reputation for openness and liberalism.[18]

Schwartz was active in student organizations, including Vassar's student government and, ironically, was even elected to the Christian Association Board. She later stated that she never "felt the least bit uncomfortable as the only Jew" on the board. Schwartz graduated in 1920 with a degree in economics and psychology and that same year married Charles, whom she had met during her junior year while at home in Chicago on a school break.[19] Charles' attitudes toward women had been shaped by Jane Addams and Julia Lathrop of Hull House, two powerful, independent, and politically active women. It was because of them that he held no expectations that his wife would stay at home as her mother had.

Schwartz, on the other hand, was fully aware that her parents expected her to become a good housewife and bear her husband children. And being the dutiful only child, she obliged, for a while. She and Charles had three children, and it was while caring for them that Schwartz realized how lucky she was. Charles was not only an understanding husband; he was also quickly establishing his legal practice. Not everyone had the advantages she did. Recognizing a need, she helped found the Association for Family Living in Chicago, a neighborhood organization assisting young mothers cope with problems for which there were no family-service agencies at the time. She also co-chaired the Women's Division of the Community Fund, which later became the Crusade of Mercy, Chicago's United Way, and was an active member of the Jewish Federation of Metropolitan Chicago.[20]

Difficult financial times for the family in 1938 forced her to seek full-time employment. Fortunately, Schwartz had gained a name for herself in the city through her involvement in the various nonprofit associations. Seeking to capitalize on that reputation and her momentum, the owner and manager of radio station WBBM, a CBS affiliate, offered her a job on the understanding that she would attend a radio management training program. She never did attend the training; instead, she developed her own position at the station, becoming CBS's first director of education and public service. Charles was happy for his wife, but her success was not always easy on him. His friends criticized him for allowing her to work. Nor was it easy on her parents. "I was not being the wife and mother they had raised me to be," she would say much later.[21] Yet, none of it slowed her down.

Perhaps because of her work at the station in the area of education, when World War II started, Schwartz was installed as the Midwest chief of the Office of War Information's Radio Bureau—the only woman deputy chief in the country at the time.[22] In that role, Schwartz worked closely with the War Advertising Council. When the war ended, the War Advertising Council became the Ad Council, developing public service campaigns to raise awareness of issues, inspire action, and save lives.[23]

On February 1, 1946, the Chicago branch of the Ad Council opened its doors with Schwartz as manager. It was one of four offices, the others being in New York, its headquarters; Washington, D.C.; and Los Angeles. At the time, Chicago was the center of network radio programming, and advertisers had a great deal of control over the production of that programming. Thus, a presence in Chicago was a must for the Ad Council. But as television overtook radio in programming popularity in the early 1960s, the networks shifted their efforts to New York, and broadcasters, not advertisers, took control. When the Chicago office of the Ad Council was finally closed in 1969, Allan Jaklich of the *Chicago Tribune* said of Schwartz, "she was the Chicago office." Until the final decision to close the bureau, Schwartz continued to work "at top speed, bringing what has been called her most outstanding business ability—follow thru [sic]—to bear."[24]

By the time Plank was introduced to her in late 1947, Schwartz was a force to be reckoned with in Chicago. At their first meeting, Plank found Schwartz to be "bright-eyed, a small, slender slip of a thing with a telephone growing out of her ear. She wore sensible shoes and sat behind a big, second-hand desk in a modest office." Schwartz probably saw something of herself that day in Plank, who was "young and thin and gussied up pretty smartly on the outside," but was "really discouraged, getting a little desperate, and very hungry" on the inside. The two women, although generations apart, were strikingly similar in many ways. Both were only children and had high expectations put on them. When Schwartz made Phi Beta Kappa at Vassar, for example, she telegraphed her parents to tell them the happy news. Her mother wrote back that, of course, they were pleased but wondered why she had sent a telegraph. "That I should excel was expected. To be extravagant was not," Schwartz explained.[25] And they both believed in giving back through civic and philanthropic causes.

After taking Plank's measure that first day, Schwartz told her that an agency handling the major nonprofit campaigns in Chicago, including for the Red Cross, the Community Chest (later the United Way), the March of Dimes, and the Girl Scouts, had a six-month opening in radio and television public relations for the upcoming Red Cross Campaign. Plank hesitated at first; she did not know anything about public relations or even what it was, which was not surprising.[26]

LANDING IN PUBLIC RELATIONS

Public relations as a business was still relatively young and not well understood, but that was about to change. Peace had brought with it a period of significant growth and prosperity to the United States, as the economy shifted from war materiel to consumer products, aided by burgeoning consumerism and rapid advances in telecommunications. With its focus on communication, public relations was primed to take advantage of the situation and did, experiencing an "unprecedented expansion" during the 1950s. According to the U.S. Department of Labor, there were just nineteen thousand "public relations specialists" in 1950. Ten years later, the number was thirty-one thousand, a sixty percent increase. The number and size of public relations agencies grew as well in this period. Edelman, Burson-Marsteller, and GolinHarris were all established in the 1950s and rapidly became large agencies with executives and staffs handling all aspects of the business.[27]

While public relations was decidedly male-dominated at the time, women were able to find some success in the field in the late 1940s. One reason for the relative openness of public relations to women was that "it was free from the prejudices found in more traditional professions such as law and medicine."[28] Many medical schools had quotas on the number of women admitted each year, and as late as 1937, women were still excluded from practicing law in New York City.

Intelligent and ambitious women who did not want to enter the traditional female fields of nursing or teaching, found public relations an attractive alternative and were optimistic about their future as practitioners. Despite that optimism, the actual number of women in the field suggests that public relations could be considered welcoming only relative to other professions. In 1951, readership of the *Public Relations Journal*, the news-letter of the Public Relations Society of America, was ninety-five percent male. And of the 732 new regular members admitted to PRSA between 1945 and 1952, fewer than thirty were women.[29]

Still, if a woman were good at her job, had experience in journalism or business, and was determined, a public relations agency would take a chance on her. A journalism background was especially important since much of the public relations work in the postwar era involved media relations. Plank was not a journalist, but with her radio background, she was in the right place at the right time for the growing field. She had skills that were becoming increasingly important. She had written for the voice and ear and had gained production knowledge, skills that many of the public relations practitioners who came from print journalism did not have.

Plank did not recognize the value of her abilities at the time, of course, and was reluctant to move from the media side, where she was grounded and felt comfortable, to the agency side of the business. In considering the position with the Illinois Association for the Crippled, she thought of it only as a way to get back into broadcasting. She did not see it as a change in career path. But here was Schwartz, suggesting she jump ship and swim in the uncharted waters of public relations, not even knowing what it en-tailed. Ever the pragmatist, Schwartz simply said, "you're hungry, aren't you? Go over and get the job." Schwartz assured Plank that she would tell her exactly what she needed to know.[30] And she did.

On Plank's triumphant return with the job in hand, Schwartz presented her with a to-do list of about five, single-spaced, typewritten pages and four arm's length boxes of 3x5 cards of contact information for everyone who was anyone in radio-TV, advertising agencies, and corporations in Chicago. For the next five months, Schwartz patiently coached and coun-seled Plank:

> Occasionally we went to meetings together with sponsors and agency and media people and those men—and they WERE all men!—would sit there and listen intently to Duffy because they knew that she knew what she was talking about—and that she had the tenacity and professional mother-deafness to persist until they did right by the campaign.[31]

Fig. 9: Plank, on the left, presenting her mentor, Duffy Schwartz, with Chicago's
Advertising Woman of the Year Award on April 22, 1959. Courtesy of the Plank Papers

Plank had been hired to assist with the American Red Cross annual
fund-raising drive. For the first time, the national kick-off was to be held
in Chicago, and the local chapter, the largest in the country, had retained
the services of the Mitchell McKeown firm to plan the special event
for the sixty-million-dollar drive. It was a job for which McKeown was
well qualified, having trained under some of the best in the country in
nonprofit fundraising.

McKeown started as a journalist and then became a freelance publicist
before being hired by New York's Tamblyn & Brown as public relations
director in 1929. George Tamblyn had joined the pioneering fundraising
firm of Ward & Hill Associates in early 1920 after working with Harvey
Hill on Red Cross membership drives. Hill's partner, Charles S. Ward, was
renowned in philanthropic circles for his fundraising prowess.[32]

Ward and Hill recruited talented men to their firm, such as brothers,
Carlton and George Ketchum, and Tamblyn, but ambitions ran high, caus-
ing internal strife. Before the year was out, Tamblyn struck out on his own
with John Crosby Brown.[33]

The new Tamblyn & Brown firm put a greater emphasis on publicity, essentially media relations, than the Ward agency had. Tamblyn handled the

organization side while Brown took care of publicity. When first hired by Tamblyn, Brown had no fundraising experience, nor publicity experience for that matter. But it did not take him long to develop a rather modern understanding of public relations. For Brown, a good public relations program consisted of 1) "surveys and studies to discover the lay of the land and mind of the constituency," 2) "the willingness to set one's house in order if intelligent criticism reveals the necessity," 3) "development of a definite plan and policy," and 4) "dissemination of constructive information through use of every legitimate vehicle."[34]

The partners professed that both organization and publicity were necessary for fundraising. As Brown described it, "There are two oars on a boat and you both have got to pull the same way and you have got to pull in harmony." Yet because of their backgrounds, they continued to think of organization and publicity as separate functions. A later president of Tamblyn & Ward suggested that as a result, "it was difficult for them to gain a concept of 'public relations' as an exercise which would, in fund raising, embrace both organization and publicity."[35]

One thing the partners did agree on, however, was staffing. Unlike Ward who brought directors on board temporarily for specific campaigns, Tamblyn thought it in the agency's best interest to hire a permanent staff, believing that steady and regular employment would attract a deeper talent pool. And it did. Five men and five women, "college bred and widely experienced in various fields of publicity and campaign work," were on staff in 1920. McKeown was an example of the kind of individuals they were looking for. He was "college bred," had worked for five years as a reporter for the Brooklyn *Daily Eagle* and had served as a freelance publicist for another five before joining the firm.[36]

McKeown was a good hire and a quick study. When Tamblyn & Brown opened a branch office in Chicago in 1929, they sent McKeown to run it. Four years later, McKeown left the firm, opening his own competing agency for nonprofit organizations. McKeown's clients included the American Library Association and the Chicago Chapter of the American Red Cross.[37]

It was for the Red Cross's national kick-off that McKeown, needing extra hands for such a large event, had taken on Plank, who fit the mold of the Tamblyn & Brown employees—college-educated with media experience—forever changing the direction of her career. The campaign was high profile and heady stuff for an introduction to public relations. For the keynote speaker, McKeown and the Red Cross had managed to secure General Dwight D. Eisenhower, who was riding high on a wave of positive public opinion, fresh off his successful stint as the Supreme Commander of the Allied Forces in WWII. The actor Jimmy Stewart agreed to act as the master of ceremonies, and the actress Helen Hayes was to appear. Writing copy for the three high-profile individuals was a thrill for the twenty-four-year-old Plank.[38]

Approximately five thousand Red Cross volunteers crammed Chicago's Medinah Temple the night of February 28, 1949, to see and hear the speeches, which were also aired live. During the last five minutes of the broadcast, President Truman made his own on-air appeal from the White House in support of the campaign. For his part, Eisenhower declared the Red Cross to be "the warm heart of a free people," and said support for the organization revealed what individual efforts could accomplish.[39] Newspapers around the country carried coverage of the event, most of it taken from an Associated Press story, but some may have come from Plank's news release, a copy of which she saved. By all accounts, it was a successful launch for the Red Cross, McKeown's firm, and Plank.

Even before the campaign was over, McKeown hired Plank as a full-time account executive. She proudly reported the good news back to Schwartz, who simply said "of course." When Plank reminded her that she had just been doing what Schwartz had told her to do, Schwartz responded that she had given the same advice to lots of young people before, but Plank was the first to follow through on it.[40]

Next to her father, Schwartz became the most influential person in Plank's life. She mentored Plank and guided her through the rocky shoals of a new career. Like all mentees, Plank eventually outgrew her mentor, but the two remained close friends until Schwartz's death in 1991. In her eulogy, Plank warmly remembered the lessons the older woman had taught her:

> So I learned early how smart it was to do what Duffy told you. And I learned how good it felt when she thought you performed up to her standards. And I learned that when you succeeded in doing well what she told you to in the first place, she would—at all costs—avoid taking any credit. That was just her native style.[41]

Plank also learned small things like always making lists and using 3x5 cards, as well as big things like paying it forward and becoming a mentor. As Plank explained, "I learned to be kind to hungry young strangers looking

for employment. It's one of the only ways she would ever allow me to acknowledge my debt to her generous spirit and abiding friendship." And
perhaps most importantly, "I . . . learned well that when one door closes,
watch out for the next one God opens for you because there may be some
stubborn angel like Duffy waiting there to take charge of you."[42]

In those early years, Plank thrived under Schwartz's and McKeown's tutelage as they laid the groundwork for her future in public relations. From
McKeown, whom she described as having a "genius for fund-raising," she
was learning the craft of the field, including "publicity, promotion and organization; how to write and edit brochures, annual reports and proposals"; and
how to use her skills to bring about social change. From Schwartz, she learned
the importance of professional associations and how to build relationships
within them. It is no coincidence that in the late 1940s and early 1950s
Plank joined associations, such as the Publicity Club of Chicago, the Welfare
Public Relations Forum, and the Chicago Chapter of the American Women
in Radio and Television (AWRT), and became a volunteer with the Chicago
Council on Foreign Relations; they were all organizations that Schwartz was,
or had been, involved with.[43] As Plank had done in high school and college,
she did not just join these organizations, she became an active member of
them, volunteering for committees and helping with events.

Of all her affiliations at the time, Plank felt most at home with the
Publicity Club of Chicago (PCC). Formed in 1941, the PCC's purpose
was to provide Chicago-area communication professionals with the tools
necessary to excel in public relations. By the time she joined in the early
1950s, the PCC had an established tradition of performing skits at its annual President's Dinner. Ever the performer, Plank loved everything about
the evening, eagerly helping write skits and song lyrics and then topping
it off by volunteering to perform them. The 1961 President's Dinner, for
example, included skits with themes such as "the smoke-filled room—the
corporate image, and—the wire tap, or the PR man's unbuttoned lip."[44]
The finale to the 1958 dinner featured a song parody sung to the tune of
"Seventy-six Trombones":

Two seventy-six PC'ers just can't be wrong,
We've gotta be right to work with the press!
You can always depend that we'll
Write the story with zeal
We just won't be satisfied with less.[45]

Plank immediately felt an affinity for public relations. She loved puzzles as a child and saw public relations as problem solving on a large scale. It was her drive to solve problems that in some ways helped buffer her gender disadvantage because she kept the focus on the problem and not on the politics. She had first learned that lesson from her run-in with the *Bethanian* general manager and then had it reinforced by Miss Ruland at the summer camp.

Now, she threw herself into her work and the profession itself. She read everything about public relations that she could get her hands on, although the literature was relatively scarce at the time. Edward Bernays published *Crystallizing Public Relations*, one of the first book-length treatises on the practice, in 1938. Other books available included *Profitable Public Relations*, also published in 1938; *Public Relations at Work*, which appeared in 1948; and *Your Public Relations: The Standard Public Relations Handbook*, written by Glenn and Denny Griswold who also published the trade publication, *Public Relations News*. Other trade publications such as *Ad Age*, *Editor & Publisher*, and *Printer's Ink* on occasion also ran articles on public relations.[46] Plank attended seminars and lectures to find out more about the field, developing her own definition of public relations along the way and creating her own ethical code of conduct, one she adhered to strictly.

Plank found her purpose in public relations and the gratifying work she did for her clients, which included the Red Cross, March of Dimes, Mayor's Youth Foundation, and the Girl Scouts. Her work with nonprofit organizations at McKeown provided her with an opportunity to meet and interact with prominent leaders in the city. The boards of her clients were made up of successful, powerful people, people she may never have met had she been in an entry-level position at another agency. That exposure taught her early on how to relate to such individuals and how to voice her opinions effectively to get results. Having these influential people listen to, acknowledge, and validate her views, empowered her.

During Plank's seventh year with the firm, McKeown died suddenly. The agency was a proprietorship and forced to close after his death. Plank was the last person out the door, leaving at 2:00 a.m. after boxing up files and taking care of loose ends. This time when she found herself out of work, she had the security of a safety net in Sherman (Sherm) Rosenfield, the man who would become her second husband a month later on April 10, 1954.[47]

Fig. 10: Plank, aged 30, smiles at her father following her wedding to Sherman Rosenfield (right) on April 10, 1954, in Chicago, Illinois. Courtesy of the Plank Papers

THE END OF ONE MARRIAGE AND START OF ANOTHER

While Plank was busy developing her professional life at the McKeown agency, her home life had been falling apart. Kirk was drinking excessively and was often belligerent. If he thought by moving Plank away from her family he would be able to control her, he sorely underestimated his wife. The petite, red-haired Plank was a fighter. She did not sit around waiting for him to fulfill her. She went out, made contacts, met Schwartz, and landed a job she enjoyed. As she became more independent, Kirk tried harder and more desperately to regain his power over her.

It was a difficult time for Plank, who blamed herself for their troubles even though it was Kirk who did not live up to her expectations. She prayed for help in being kind and in having a happy marriage. But by early 1950, she could no longer handle the stress. Still, she hesitated to tell her parents. No doubt, they had not been pleased when she married Kirk in the first place. Now, she had to admit to them that they had been right, that he was making her life miserable. Finally, she gathered the strength to do so, and with their support, she told Kirk she wanted a divorce. But he did not leave quietly. Eventually, she had him involuntarily committed to a psychiatric facility. The divorce papers filed on her behalf cited Kirk's extreme and repeated acts of cruelty on May 5 and May 11, 1950, as grounds. Their divorce was finalized on July 17, 1950, closing a painful chapter of her life.[48]

Freed from a psychologically abusive home situation, Plank focused on her work, which she loved. But the old loneliness she felt as a child returned. Fortunately, she would not be lonely for long. Treating herself to a much-deserved vacation, she spent two weeks at a dude ranch where she met Sherm Rosenfield who was two years older than her and a Chicagoan.

The son of Russian immigrants, Rosenfield was an industrial film producer and editor. With her radio background, the two felt an immediate professional kinship that blossomed into a loving relationship. Their religious affiliation, however, was very different. Plank was Presbyterian, and Rosenfield was Jewish, although he was not raised in an orthodox household. His family welcomed her with open arms, but Plank's family, her mother especially, was not as understanding, partly because the memory of Plank's failed first marriage was still fresh in their minds, and partly because they thought the cross-cultural marriage would be difficult for the couple to overcome. Despite the Allies' noble victory over the evils of fascism, considerable prejudice still existed against Jews in the United States in the 1950s.[49]

Plank and Rosenfield were not oblivious of their cultural and religious differences; they explored them thoroughly before marrying, deciding ultimately that their shared bedrock of faith and similar value systems were more than enough to sustain them. As she had with Rap, Plank put Rosenfield through a series of "tests" before she committed herself. One such test was to introduce him to the group of ten-to-twelve-year-olds in her Sunday school class at the Fourth Presbyterian Church to see how he would be with children. He passed with flying colors, loading them all in his car and taking them out for the day. She described him as "marvelous" with the children.[50]

When asked years later why she had kept her own name after their marriage, Plank said the decision about whether to change her name never came up. She was thirty at the time and had worked for ten years as Betsy Ann Plank, which was her given name because "according to God and [her] Mother no Southern girl exists without a middle name." She simply kept on using that name for business. At home and for personal matters, she was Mrs. Sherman Rosenfield, she told the interviewer.[51] But it was more complicated than that. Even her first name changed according to the cont

Professionally, she was known as Betsy Ann. To Rosenfield and their closest friends, she was Bets. To yet other friends, she was simply Betsy. Taking on different names was an outward manifestation of her ability to adapt to situations as well as to compartmentalize her life, defense mechanisms she had carefully crafted as a child. Seldom did she allow the various aspects of her life to intermingle.

Plank was, perhaps, her truest self only with Rosenfield, who was clearly not threatened by her strong personality. She described him as a man "who has no peer." He was a man who really did have the qualities she thought she had found in Rap and Kirk: an even temperament and an easy-going attitude, combined with maturity, integrity, and patience. And more importantly, unlike Rap and Kirk, Rosenfield was comfortable with himself and fully capable of handling Plank's volatility and impulsiveness, for which she called him a saint. Much like Schwartz's husband, he was proud of her work and did not expect her to be the perfect wife. It helped that Rosenfield had a work schedule like Plank's, which meant long days, even stretching into weekends. Successful women of Plank's day often found it difficult to find balance between their careers and society's expectations of how a wife should behave. But Plank was freed from that inner struggle. Rosenfield accepted her and loved her for who she was.[52]

In 1984, looking back on thirty years of marriage, Plank said she could not recall that their marriage had had any great difficulties, but then she admitted she forgot things. It's "one of the ways I survive," she said, which was true; she was quick to anger, but equally quick to forgive and forget.[53] They also rarely discussed business problems at home—"living through them once was enough," she said. Rosenfield gave her the security and stability, both financially and emotionally, that she had been seeking. For the first time, truly no longer lonely, Plank could move forward with her career and take chances she might not have been able, or as willing, to take had she been alone or still with Kirk.

Thus, when the McKeown agency closed, shortly before she and Rosenfield married, Plank quickly took on a freelance position as a public relations consultant for the Chicago Chapter of the Red Cross. Of course, they knew her well from the work she did for them while with McKeown, and likewise, she felt comfortable with them. Her role as a consultant included responsibilities for "audio-visuals, annual reports, orientation program development, annual meetings and special events, public relations counseling for and work with volunteer committees."[54]

During her three-year stint with the Red Cross, Plank and Rosenfield settled into a comfortable lifestyle. For their first wedding anniversary, they bought the Yearling III, a wooden boat, which they berthed at Burnham Harbor in Chicago. They spent many warm summer evenings sitting on the Yearling, watching the crowds head toward Jackson Park, the location of the city's first (1893) and second (1933) World's Fairs. Plank recalled attending the 1933 Fair when she was nine. Plank, her parents, and her grandmother Annie had piled into Annie's old Buick and made the more than seven-hundred-mile trek from Tuscaloosa to Chicago because it would be educational for "young Betsy." As is typical of such summer excursions when one is young, Plank remembered little of the trip itself other than the sound of the Fair's criers enticing people to enter their tents of intrigue. She did remember stopping at one point, overtaken by curiosity by what looked like human fetuses in a glass jar. Her mother quickly grabbed her arm and pulled her along, saying that what Plank was looking at was "not nice." Rosenfield, on the other hand, had grown up in Chicago. As they sat on their boat, he regaled her with stories of his childhood exploits at the park.[55]

Boating became a serious hobby for the couple. Rosenfield joined the Chicago Power Squadron, a group dedicated to "high standards of navigation and seamanship" and later became an instructor in its boating class, even receiving an award from the Squadron in the late 1960s for rescuing five people from a sinking boat in Lake Michigan.[56] For her part, Plank joined the Squadron's Women's Auxiliary, serving as its president in 1958. The pair worked hard, played hard, and lived life to its fullest.

In 1956, Plank suggested to the wives of three of their closest couple friends that they establish a gourmet dinner club like one to which she had belonged while attending The University of Alabama. Her friends loved the idea. For the next several years, every six weeks or so, one of the couples would host a dinner for the group, serving food from another country. The host couple was responsible for "selecting the type of meal, choosing the menu, scouting ingredients for recipes and decorations for atmosphere." When it was their turn to host, the wives even went so far as to locate "experts on the country of their choice for help in locating recipes and ingredients." The night of the dinner, the cooking was done by all four women together, because that was the fun part. At first, the men just went along to humor their wives, but soon they too embraced the adventure.[57]

The couples originally called themselves the Gourmets, until one of them remarked that a gourmet enjoyed good food, while a bon vivant enjoyed good company and conversation while enjoying good food. They quickly changed their name. The Bon Vivants suffered through eleven tries to "get the sugar caramelized for the French orange sauce," "awful green noodles" for the Italian dinner (no one told them they needed a noodle maker), and two backed-up sinks. But of course, that was all part of the fun. When one couple decided to host a Hawaiian luau, Plank and Rosenfield arrived the night before to help dig the pit for the pig roast, a hole three feet in diameter in the middle of the couple's back lawn.[58]

While Plank's marriage to Rosenfield brought her great joy, she also experienced personal heartbreak in the fifties. Her mother, Bettye, had been ill for some time, and on Valentine's Day, 1958, she died at the age of fifty-five. Plank's relationship with her mother had been a complicated one, but the loss of a parent is always difficult. She did not write of her mother's death, although she did sketch her mother lying in bed, a tiny, frail woman. Adelyne, whom Plank adored, died suddenly just six weeks later at the age of sixty-one.[59]

AN UNSETTLED WORK LIFE

At the same time, Plank was experiencing changes in her professional life. After three years with the Red Cross, Plank left to become the public relations director of the Chicago Council on Foreign Relations.[60] Formed after World War I by a group of influential men and women in the city, the Council was to serve as an impartial forum for the discussion of foreign matters and to educate citizens in world affairs. Plank had been a volunteer with the organization since Schwartz, who was a board member at the time, first introduced her to the group.

The position provided Plank with the opportunity to transition from the realm of cause-related nonprofits, or health and welfare as it was called at the time, to one focused on politics and policy. As the public relations director, she was responsible not only for media relations and promotion, but also for working with community and business groups on cooperative projects.[61] The position seemed a natural fit for her; Plank had always been interested in politics and world affairs. But unfortunately, the Council struggled financially and had difficulty funding her salary. After just a year, she left, moving to the Ronald Goodman Public Relations Agency.

Goodman had been with the McKeown firm for about two years when Plank was hired to help with the Red Cross campaign. Goodman

subsequently moved to the Red Cross in 1952 where he served as the
director of public information until he opened his own agency. Despite
his nonprofit work experience, Goodman's firm specialized in corporate
public relations. Plank's move to the agency provided another opportunity
for new experiences in the practice. As Goodman had done, she, too, left
nonprofits behind to focus on financial and stockholder relations, external
and internal communication, and community relations, with clients such
as Oscar Mayer, a meat and cold-cut producer; Burgess Battery Company,
a manufacturer of dry-cell batteries; UARCO, an Illinois-based printer of
business forms; and American-Marietta, an industrial conglomerate based
in Chicago. Here, she received "a baptism in corporate management, strategic planning, and finance. It taught [her] to understand financial statements, product codes, the corporate vocabulary."[62]

Plank was hired as an account executive but quickly proved her worth.
Initially, she would attend new client meetings with a male colleague from
the agency because clients were not used to dealing with a woman. But
soon, they warmed up to the feisty redhead who kept the spotlight on
where she thought it should be—taking care of them and their problem.
After three years, she was elected vice president of the agency and named to
a newly created post of assistant to the president. As such, she was responsible for external and internal print communications and women's interest
programs. In addition, she supervised the firm's radio, television, and film
functions.[63] Within days of being promoted to vice president, however,
Plank quit over a dispute with Goodman. No record exists in Plank's files of
what caused the split, although Plank later said it was over an ethical issue.
She could not endorse Goodman's position on some matter and resigned.

Although Plank had described herself as neither moral nor amoral as a
student at Bethany College, she did find her moral compass as she matured.
During her first thirteen years in public relations, Plank had developed her
communications skills and grown proficient in the practice through a variety of experiences. The quality and diversity of those experiences provided
her with skills, knowledge, and wisdom that she would bring to bear in the
future as a public relations leader. She increasingly used her competence
as a means of managing her clients and finding her way in a man's world,
networking and building relationships.

With a solid reputation for achieving results, potential employers came
calling for her services as soon as word got out that she was no longer with

Goodman. She considered teaming up with two colleagues she knew from the Red Cross who were launching their own agency to serve nonprofits. But instead, she decided to accept Dan Edelman's offer to join his firm, which specialized in marketing public relations. Plank found the position intriguing. From her experience with Goodman, she concluded that she could serve nonprofits better by working to influence corporate executives from the inside rather than by working for nonprofits directly. Plus, she liked Edelman's style. As she put it, "his troops ran fast; he ran faster."[64] And in 1961, at the age of thirty-seven, she joined Daniel J. Edelman, Inc. It was a move that would solidify her reputation as a force in public relations.

CHAPTER 3

The Emergence of a Public Relations Leader

[The glass ceiling] is there for people who think it is there. I
think it is in the mind's eye and can be shattered.
> —Betsy Ann Plank

PLANK ACCEPTED DAN Edelman's offer to join his firm in August 1961 because she liked his style, perfectionism, and demanding nature. And having
left the Ronald Goodman agency on a sour note, she found Edelman's high
ethical standards refreshing. In such an atmosphere, Plank excelled and
found her rhythm, flourishing at work and in the community.[1]

DANIEL J. EDELMAN & ASSOCIATES

Like Plank, Edelman was not a native Chicagoan. Originally from New
York, he moved to the city in 1948 to assume the position of public relations manager for the Toni Company. Toni was a significant player in the
home hair permanent kit market, thanks to a successful Foote, Cone &
Belding advertising campaign, which featured identical twins with identical
hairstyles. The twist was that one had a salon permanent while the other
had a Toni home permanent. The ads posed the question, "Which Twin has
the Toni?" Despite the campaign, competitors were beginning to cut into
the company's market share.[2]

That's when Edelman came up with the idea of taking Toni's "twins" on
a several-months-long media tour. He lined up six sets of good-looking
twins and sent them around the country. The tour was wildly successful,
garnering media attention at every stop, as people tried to guess which
twin had the Toni. Toni's twins became a cultural phenomenon, for which
Edelman was hailed within the company as a genius. But the campaign's
success did not translate directly into market share and sales. The problem
was inherent in the nature of the product itself. Once a consumer purchased
the original kit, refills were needed to keep up the curls, which significantly

reduced sales potential. In addition, beauty salons around the country felt
threatened by the "at home" permanents. In lawsuits, salon owners argued
that users were operating beauty parlors without a license. Faced with these
challenges, Gillette, which had purchased the Toni Company in 1948,
put a halt to the campaign. Unfazed, Edelman responded by opening his
own agency.[3]

Chicago was a largely untapped market in terms of public relations
despite its growing economy and strong media presence when Daniel J.
Edelman & Associates was established in 1952. In fact, only seventeen
thousand men and two thousand women in the nation classified themselves
as public relations practitioners in 1950, according to the U.S. Census.
Many of those probably practiced in New York City, which had a more
robust public relations scene at the time with Carl Byoir & Associates
(1930), Hill & Knowlton (1934), and Ruder & Finn (1948), among other
agencies, active.[4]

The Chicago landscape was not all positive, however. Clients, especially smaller businesses, were accustomed to advertising and did not really
understand the nature of or see the value in public relations. That made
things more difficult for entrepreneurial practitioners like Edelman who
initially struggled to gain a foothold in the city. Ultimately, he was successful, of course, aided by the booming postwar economy and the emergence
of television.[5]

With few barriers to entry, such as educational requirements, standards of
practice, and start-up costs, the field had the potential for greater diversity
in its ranks than other professions, such as law and medicine.[6] Good writers
with creativity were in demand, regardless of age, experience, or even race
and gender. But at the same time, those low barriers to entry meant that
anyone, including the unqualified and unscrupulous, could claim to be
public relations practitioners. Ethical lapses and questionable tactics on the
part of such practitioners sullied the field's reputation.

Edelman, who always held himself and his firm to high ethical standards,
joined other industry leaders in pressuring the Public Relations Society
of America, the national association for public relations practitioners, to
strengthen the ethical code it had initially adopted in 1950 to help combat
ethical breaches by practitioners. Of ethics in public relations, Edelman
wrote, "all of us in P.R. must bring to the office our own sense of morality
and live by it every day," to maintain and achieve greater respect. Here was

a man Plank could relate to. Fresh from a situation that had forced her to draw an ethical line in the sand, Plank saw in Edelman a kindred spirit. Apparently, the feeling was mutual as Plank quickly became "synonymous" with the agency.[7]

Edelman and Plank had more than just ethics in common. Both were children of the Great Depression, were hard workers, and set high standards for themselves and others. Edelman's biographer, in discussing Edelman's efforts to elevate the industry's ethics, described Plank as "a red-headed sprite of [sic] woman" who was "a natural, taking up the causes of her clients as well as the industry banner as a whole. . . . In Plank, Dan found a colleague who would stand up for the profession, even if it meant offending violators."[8]

For more than a decade, the Edelman/Plank relationship was a success, with Edelman describing Plank's contribution as "invaluable." It was also a decade during which the fabric of American society seemed to fray at the edges. Civil rights, feminism, consumerism, the environment—all were issues public relations practitioners now had to deal with. Issue identification—anticipation of problems that could affect the client—and issues management, a term Plank was not fond of because it sounded too Machiavellian, became important tools in the public relations arsenal, followed closely by crisis management.[9]

Plank began at Edelman as an account executive but soon progressed to account supervisor and then to vice president. Initially, her primary responsibilities were media relations, by which public relations was largely defined at the time. Within five years, Edelman named her executive vice president, telling his staff that the promotion was in "recognition of Betsy's great achievements for our agency in recent years and the areas of responsibilities which she has assumed for me and for all of us."[10]

As executive vice president, Plank's duties included serving as operations director "(assignment of personnel to accounts; evaluation of profitability of accounts; and all administrative responsibilities)"; structuring and heading up a Plans Board; and serving as chair of the vice presidents committee. In addition, she was responsible for the overall operations of the Edelman offices in Chicago, Los Angeles, New York, San Francisco, and Washington, D.C., and served on the agency's board of directors that oversaw its U.S. and U.K. offices. It was all work that needed to be done given the growth of the agency but work for which Edelman himself had no taste. He preferred working directly with clients. Administration was not something Plank necessarily aspired to, but her organizational skills and ability to get things done meant she fit her new responsibilities well. The result was that she spent less than fifty percent of her time supervising accounts.[11]

Fig. 11: Plank, aged 46, in her office at the Edelman public relations agency in Chicago in 1970, three years before she left the firm for AT&T. Courtesy of the Plank Papers

WORK THAT MATTERS

The Kimberly-Clark account was especially important to Plank although the company was not technically her client. The advertising agency of Foote, Cone & Belding had the Kimberly-Clark's Kotex brand account and had brought Edelman in to develop a public service program to supplement the marketing campaign. Promoting Kotex presented an interesting advertising challenge. Although the 1960s were known as a time of sexual liberation, the topic of menstruation remained taboo in many ways. Women's magazines carried advertisements for sanitary napkins, but television was considered strictly off limits. It was believed viewers would be offended by an ad on the subject.[12]

Kotex, so named because of the product's cottony texture (co-tex), first appeared on the market in the early 1920s. But it had an inauspicious start. Stores were reluctant to put it on their shelves, fearing it would offend shoppers. Some kept it behind the counter, which further complicated matters because women had to ask the male clerks for it, putting everyone in an uncomfortable situation. To solve that problem, Kimberly-Clark branded the product so that women would no longer have to ask for sanitary napkins. Instead, they could ask simply for Kotex, lessening women's embarrassment, but probably not doing much for that of the male clerks.[13]

Beginning in 1932, the company included in boxes of Kotex a free educational booklet titled, *Marjorie May's 12ᵗʰ Birthday*, designed to teach pre-adolescent girls about menstruation. Kimberly-Clark advertised the booklet as helping "ease the task of enlightenment" for mothers. As Plank described it, most mothers, probably even her own mother, at the time "didn't know enough about the subject to discuss it." Many women just handed "that booklet and a box of Kotex to their daughters—*very* grateful to the company for helping them avoid the topic."[14]

Plank's own experience being sexually active in college and going through the anguish of being "late" on occasion made the account personal to her. When she took it on in the 1960s, not much had changed. Ads still appeared only in magazines because it was believed that television and radio ads would offend viewers and listeners. With these channels closed to the company, Kimberly-Clark searched for more creative ways to deliver its message about Kotex to the public. In terms of public relations, it had moved beyond the *Marjorie* booklets and into schools. Plank worked with curriculum designers at secondary schools, encouraging the "fledgling effort toward sex education, developing useful teaching programs to supplement it—and supplying [Kimberly-Clark] educational materials for students." But teaching sex education in schools was controversial at the time. Plank reported that "it was uphill all the way." Still, she found it "very worthwhile and satisfying work—and I'm proud of it."[15]

At the same time, the company knew from the mail it was receiving that the increased focus on women and sexuality in the 1960s was also expanding the type of information women needed. It had gone beyond menstruation to such topics as "developing sexuality, physiological and sociological development, personal relationships, attitudes and behavior as well as the role of women in society." To address the new demand for information about female development, Plank worked with Kimberly-Clark to establish the Life Cycle Center in 1967. The Center's purpose was to support the company's basic sex education program while producing authoritative materials geared to answering the new questions women were asking. She was proud of her work on the Center, "because we made a genuine contribution to the enlightenment of that generation."[16] It was this kind of work—making a difference in people's lives in areas of importance to Plank personally—that she enjoyed the most.

Another client at Edelman from whom she took great satisfaction was Playskool Toys, which made toys aimed at developing children's minds and hand-eye coordination. Its early slogans included "Learning While Playing" and "Playthings with a Purpose." The company took advantage of the educational aspect of its toys, advertising to conscientious parents in magazines such as *Redbook*, *Parents*, and *Psychology Today*, rather than marketing directly to impressionable preschoolers through television, the way most of its competitors did.[17]

Plank and her team set several objectives for Playskool's public relations program: to convince the parents of young children of the importance of preschool play in the development of their child's learning; to project Playskool as a concerned authority in the area; and to further the company's marketing program. One of Plank's successful tactics was a feature story on Playskool's chief toy designer, Jerry Rockwell, the brother of the artist Norman Rockwell. The Christmas buying season was and continues to be prime time for toy manufacturers. Most of Playskool's publicity at this time focused on toy-buying tips and instructions on how to provide a positive play/learning environment for preschoolers. The Rockwell feature story was an additional way to emphasize the value of educational toys through a human-interest story. The feature first appeared almost word for word in the *Chicago Tribune*. Later, it was picked up by other newspapers and 163 radio/television stations. Sales of Playskool toys jumped from $12 million to $23 million during Plank's time on the account, although the company itself credited the rapid growth to the federal Head Start program, which launched in 1965 and emphasized the kind of play-learning that was associated with Playskool.[18]

Regardless, Plank enjoyed researching early childhood education and learning from child psychologists such as Dr. Bruno Bettelheim, at the University of Chicago, for the account.[19] Little was known about preschoolers in the early 1960s. But Playskool Toys' vice president of research and development, with whom Plank worked closely, believed that children's play was their work, and their work, in turn, was their play. If preschoolers could develop the right attitudes toward play, then in adulthood, their work would become play, he argued. It was a position with which Plank did not disagree. Of her chosen profession, she once said, "Despite the pressures and the erosion of my personal life, it's still play. I happen to be in love with communications. When I sit down at the typewriter, it's akin to playing the piano, and I enjoy it."[20]

Plank saw public relations as facing, meeting, and resolving problems in an ethical and responsible way. Thus, when she was brought in to consult on the 9 Lives cat food account, she insisted on maintaining her ethical values. Leo Burnett Advertising had created Morris the Cat as a "spokescat" for its client, 9 Lives. Everyone loved the "World's Most Finicky Cat," a big orange tabby that had been discovered in an animal shelter in 1968, and 9 Lives wanted to capitalize on his notoriety. The Edelman agency was brought on board to turn Morris the Cat into a cultural phenomenon akin to what Edelman had done for the Toni twins. The result was a Morris look-alike contest held in several cities around the country with the real Morris attending each event to help choose the winner. A biography, *Morris, An Intimate Biography*, was even written.[21]

Plank recalled the day she first met Morris. She was working in her office, amidst a mass of papers, books, mementoes, etc., two photos of Rosenfield, and other sundry items. Between her office and Edelman's was a small conference room with sliding glass doors, which were kept closed when the room was in use so as not to disturb Plank and Edelman who tended to work with their office doors open. On this day, Plank could hear voices coming from the conference room. Someone had forgotten to close the sliding doors. Not pleased with the disruption, she got up from her desk to give them a piece of her mind. It was then she saw "practically the entire agency staff—making sounds of idiot's delight at something."[22] Making her way through the crowd, she found Morris the Cat at its center.

With all the attention Morris was receiving, Judith Rich, the lead on the account, called a special meeting of some creative minds, including Plank. The purpose of the meeting was to strategize about what to do in the event something happened unexpectedly to Morris. The assembled team decided two avenues were open to them. The first was to find a substitute for the orange tabby now, start training him, and have him ready to go at any time. The second option was to be transparent and tell people when Morris died and that they were in the process of finding a replacement.

As Plank recalled it, everyone in the meeting, except for her, voted for option one. They figured that with good preparation the replacement Morris would just fit right in, and no one would notice the switch. But Plank was a cat lover and told the group that she would indeed know it wasn't Morris, as would all 9 Lives customers. They would know, and they would resent that 9 Lives tried to fool them. Public relations was never about marketing or selling to her. She saw it as personalizing businesses amid the give and take of the democratic process. She sought to help businesses like 9 Lives recognize that they depended on good relations with their customers "whose opinions, decisions, and actions affect the vitality and survival of those organizations." Plank held her ground and transparency prevailed. When Morris died in 1978, the *Chicago Tribune* reported that "an understudy had been in the wings for some time."[23]

BUILDING A NETWORK

As Plank was busy rising through the ranks at the agency, she was simultaneously becoming known in public relations circles and in the community. In 1961, she took on the responsibility of planning and coordinating the Publicity Club's 20th Anniversary Dinner for more than three hundred attendees. Little did she know at the time that she would be honored that evening with the Pub-Clubber Award, which was awarded to the single most valued Club member of the year. According to the group's newsletter, Plank received a standing ovation when it was announced she was the award's recipient. Typical for the Publicity Club events, the night's entertainment "consisted of five skits, 'Astro-Naughties of 1961,' which satirized the moods, methods and mores of publicity and public relations.'"[24]

Having been a performer for most of her life, Plank loved writing and producing the skits and songs for the Publicity Club's annual dinners, which were elaborate affairs. One such show that she and another member wrote, produced, and directed included skits on Vietnam, the Peace Corps, Automation, and President Johnson's War on Poverty. In typical Plank fashion, she orchestrated every aspect of the dinner and show. In a letter to her "cast" before the big night, she described what they could expect. "At some point in Friday's festivities, the nomination adventure of Peak for President will commence. In 'place' will be Herb Bain at the piano, Bruce Butterfield at the guitar. . . . Pat Foley will be the 'assistant' and 'escorter' on the platform. At every possible 'punctuation point,' Bruce and Herb should make musical chords—in addition to accompanying the two campaign songs," she wrote. She went on to say that the nominators would find on the platform, "Derby hats awaiting you. Please put them on. (If anyone feels like smoking a cigar, please do)." The General Campaign Song would then be sung by everyone. "We may try to march around the room (led by Pat), as kind of a high-stepping Majorette. Hope all goes well . . . Be loud, rowdy, political—and cheer a lot for our candidate!"[25]

In the fall of 1961, Plank became chair of the Publicity Club's admissions committee, which was charged with vetting applicants and making recommendations about their membership to the Board. Following a luncheon meeting not long after, as she and fellow practitioner Herbert Bain were walking back to their offices, Bain suggested that Plank run for president of the Club. She thought he was being absurd. "They would never consider having a woman president of this important organization," she said. But Bain insisted that he and others in the group saw her as the ideal candidate. And by the next summer, Plank was sitting on the beach in Michigan looking at the Club's by-laws because she was to become its vice-president that fall and president the following year.[26]

The Publicity Club's response to Plank's presidency suggests that its membership was satisfied with the job she did. At the end of each president's year, the Club toasted the person with a Past President's Dinner complete with skits and a song in the person's honor. Plank's song was sung to the tune of "These Foolish Things":

We found a girl we wanted for our leader
We finally made her see how much we need her
To Betsy Ann we sing
She's everything
We've wanted for years

We love the way she handles all our troubles
She punctures them as if they're just air bubbles

To Betsy Ann we sing
She's everything
We've wanted for years

She's firm, (ask Sherm) she gets her way!
But when she smiles at you
You know just what you're going to do

For P.C.C., our Betsy is a winner
We always knew she really had it in her
So here's to our Betsy Ann
She's no mere man
Let's give her our cheers[27]

The traits highlighted in the lyrics—her ability to handle problems and solve them by seeing through the details and cutting to the chase; and her ability to always get her own way, not by cajoling or browbeating people into submission, but through subtle persuasion, by getting them to do willingly what she wanted or needed done—would remain important components of her leadership style for the rest of her life.

Because "the sky did not fall" when Plank took office, her presidency proved to be an important milestone for women in public relations. Her success in the position gave permission to other public relations associations in Chicago to take a chance on women in leadership roles. It certainly allowed others to take a chance on her. During her tenure as the Publicity Club's president, Plank was elected to the executive committee of the Welfare Public Relations Forum, a group consisting of individuals in private and public agencies who were concerned with the study and improvement of "educational, public relations, and fundraising programs and techniques" used in the field of public welfare.[28] She served as chair of the Forum's Committee of Judges and its Program Chair before becoming the organization's president two years later. Two years after that, in 1968, she became the first woman president of the Chicago Chapter of the Public Relations Society of America. As she had with the other associations to which she belonged, she worked her way up in PRSA at the chapter and national level after she joined in 1958, establishing herself as an indispensable worker.

Her dedication to PRSA was rewarded in 1972, when she was tapped to chair its newly created national Education and Research Council. She and the Council's eleven members, all men, were charged with looking at PRSA's "cradle to grave requirements," including the student organization, the accreditation of college courses, and the Society's own internal professional advancement program.[29]

A LATENT FEMINIST

Although Plank was blazing trails for women within public relations associations in the 1960s, she did not set out to do so. In fact, she was careful not to publicly promote a feminist agenda. She rarely spoke about being a woman in public relations, even as she became a sought-after speaker, instead opting to keep her speech topics gender neutral. She knew that business was still a man's world, and not everyone was used to women in positions of leadership or happy about it.

In one instance, she was described as a "secretary" in a *Chicago Tribune* column titled "White Collar Girl," even though her real title—vice president of the Ronald Goodman Public Relations firm—suggested otherwise. And when she was first promoted to executive vice president at Edelman, Dan Edelman defended that decision to a client, arguing that she was deserving of the position because she had "demonstrated impressive capabilities in creativity, writing skill, account planning and management."[30] Plank wasted no energy on such discriminatory attitudes. She just put her head down and continued to work hard as usual.

In that regard, Plank was different from some of her female contemporaries, many of whom became part of the National Organization for Women (NOW), established in 1966 to form an "NAACP for women." The group was fueled in part by frustration that women were still barred from equal employment and higher education opportunities despite Title VII of the Civil Rights Act of 1964 prohibiting discrimination on the basis of sex. Despite Plank's stated desire after college for an "activist" lifestyle, championing the cause of women was not, apparently, something she was interested in doing. Even as late as 1977, Plank proudly proclaimed that she didn't belong to any women's groups.[31]

When asked by a *Chicago Sun-Times* reporter in 1965 to comment for a story on the treatment of women executives in the city, Plank experienced a "whole tide of impressions." Coming to mind were the raised eyebrows at

initial client meetings when they saw her enter the room; "constant struggles within [Edelman] to bring salaries of women account executives up to
a comparable level with men"; and frustration at not being able to assign
women to certain accounts because they were "unsuited" for them. But
as the reporter began her questions, Plank found "the answers weren't as
ready" as she had assumed they would be and that "prompted a very curious
and interesting" reaction from Plank. For the first time, she stopped to
really think about her experiences. Some of her conclusions surprised her.[32]

She acknowledged that discrimination did exist, even in public relations,
which was more receptive and open to women than other professions. But
complaining about the situation, she wrote, "seems to me to be a need-
less waste of energy and time; today's executive—whatever the gender—
doesn't have much of either to spare." Discrimination was both unfair to
the woman and unfortunate for the organization, robbing the latter of
"talent and experience." But she understood it. "The skirted executive is
still a novelty; like it or not, she's still on trial in business. The burden of
proof—for performance, for ability to sell ideas and motivate people—rests
with her. If this often requires tact, sensitivity, emotional self-discipline,
and understanding, why should she resent the challenge? Those qualities are
well worth nurturing, both in business and in personal life."[33]

Plank admitted that she had faced discrimination and that some doors
were closed to her because of her gender, but being an optimist, she focused
instead on the doors that had opened. After all, it was her choice to enter the
man's world of business. "It's up to me to earn the respect of the men—and
women—with whom I work," she wrote. She also recognized that while it
was courageous for women to fight the good fight, it was just as courageous
for managements to take a chance on women. Until courage was no longer
needed, she suggested women executives should keep their sense of humor
about "1) long distance operators who insist that you 'put your party (male,
of course) on the phone'; 2) the airlines' 'executive flights' which literally
translate 'for men only'; and 3) the classic myths that all women have exclusive claims to emotional outbursts, gossiping, and chronic illness."[34]

Plank might have been called a "latent feminist," as one managerial
woman described herself in 1976. "I believed in the essence of feminism all
along, but I had failed to recognize it within myself," Marcille Gray Williams
wrote. "I arrogantly felt that I did not need the feminist movement for I had
made it on my own." Plank appears to have felt the same way. She did not
understand what all the fuss was about. She had worked hard and had gotten

ahead; nothing was stopping other women from doing the same. But as the women's liberation movement gained traction in the late 1960s and early 1970s, Plank became more conscious of how she and other women were treated. By then she found less humor in a flight attendant offering the men copies of *Business Week* and *Forbes* and her, the *Ladies Home Journal*, after she had "just lugged two briefcases of paperwork aboard."[35]

Still, only three of the seven organizations Plank belonged to in the 1960s can be considered women-centric: the Girl Scouts of America, the YWCA, and the American Women in Radio and Television Association. Plank had been a Girl Scout as a young child and, as she once noted, would be until the day she died. But she hadn't given much thought to the organization as an adult until she went to work for Mitchell McKeown in the 1950s and the Girl Scouts of Chicago became one of her clients. After volunteering on several of the organization's committees, Plank was asked to serve on the chapter's board in 1968. She would ultimately serve on the board of the Girl Scouts of America as well. Around the same time, she also became a board member of the YWCA in Chicago and served in that capacity for five years.

Similarly, in 1966, Plank was chair of the East Central Area Conference for the American Women in Radio and Television Association (AWRT), which was formed in 1951 in reaction to the National Association of Broadcasters' decision to dissolve its women's division. Schwartz was a member of the AWRT when it made the transition to an independent entity and recruited Plank to the organization.

COMMUNITY WORK

More typically, Plank's community service activities, such as her work on behalf of the Association House of Chicago, involved broader societal issues than gender discrimination. Originally conceived as a "port of entry" for new immigrants from Eastern Europe in the early 1900s, Association House had tailored its services over the years to meet the needs of the changing immigrant population. By the time Plank became the president of its board in the late 1960s, the organization served more than forty-five thousand individuals from twenty-four nations and ethnic groups. It provided English classes, tutoring, and programs for senior citizens. It also worked with teenage gangs and school dropouts, and counseled families.[36]

At about the same time, Plank served on the communications committee of the Presbytery of Chicago. Plank had been active in the Fourth

Presbyterian Church since her arrival in the city, teaching eleven-year-olds Sunday school and serving on the church's Christian Education Committee. It was not surprising that the Chicago Presbytery recognized her public relations expertise and asked her to serve on its communications committee. She could not have anticipated that she would need to use her skills to help handle the Presbytery's public relations efforts surrounding the controversial "trial" of the Rev. John Fry, however. Fry, who was white, had become the center of national attention when the Senate Permanent Investigating Subcommittee held hearings into the activities of Chicago's Blackstone Rangers, a Black gang.[37]

By 1968, thousands of young men in the city identified themselves as part of the Rangers. But an ensuing gang war between them and a rival gang, made it "unsafe for man, woman, or child to be on the streets after five in the afternoon."[38] According to Fry, the Chicago police for the most part ignored the Black-on-Black violence in the area. As a result, Fry began working with the Rangers, allowing the young men to use the Church's gymnasium for some of their activities, and bailing them out of jail after several were arrested on what Fry considered trumped-up charges. They were decisions he would come to regret.[39]

One of the Rangers told authorities that Fry's Church was being used as "an arsenal for the Rangers to store their guns and a place where they sold and smoked marijuana, had sexual activity, and held their secret gang meetings."[40] Because a nonprofit organization had received a government grant of nearly $1 million to work with the Rangers to reduce the violence, a Senate investigation into the affair was conducted, during which a former member of the Rangers testified that Fry knew what was going on and had even advised them to start extorting merchants in the area.

To save its reputation, the Presbytery of Chicago conducted its own investigation, releasing the results in a 227-page report that ultimately cleared Fry of "charges of illegal, immoral, and improper conduct in relation to his work with the [Blackstone Rangers]." Plank handled the media relations involved in publicizing the report, including sending out news releases and organizing a news conference, at which Fry and two senior clergymen challenged the allegations and questioned how the Senate hearing was being conducted. The media coverage of the report and news conference was generally positive with articles appearing in the *Chicago Tribune, New York Times, Washington Post, Wall Street Journal,* and even the *Los Angeles Times.*[41]

MARCHING TO MONTGOMERY

As a racial issue, the Blackstone affair was relatively mild in comparison to what was happening in the South, however. Along with most Americans, Plank watched in horror at the scenes coming into her living room via the nightly news--African-American children blasted with fire hoses and attacked by police dogs in Birmingham, and marchers beaten crossing the Edmund Pettus bridge in Selma. Plank had left the South when she was just a child; yet, she always thought of herself as a Southerner. Thus, these scenes held special meaning for her. They were coming from her South, her Alabama, her people. On impulse, she headed to Selma, making it in time to join the final leg of the 1965 march to Montgomery. She would be the first to acknowledge that sometimes her impulsiveness got her into trouble, but this time she did not regret her actions. In fact, it is one of the things of which she was proudest. And she did it because she believed it was the right thing for a Southerner to do, heeding Dr. Martin Luther King, Jr.'s warning that "A man dies when he refuses to stand up for that which is right. A man dies when he refuses to stand up for justice. A man dies when he refuses to take a stand for that which is true."[42]

But as a Southerner, Plank did not question her own role in the perpetuation of systemic racism. Her mother's family was deeply entrenched in the segregated and racist culture of the Old and New South. Her great-great-grandfather became a wealthy landowner in Alabama on the backs of slaves. His son, who was her grandmother Annie's father, fought for the Confederacy in the Civil War. Annie herself was born just seven years after the war and was tended to by Black servants for most of her life. And then there was Plank's Aunt Adelyne who performed in blackface into the 1940s and displayed the paternalistic attitude toward African Americans that was prevalent in the South in the early twentieth century. Adelyne claimed she knew African Americans because she had lived among and worked with them all her life and that they were made of "religion and love and a great room for happiness." A Northerner described Adelyne as loving "them in the real old-time down-south way." Adelyne even wrote letters to Plank in character as Aunt Caroline, her radio alter ego.[43]

As a teenager and into her early twenties, it does not appear that Plank ever challenged her aunt's racism. In fact, she and her mother both loved the Aunt Caroline show, as did most whites in Pittsburgh at the time. Plank certainly came to be concerned about civil rights in the 1960s, but she did nothing specific to support racial diversity in public relations. The field was predominantly white, as were most professions in the 1950s and 1960s. Just as she did not "see" gender discrimination in the workplace, she did not recognize race discrimination either. She helped women and people of color alike get established in the profession, but on an individual basis. It appears that the first time she talked about racial diversity as a systemic issue in public relations was in 1991 when she was asked to participate in a panel on "Diversity in the Workplace." As Plank always did, she threw herself into the literature on the topic, concluding that the answer to the question of diversity's worth to public relations is: "it's worth plenty."[44] Even with that knowledge, however, she did not use her influence at PRSA to promote greater diversity in the profession's ranks.

Reflecting years later on the experience of joining the Selma-to-Montgomery march, Plank contemplated what might have been had she not found public relations. "I have a feeling because I was concerned about civil rights and I'm a native Southerner and cared very much about that whole issue and it's [sic] many facets, I probably would have been a writer and a troublemaker in some respect."[45] Given her failure to take on an activist role in the sixties with respect to either gender or racial issues, her comment probably came with the benefit of hindsight and perhaps wishful thinking for what might have or could have been.

FACING THE INEVITABLE

Despite her successes personally and professionally during the 1960s, Plank was beginning to question her worth in Edelman's eyes. It was true that Edelman had treated her well and had rewarded her for her contributions to the firm. She was, after all, executive vice president. And yet, she felt dissatisfied and realized her growth within the agency had its limits. In fact, she had "'heard it' [from Edelman] in so many discussions and actions that I could no longer deny it to myself." Leaving was becoming "inevitable." In 1968, when she first began to face up to the reality of it all, she put a handwritten calendar on her bulletin board. For five years, she crossed off the days, one-by-one, then the weeks, which turned into years, knowing that eventually, the end would come.[46]

When the "end" did come, it was in the form of an offer from AT&T. Paul Lund, vice president of public relations and employee communications at AT&T, and Plank had crossed paths over the years on community service projects. At one meeting over lunch, Lund made a business proposition to Plank. He wanted her to come over to the client side and join AT&T. Intrigued by the offer, she visited the company's headquarters in New York and saw firsthand the positive energy generated around the Bell system in the early 1970s. She would later say that Lund "was a great salesman and difficult to say no to."[47] That no doubt was true, but the offer also came at a time when Plank was reaching her limit with Edelman.

In reflecting on why she should leave the agency, Plank made a list of reasons:

"No place to go at DJE; Dan's 'clutching it all.'"

"Frustration at not being able to move the mountain sufficiently to institutionalize the business."

"Constantly being a 'what have you done for me lately' situation; risk of coming to point-of-no-return, i.e., it was really a question of Dan's choosing or yours, so better yours."

"Lack of security; questionable financial position of firm with no measures being taken to improve it. Slow personal financial growth— bypassed erratically by men."

"Prospect of practicing p.r. [sic] always 'the same as before': nothing much new or learning or mind-stretching."

"Constant pressure and responsibility without much authority which really counts."

"Not much progress for firm or self no matter whether you worked 24 hours a day, i.e., weariness without much satisfaction or appreciation or light at the end of the tunnel."[48]

Still, leaving was not an easy decision for her. Plank was proud of the Edelman agency, proud to be part of it, and proud of the work she had done there. At the same time, she knew the end had come. In her August 1973 resignation letter to Edelman, she told him she would be leaving to join AT&T, an announcement that must have stunned him. The deal had been finalized that morning, she wrote. She hadn't told him earlier because "to have done so would have implied a threat or a challenge to negotiate. That would have been a totally incorrect inference. I believe you know me well enough to realize that I have not—nor would I ever—make any demands on you under pressure." That was, she said, a "lifelong personal principle."[49]

Subtle things over the years had finally confirmed for her that she and Edelman did not share the same viewpoint about her future with the firm.

She hoped he could understand "why I finally cannot continue to accept and live and work within a limitation which no amount of work and commitment on my part could ever change. That would begin to erode my self-respect. I could not let this happen for myself, for you, or for this firm."[50] In contrast, AT&T offered her the chance to grow professionally and financially, and to find fulfillment. That she was almost fifty years old was also not lost on her. The time she had left to make a major life change was narrowing.

At first, Edelman thought Plank was just overworked and needed some time to reconsider. He had received a letter from her assistant begging him not to accept the resignation. She was convinced Plank's decision was based on mental fatigue from serving as PRSA national chair while maintaining her position at Edelman, and that Plank would change her mind once her tenure at PRSA came to an end and everything settled down. Plank was sincerely touched by her assistant's concern but reiterated to Edelman that her decision had been five years in the making. It was not one she had made lightly or quickly.[51]

At the same time, Plank wanted to leave on good terms and worked with Edelman to decide on when best to announce publicly her resignation. The timing and tone of the message would be tricky because another senior executive, Thomas Harris, had recently left the firm for a second time. Harris was executive vice president when he left the first time in 1966, at which time Plank assumed his position. But in February 1973, Harris had rejoined the agency, this time alongside Plank as an executive VP. Edelman's response to Harris' return had confirmed Plank's belief that it was time for her to go. But now, just six months later, they were both leaving; Harris for the second time.[52] She was sensitive to how that would look to outsiders. She did not want anyone to think the firm had issues internally.

Originally, Edelman and Plank planned to release the news in late September, but people were already beginning to talk. To stop the rumor mill and to maintain relationships with both her new and old employer, Plank suggested they move up the date and bring AT&T in on the plans. "The fact that I'm going to a corporation, not another agency, and not another firm in Chicago, can help cool the situation if it's handled forthrightly. In any case, if the question should arise, we all should be in sync on the comments so that the truth of mutual good grace is projected" she wrote to Edelman.[53]

Plank even challenged Edelman on the wording of his announcement to the staff. She was disturbed that his draft memo made it sound like she was leaving because she could not practice the kind of public relations at the agency that she wanted to. She wrote, "On behalf of everything that's holy to me in this firm, please accept a deletion of the idea that it's 'there' but not 'here.' It is simply wrong to infer that people can't practice that kind of public relations here." It was just a question of making a move "to a fine corporation from a fine agency. . . both of which practice the best public relations."[54]

Despite Plank's protestations to Edelman about why she was leaving and what the wording implied, Edelman's statements were true to an extent. Edelman had built a successful public relations business assisting the marketing efforts of his clients. One only must look at the Toni Twins campaign to realize his genius in marketing public relations. A Plank contemporary at Edelman in the 1960s described the firm as "heavy in product publicity but light on counseling and issues communications."[55] It was this latter aspect of public relations that Plank enjoyed the most. For her, public relations was communication on behalf of organizations in the furtherance of democracy.

Of course, Plank recognized that public relations "sells," but she saw it as broader than simply the promotional arm of marketing. She acknowledged that product publicity was fundamental to the role of public relations in the marketing mix but viewing it as simply part of the publicity arm of marketing took a narrow view of public relations as a whole and relegated it to a subservient position.[56]

At a 1968 PRSA workshop, Plank argued that if marketing were viewed from the standpoint of the customer's self-interest rather than the company's, a new role for public relations would open up: Defining and understanding the interests of the audiences; identifying the product or service with those interests; and relaying that information to the marketing team. Of course, that inferred that public relations practitioners understood the audience. And she questioned whether they did. The "mass market" no longer existed after all; it had become fragmented. "There is the burgeoning youth market—some 92 million Americans under 25 revolutionizing our attitudes and values . . . the Negro market . . . the ethnic market . . . older people, living longer, approaching older years with entirely new goals . . . the education market . . . the medical community and countless other opinion leader groups."[57]

In a paragraph from her speech that sounds presciently modern, she wrote about the other factors within marketing public relations that needed to be researched:

> the Knowledge Explosion—can you present your product or service within the context of the expanding desire to learn more—faster—better? . . . . Social Responsibility—can we identify with larger national concerns, social values, public problems and solutions. Are your industrial products being used, for example, to help solve housing or transportation or pollution problems? Your food products—what are they doing to solve some of the problems of nutrition? Cosmetics and clothing—what about good grooming aids for inner city youth?[58]

What Plank was proposing was that marketing public relations should focus on concepts rather than products or services. For example, one of her clients at Edelman was in the business of overhead projectors and wanted to sell projectors to educators for classroom use. Focusing on the self-interest of educators, the theme became "creative teaching." Teachers themselves were encouraged to submit ideas on how they could use overhead projectors as a tool in their classroom to foster learning. The result of such conceptual positioning, identifying the product or service with the targets' self-interest, was that it led to highly successful marketing programs. But more importantly, according to Plank, it secured public relations a place in the marketing mix. Instead of simply playing a supporting role to advertising, public relations would assist marketing by sensing, analyzing, interpreting, and influencing consumers. The job of public relations practitioners within the marketing sphere was "to position our products and services within the context of consumer interest—and it is to this objective that we must constantly direct our professional attention, our study, imagination and creativity—and our persuasiveness with management."[59]

Plank had always been more concerned about the conceptual approach, as she called it in this speech, than with selling products or services. She wanted to help people live better lives, and she believed that public relations was especially suited to such a role. Thus, when given the chance to move to a company that was known for its community relations and social responsibility, she could not say no. It was closer to her heart and to her understanding of the value of public relations than was marketing public relations.

The 1960s had shown Plank to be a public relations leader. She had risen to executive vice president of the Edelman agency and had managed its successful expansion throughout the United States and overseas. She was active in the Chicago community and had broken barriers by being elected president of the Publicity Club and of Chicago's PRSA chapter, among other associations. For her, public relations leadership meant listening to others, sketching out various scenarios, deciding on the best course of action, and then rolling up one's sleeves and going to work.[60] Her professional experiences had given her a quiet confidence in her ability to get things done and done well.

Although letters in support of honors and awards tend to be highly complementary and their sources should be considered, Edelman's own words perhaps sum up Plank's leadership style at this time best. His letter, supporting Schwartz's nomination of Plank for Chicago's Ad Woman of the Year in 1968, described Plank as having "an uncanny ability to lead you to a decision yourself, and she rarely, rarely tells you point blank that 'this is wrong.'" She, on the other hand, was quick to admit when she was wrong, but she also would not back down if she believed the decision was the correct one. The letter went on to say that standing up for what you believe is right even in the face of opposition, "can make life lonely sometimes," but in Betsy's case, "it also contributes to the growth and development of the people she works with."[61]

Here he repeats themes contained in the Publicity Club song lyrics about Plank, such as her ability to quietly lead people to the decision she wants, and reflects other themes that would emerge in later years, for example her refusal to back down even if it meant being on the unpopular side of a decision. All of these suggest the development of a servant leadership style with its emphasis on the development of others.

In the memo that Edelman finally sent to the staff, he announced with "deep personal regret" that Plank would be leaving, describing her as "an invaluable member" of the firm. "Her great strength of character, integrity, loyalty, conscientiousness, good judgment, and her outstanding professional skills will certainly be missed."[62] And no doubt they were.

CHAPTER 4

Leading by Example

Our goal is not to be loved, or liked, or necessarily admired, but to be respected. (The rest may come in time.)
—Betsy Ann Plank

AS PLANK WAS ending her time at Edelman in the fall of 1973, she was also winding down her tenure as chair of the Public Relations Society of America. It had been a somewhat turbulent and eventful year for Plank, but one that came to define her as a leader.

TURBULENT TIMES

Plank's ascendance to the height of PRSA's leadership began on a hot summer day in 1972, when she ran into George Hammond at Chicago's O'Hare Airport. Hammond, the chairman of New York's Carl Byoir Public Relations Agency, had been president of PRSA in 1969, the year Plank was president of the Chicago Chapter. Much as Herbert Bain had done ten years earlier with respect to the Publicity Club, Hammond asked Plank if she would consider running for the national PRSA presidency. Flattered and honored, Plank was quick to say yes but privately had her doubts it would ever happen. If elected, she would become the first woman to lead the Society in its twenty-five-year history.[1] She wrote her father both the good news—she had been nominated—and the bad—it might never come to fruition because of her gender.

Despite advances made in the 1960s, women still faced discrimination in the workplace. Taking its cue from the civil rights movement and the Vietnam War protests, a rejuvenated women's movement found its footing and gained traction in the 1970s. The activism, and often radicalism, of the movement took many men, and some women, by surprise. The National Organization for Women, formed by Betty Friedan, was already four years old, but the 1970s seemed to usher in a new militancy captured perfectly by the refrain "I am woman; hear me roar." The Women's Strike for Equality came at the beginning of the decade, as did the publication of Kate Millet's *Sexual Politics* and Robin Morgan's *Sisterhood is Powerful*, both consciousness-raising and controversial feminist treatises. The organization of the National Women's Political Caucus followed in 1971 and the Coalition of Labor Union Women in 1974. In 1973, the year Plank became chair of PRSA, the Equal Rights Amendment was finally ratified and the U.S. Supreme Court constitutionalized abortion with its *Roe v. Wade* decision. The timing was right for a woman to lead PRSA, but that would still require, as a male Equal Employment Opportunity director put it about women leaders in general at the time, "a man in her life who believed it's the right thing to do," a sentiment Plank herself had expressed several years before.[2]

As for her father, he hoped her "qualms about being a woman in a man's organization were unfounded." But, he continued, "I wouldn't worry about it if I were you. In this day of Women's lib, yes, there is a natural hostility or resentment among the male of the species but that is attributable to the militancy of the female when it occurs and certainly you are not militant as far as your friends and associates are concerned."[3] Her father was correct; Plank was not militant when it came to gender. In fact, it was her apparent lack of feminist awareness that helped propel her to success and allowed Hammond, the chair of PRSA's Nominating Committee, to assure her the Committee's recommendation would be accepted despite her "qualms."

To prepare herself for the daunting task of taking on the presidency, she sent a letter to each of the living PRSA past presidents seeking their advice. She knew they would appreciate the "mixed emotions" of "anticipation and trepidation" she felt on the eve of her administration if elected. Plank recognized that they were uniquely situated, having been president, to provide her with wise counsel. Thus, she sought their advice about what the president should do first, the pitfalls to avoid, the issues needing attention, what they saw as the overall priorities for PRSA, and finally their vision for the Society. In short, she wanted to know, "if you had it to do all over again—today—what would you do—or avoid?" Concluding, she wrote that she hoped to contribute as much as she was capable of—"and even beyond my limitations, God willing."[4]

Plank received a number of responses to her letter, but not as many as she had hoped. Several told her they would think about it and get back to her but never did. Averell Broughton, PRSA's second president, was one who did write, giving her insight into the early political machinations of PRSA. Broughton did not know her personally, being of advanced age by this time. But from her letter, he determined her to be a "naïve optimist" and recommended that she get a copy of his 1943 book, *Careers in Public Relations: The New Profession*, because "the answers are all there," even though the book was, by this point, thirty years old, and Plank had been in the profession for nearly as long. Regardless, he used the opportunity to set the record straight. He informed her that he was the first, not the second, president and that Virgil Rankin, the first president according to PRSA, was "a phony . . . a tinhorn . . . who wrangled the title of president." According to Broughton, he fired Rankin, who "was in fact the Paid Secretary [sic]." But much to Broughton's dismay, he could "never destroy the myth" of Rankin's presidency. Plank was probably rid of Milton Fairman though, which, in Broughton's mind, was a good thing. "He was hard luck for the Society." Regardless, he wished her the best because she sounded "fine and vulnerable," which was "so much the better."[5]

Others provided more sage advice although all tended to take advantage of her sympathetic ear to pontificate about the sorry state of the profession and/or the association. Dan Forrestal, the 1957 president and former corporate public relations executive of Monsanto Chemical, wrote that he was "nauseated by PR people who say they're engineers of consent, guardians of morality, insurers of justice, 'saviors' of the free enterprise system, moudlers [sic] of men's minds and choreographers of corporate behavior. . . . All this mountaintop language is especially silly when I know many of the ballroom orators can't even make a small dent in the attitudes of their own managements!" In closing, he advised her to get PRSA back on track and reassure its members; to identify public relations with business objectives; and above all to be herself. "Be Betsy Ann Plank and you'll be great," he wrote. The Old Guard have had their chance. "It's the new batter in the box who best knows how to hit the booming home run under today's circumstances."[6]

J. Carroll Bateman of the Insurance Information Institute, who served as PRSA president in 1967 and co-founded the Public Relations Student Society of America, responded that he believed the most important function of the association was professional development through the educational process, a sentiment he had outlined in a column for the association's *Public*

Relations Journal. The column, which he included for Plank's information, was supposed to be a review of the book, *Mass Media in the Marketplace.* But rather than writing a traditional book review, Bateman discussed instead a question that had long been on his mind: "What are the characteristic activities of a truly professional society?" He wondered whether PRSA bothered to engage in such activities anymore and for that matter, whether its membership even cared. The roughly seven thousand members were at a crossroads and needed to decide whether to go up "to a meaningful level of professionalism—or down, to a level of innocuous and aimless activity leading perhaps to dissolution."[7] Bateman's musings fit with Plank's own evolving sense of PRSA and the future of public relations.

Bateman was not alone in questioning the role of PRSA in the early 1970s. When the Society was originally established in 1948, its emphasis was on professionalism, but that focus was soon challenged as the postwar economic boom created a demand for practitioners. The result was a flood of untrained and unqualified individuals offering public relations services. How best to deal with this issue created fissures within the Society's membership. Some saw PRSA's role as providing professional development to those who had entered the field unprepared; others thought that doing so meant an abdication of the Society's focus on senior practitioners and professionalism.

At the same time, American society was experiencing seismic shifts resulting from the civil rights, women's, environmental (then called conservation), and consumer movements. With new publics gaining influence on what seemed like a daily basis, the organizational need for public relations was great, but the profession did not appear to be up to the challenge.

For most of the 1950s, public relations had supported marketing. As Plank described it, "Those were halcyon days of product publicity—primarily through the mass media, which was being fueled by a miracle called television." But as the economy grew, so did the demands on public relations as the concept of "publics" expanded. In 1956, the number of white-collar workers exceeded the number of blue-collar workers in the United States for the first time. Sixty percent of Americans were now in the middle-class, up from thirty-one percent before the Great Depression. This spreading of the wealth brought an increased democratization of the stock market among other things. The term "stockholders" now included not only traditional financial players, but also individuals holding stock for the first time, requiring a change in what and how corporations communicated to their shareholders. Thus, financial relations was added to the public relations purview.[8]

The unrest of the 1960s and early 1970s brought even greater change to public relations and with it, greater responsibility. Businesses were being drawn into the social turmoil often unwittingly. As one CEO said, "I don't understand it. I'm doing the very same things now that I did in the early 1960s. Yet, then, I was applauded as an enlightened and progressive business statesman; now I'm vilified as a stubborn defender of the status quo." The difference, of course, was that the environment in which businesses operated had changed radically. Sit-ins and protests could thrust a company into the national spotlight and not in a good way. The initial reaction of business to it all "has been one of indignation and no little paranoia—sort of a plaintive 'Here I am folks, still that same, giant-sized lovable rubber ducky you once loved,'" as Plank put it in a 1977 speech.[9]

Many of those companies looked to public relations for help, which meant public relations practitioners could no longer be "simply the firefighters and purveyors of 'good news'—new products and new services, expansions and acquisitions and growth." Suddenly, they were expected to anticipate new threats and opportunities, evaluate situations, and strategize how best to minimize the potential damage to their clients' reputations.[10] It meant a dramatic leap forward for the still-fledgling profession. The question was whether the field could handle the responsibility and realistically address what appeared, to many, to be the disintegration of American civil society.

In some ways, it all seemed to culminate in Watergate, a symbolic changing of the guard. It was a dark time in American politics, and unfortunately, public relations found itself at the front and center of it. President Nixon had surrounded himself with campaign strategists and aides who were sharp and slick and fresh from Madison Avenue with backgrounds in advertising and marketing, not public relations. In fact, the only Nixon aide who understood public relations was Herbert G. Klein, who served as director of the Office of Communications, although he was quickly discredited and pushed aside by the rest of the President's inner circle.[11] But in the media's eyes, and therefore the public's, it was all public relations. Thanks to Watergate, people equated public relations with an "ends justify the means" kind of profession.

BECOMING CHAIR

Thus, Plank came to power at a critical juncture for public relations and PRSA. The discontent among the Society's members had escalated to a near revolt with the membership about evenly divided "between those who were hot to storm the palace and those who had given up on the Society's future." Young practitioners held negative attitudes toward PRSA. One described it as a "worthless, self-serving, hollow and purposeless" organization; another as "a do-nothing group."[12] PRSA just did not seem capable of dealing with a field that was changing all too quickly.

To make matters worse, corporate communicators had made little head-way convincing chief executive officers that their skills were needed to help businesses deal with the societal change. In a survey of 810 CEOs of com-panies with more than one thousand employees, 86 percent said the head of public relations did not report directly to the CEO. Only 21 percent thought the CEO should share more corporate information with the public relations department, and a full 46 percent of the respondents said their company's public relations program was "significantly worse" than their competitors.[13]

It all weighed heavily on practitioners. A 1972 survey of some 354 prac-titioners revealed that they suffered "from strong feelings of inadequacy." As individuals and professionals, they took a great deal of pride and satisfaction in their work, but 84 percent were convinced "the outside world frowns upon our occupation." And a whopping 98 percent felt that "most people do not understand what public relations is." For the author of the study, the results indicated that "PR people have very mixed emotions about them-selves and do a great deal of professional soul searching."[14] It was not a time for the faint of heart, but perfect timing for Plank with her strong ethical compass and her passion for public relations.

When addressing her constituency for the first time as chair-elect, Plank zeroed in on the identity crisis public relations was facing. "Our conven-tional wisdom is being challenged. Where, for example, was our touted two-way channel of communication when the turbulence of the late sixties erupted? Where today is our research that accurately delineates public opin-ion and anticipates trends?" she asked rhetorically. Public relations practi-tioners were no longer invisible, able to hide behind their organizations and clients. "Our management knows we're there. The media know we're there. So does the increasingly sophisticated consumer and the public."[15]

Accountability was the new watchword for public relations. It was, she said, "the rapidity of change, the distemper of our times, and the impudent—and often successful—co-opting of communications by amateurs," that had caused the crisis of identity. The movements of the day, arising from discontent, had convinced management that public relations had an impact on the bottom line and that listening was as much a part of communication as was talking. Whether public relations practitioners answered the call to be "problem-solvers and not mere courters of management messages; to become professional in fact as well as in title," remained to be seen.[16]

Plank hoped PRSA could play a role in helping practitioners better cope with and take advantage of "the avalanche of contemporary problems—accelerating and affecting our total sense—our companies and organizations, our clients, our customers, constituencies and communities." Her goal for the year of her presidency was to strengthen the Society's professional development programs; further build its relationships with students and educators; expand dialogue with other associations and groups for shared learning and insights; and conduct public relations for public relations. With Plank's interest in education, professionalism, and ethics, she also put an emphasis on new membership. She wanted to reach out to those "whose basic tool was never a typewriter," recognizing the danger in individuals holding themselves out as practitioners when they did not understand the purpose or the practice of public relations. The result could be potentially devastating for the profession's reputation. It might not withstand another Watergate.[17]

In concluding, Plank affirmed her vision that PRSA had "an obligation to the human society we serve, in which we live and work. We must reach out in both directions—within our ranks and outside them—more vigorously, more often than before. . . . Our goal is not to be loved, or liked, or necessarily admired, but to be respected. (The rest may come in time.)"[18]

Once Plank officially assumed office as chair, she experienced a whirlwind of speaking engagements and meetings. She kept her word and promoted public relations and PRSA whenever and wherever she could, encouraging others to do likewise, to challenge those who painted public relations with a broad brush as the "Original Sin of Watergate." Those practitioners who did speak out in support of the profession, Plank dubbed the "Truth Squad." The result was favorable media coverage for public relations in the *New York Times* and other newspapers. Plank herself described Watergate as "no instant disaster"; it was simply a symptom of an erosion of credibility. She believed public relations could play a significant role in opening sources to the media and rebuilding that trust and credibility if its practitioners chose to do so.[19]

At the crux of Plank's thinking about public relations was her understanding of and belief in democracy. "A democratic society," she told the Pittsburgh PRSA Chapter in June 1973, "is based on consent and understanding, not secrecy and suppression—and the public's right and need to know is irrevocably linked to ethical behavior." She reiterated the sentiment in her year-end report to PRSA's membership. "In every case within the last six months, our spokesmen asserted head-on attacks against the maligning of public relations which occurred in the Watergate hearings—seeking to differentiate between the professional and amateur, the ethical and the unethical, and the professional, ethical practice represented by PRSA's 7,000 members."[20] It was a rallying cry for the troops who needed a reason to feel good about their chosen profession.

For Plank, ethics was not just a talking point; it was the essence of the practice. Always holding herself to the highest ethical standards, she found attacks questioning the ethics of public relations practitioners, especially PRSA members, particularly galling. While she was pleased with the ethical code and enforcement system PRSA had in place, she believed the code applied only to what she described as "felony" charges. She was convinced that many ethical violations were of a lesser category, occurring because the practitioner did not realize that what he or she was doing was unethical. But because the code did not provide for such "misdemeanor" charges, borderline violations went unchecked and uncorrected, making them seem acceptable. To address that problem, the PRSA Board of Directors in 1970 had given authority to the Grievance Board to warn practitioners engaged in such minor ethical lapses that "continuance of the performance in question could result in serious consequences," the most serious of which would be expulsion from the Society.[21]

Still not satisfied, Plank managed, "quietly, firmly," to expand "the policy to include other cases in which 'the importance of the matter was not proportionate to the time, money and effort required for a judicial hearing.'" In such cases, the Grievance Board could notify the practitioner of the alleged infraction and ask for an explanation. If the explanation warranted it, the matter could be dropped, but a note regarding the infraction would be

included in the member's file. Further infractions could result in a full investigation. Pleased with the added policy, Plank made sure the media were
aware of and understood what was happening. To that end, PRSA mailed
out seven hundred copies of its ethics standards to the media, even inviting
journalists to turn in violators. Even more importantly, Plank "backed it
all up by doing what had to be done in a situation when lesser 'men' might
have chosen a personally safer course."[22] In her case, that safer course would
have meant not taking on Theodore Pincus.

A MATTER OF ETHICS

The Pincus affair began innocently enough. On a Friday in July, halfway
through her presidency, Plank received a letter from Pincus addressed to
her in her capacity as the PRSA chair in which he submitted his resignation
from the Society. Pincus was the president of the Financial Relations Board
(FRB), one of the largest financial relations agencies in the country with a
staff of sixty-three and a reported net income of $1.8 million in the early
1970s. In the letter, Pincus told Plank that the PRSA Grievance Board had
brought a complaint against him alleging ethical violations, but that he had
no knowledge of the circumstances leading to the complaint. The matters
had been handled by other practitioners in his agency, none of whom were
PRSA members and over whom the Society had no power. He claimed
that as a result he was being singled out and persecuted by PRSA. To make
matters worse, in his eyes, the allegations were four years old, having long
been settled to the satisfaction of the Securities and Exchange Commission
following an investigation. According to Pincus, the firm had entered into
a consent agreement with the SEC rather than go through the time, effort,
and cost of fighting the charges.[23]

And now Pincus did not have the heart or money to fight the PRSA.
It would, he declared, cost him thousands of dollars to defend himself
against what he perceived as scurrilous allegations. The complaint was
so outrageous, he wrote, "that it serves only to dishonor the banner of
'professionalism' that PRSA aspires to wave, underscore the hypocrisy and
opportunism prevalent within our industry, and deceive those who still
harbor faith and respect for the organization."[24] He was convinced that
his competitors had conspired to bring him down, and that PRSA, to
prove it was serious about ethics, was a willing partner in the vendetta. It is
unclear from the letter exactly what he was asking of Plank, other than to

accept his resignation. But it would appear he at least wanted to state his innocence for the record and clear his name without going through PRSA's judicial process.

Having no knowledge of the situation, Plank immediately asked Rea Smith, PRSA's executive director, to fill her in on what he was talking about. Smith informed Plank that the first activity in the Pincus matter occurred after a *Wall Street Journal* article appeared three years earlier in March 1970. The article reported that Pincus's agency, FRB, had disseminated news releases on behalf of a client, U.N. Industries, that misrepresented information about U.N.'s acquisition of gas and oil leases in Texas. In the releases, U.N.'s assets were overstated by $80 million and its liabilities underreported by $5 million. FRB claimed the information in the news releases was supplied by the client, and it could not vouch for its accuracy. But, according to the *Wall Street Journal*, court records revealed that FRB failed to include in the releases negative information that U.N. Industries had provided to the agency. After reading the article, Smith forwarded it to PRSA's Grievance Board and the Society's attorney because the PRSA Code of Conduct at the time provided that a member "is obligated to use ordinary care to avoid dissemination of false or misleading information."[25]

The Grievance Board attempted to investigate the allegation but was stonewalled by Pincus who refused to cooperate. The case was finally set to move forward when a second allegation against FRB arose in a *Chicago Daily News* story. This time the client was the Pig N Whistle Corporation, but the situation was similar. Material facts were omitted and what had been disseminated to the public through news releases prepared and issued by FRB was misleading. In its defense, FRB argued that a member of its staff had written only two releases for the company during an eight-week relationship with the Pig N Whistle in 1969. For his part, Pincus claimed he did not know that the Pig N Whistle was controlled by a man who had been convicted of misapplication of federal funds nor that the company was fraudulently selling unregistered stock. At the heart of the case before the SEC was the liability of public relations practitioners: Were they simply conduits for information provided by the client, or did they bear some responsibility for verifying that information? According to the SEC, they were liable for the information they disseminated; FRB should have done independent research to establish the truth of the information provided to it by its client before releasing it to the media.[26]

The Grievance Board decided to look into the second case before making any final recommendations with regard to the first and did so in earnest in early 1972, after the SEC announced a consent decree and final judgment on the Pig N Whistle charges. By May 1973, the Grievance Board was ready to proceed with the two cases, but then PRSA's attorney discovered yet a third case. The Grievance Board filed a formal complaint on all three counts with the chair of PRSA's Midwest Judicial District panel in June, and Pincus was advised of the action shortly thereafter.[27]

After learning the background, Plank asked PRSA's legal counsel for a summary of the charges against Pincus and for clarification of PRSA's and Pincus's legal rights. The attorney advised Plank that according to PRSA bylaws, only the chair could comment on behalf of the organization concerning a resignation while charges were pending.[28] That meant Plank was the batter in the box, and it was time for her to step up to the plate. Her options were to tell the membership about Pincus's resignation and that it came on the heels of an ethics violation, or to keep the whole thing confidential. The question was which course of action would be best for the Society, especially at this juncture in its history. Remaining true to her belief in the importance of ethics and professionalism, she opted for transparency.

Once Plank made her decision, she acted quickly, in part to counteract any preemptive strike by Pincus. First, she drafted a memo for advance distribution to her "VIP" list, which consisted of chapter presidents, Assembly delegates, district chairmen, past presidents/chairs, the PRSA Board, section chairmen, committee chairmen, and judicial district chairmen.[29] In the memo, she advised them that Pincus had resigned his membership while ethical charges against him were pending. Hating surprises herself, she wanted them, as the Society's leaders, to be advised in confidence and in advance of a memo that would go out to all members the following week apprising them of the situation.

It was not an easy decision to make. In fact, it was, she wrote to the VIPs, "probably the single most difficult position and decision which the Bylaws require of your Chairman alone." But given PRSA's and her own commitment to ethics, she felt a duty to advise the membership of this situation. She believed that she had "an obligation to do so in [sic] behalf of all those professional practitioners . . . , who, through PRSA membership, bind themselves personally to the Code, its practice and enforcement."[30] It saddened Plank that Pincus had opted to resign and thus remove himself from accountability under the Ethics Code, but at the same time, his actions irked her. To her, they represented the cavalier attitude toward ethics that she had been working hard to overcome.

In her subsequent memo to the general membership, Plank outlined the grievance procedure. Had Pincus not resigned, PRSA's Judicial Panel would have conducted a full and confidential hearing. Pincus would have had the opportunity to be represented by counsel, to present his case, to examine and cross-examine witnesses, and potentially to clear his name. The Judicial Panel's decision and recommendations would have been reviewed by the Board of Directors for final action. By resigning prior to the hearing, Pincus had chosen to remove himself from the grievance procedures outlined in the ethical code by which all PRSA members were bound. Plank then gave a summation of the charges against Pincus as laid out to her by PRSA's legal counsel and a recitation of the relevant section of the bylaws.[31]

The memo quickly drew praise and criticism. One woman wrote that Pincus's resignation pointed out just how helpless PRSA was in enforcing the basic standards of ethics. She acknowledged that the ability to solve that issue was probably illusory. But one could dream. After all, why not? "It couldn't happen to a better group at a better time with a better chairwoman!" Plank's boss, Dan Edelman, wrote to congratulate her, "Quite a tough letter re Pincus—well done, Madame Chairman." Another wrote, "This kind of leadership will go a long way in further increasing the standards of the society." The president of the Tulsa PRSA Chapter also sent his congratulations, "The buck stops with the top executive, and I know it isn't always easy, but digging your heels in and following the dictates of the rules, the regulations and your own good sense and integrity makes heroes out of people like you."[32]

Others were not as supportive. Perhaps not surprisingly, Sherwood Lee Wallace, the vice president of Pincus's firm, FRB, showed his solidarity with his employer by resigning his PRSA membership in response to Plank's memo. He believed that the allegations against Pincus amounted to a smear campaign "wrapped in unproved innuendos." And by failing to include a rebuttal from Pincus in her memo, Wallace asserted, Plank was being irresponsible. Another member suggested that the allegations against Pincus were "ancient history and the leakage on the charges was most reprehensible." Pincus was at the forefront of financial public relations, while PRSA had proved reluctant to change. The member went on to say that Pincus deserved "a public apology from the entire membership. . . . If I sound angry, I am."[33]

Plank had anticipated that Pincus would not go quietly after his resignation; it was probably one of the reasons she felt obligated to send a memo about it to the general membership. And she was right. Pincus sent copies of his original letter of resignation to several influential practitioners in response to her memo. Many who received it were among the ones who criticized her failure to include Pincus's side. For example, one practitioner wrote, "I do find Ted's letter impressive—and I suspect the totally fair way to have handled the situation might have been for you to have attached Ted's letter to yours of July 30th. Then all of us would have had both points of view. . . ." Some, however, viewed Pincus's letter differently: "PRSA for too long has avoided any confrontation, large or small. In essence, it has failed us all by being mediocre, lackluster, and gutless on issues like this one. It was beautiful to see you in there swinging hard for us. As I said, Ted's letter was a shocking editorial admission of his lack of judgment and proved your points perfectly."[34]

Pincus also sent copies of his letter to the trade publications, *Jack O'Dwyer's Newsletter* and *PR News*, both of which ran stories on the resignation. *O'Dwyer's* went into more depth on the original charges and Pincus's defense than did *PR News*, which opined that PRSA did not go far enough in enforcing its ethics code and questioned why no public announcement had been made by its officers, since the allegations impacted the public, not just Society members. *PR News* was concerned that if the case reached the media, which seemed likely given PRSA's reticence, the Society would have lost the opportunity "to serve as the initial and authoritative source of information about the case. Publicity could then be garbled or even unfavorable, rather than clear and constructive."[35] Of course, under PRSA's bylaws, Plank was not in a position to make a public announcement about the matter. It was a private affair between the Society and its membership.

Apparently Pincus did not receive the support he expected from those to whom he sent copies of his resignation letter. On August 22, almost a month after his original resignation letter, he sent an open letter to the general membership outlining what he saw as "an unfair and unwarranted attack" on him and his firm. By this point, some members were thinking that perhaps the man "doth protest too much." One wrote to him, copying Plank, "If you are the innocent lamb you claim to be, petition for

re-admission and demand a trial to clear the name of your firm. If you are
the man you think you are, . . . you will settle for no less. But this crying
towel postage is a waste of your money. Stand up or shut up." Another
wrote to Plank after reading both memos, "Ted's was the most asinine,
childish thing I've read in many years."[36]

For the most part, members were happy to see PRSA taking a stand
on an ethical issue, but at least some did not like what they saw as the
one-sided message sent out by the organization. They appreciated the association's efforts at transparency but questioned why Pincus' position was
also not provided. It seemed reasonable, but Plank had no authority under
the bylaws to disclose the contents of Pincus's resignation letter other than
to say that he had resigned. As she explained in a letter to Nicholas Egoroff,
who was a former executive vice president of FRB, Pincus had three options
pursuant to the PRSA Ethics Code.[37]

The first was to resign while the allegations were being investigated. Had
he done so, the matter would have been kept confidential by PRSA. The
second was to go through a hearing and present his side of the matter.
If exonerated, the issue would be closed and kept confidential. The third
option, and the one that Pincus chose, was to resign after the completion of
the investigation and formal charges had been made to the Judicial Board
but before the hearing. At that point, the PRSA chair could advise the
Society's members of the charges, and Pincus would be free to make public
statements on his own behalf.[38] Had Plank indicated Pincus's choices in
the memo to the members, she might have escaped some of the criticism.
Regardless, she weathered the storm and came out on the other side stronger and wiser for having taken a stand.

HER TENURE AS CHAIR

Handling the Pincus affair was not the only challenge Plank faced during her
tenure as PRSA chair. She considered getting the membership to approve
an increase in dues from $72 to $96 annually, despite "deep moaning and
groaning and dire predictions of massive member attrition," the toughest.[39]

At the end of her term, Plank was able to report to the Assembly delegates at the PRSA annual conference some success with and progress on
the objectives she had set out in her opening address to PRSA members
a year earlier. She did not stop there though. Breaking with tradition, she
also published her annual report in the PRSA newsletter for all members to

see, to remedy the lack of communication from the national office to the chapters, which she knew had been an issue in previous years. Providing the report to everyone rather than exclusively to the chapter leaders at the Assembly reinforced her conviction that the Society's leadership was accountable to all its members.

Plank was pleased to report that under her watch, the Society had used an organized approach for the first time to promote accreditation; had strengthened its relationship with the Association for Education in Journalism, an academic association of journalism and public relations educators; had established a new monthly newsletter and a yearbook to improve communication to members; and had worked on external relations, with national leaders making more than twenty speeches to major organizations. Plank acknowledged that the year had not been without its problems, but she believed the difficulties had been addressed "openly and candidly" and with "a new sense of purpose, perspective, and priorities." Still, "the expectations and demands which we and others have of us—individually and through our association—often exceed our reach. But we are stretching, and we are moving." Plank's commitment to showing the members that someone at the national level recognized their concerns and cared meant constant travel at the expense of her personal life. But the result was a renewed sense of purpose among members.[40]

Rea Smith, PRSA's executive director and the person with whom Plank worked most closely during her tenure as chair, summed up her impressions of the year in a letter to Plank. Smith, too, acknowledged that the year was one of "crises, turmoil and doubts." But there were also good things, namely Plank herself. "You were the 'good thing' that happened to PRSA. And for me, the 'good thing' was the privilege of being so close to your understanding leadership." Smith said the staff had been amazed by her boundless energy and ability to deal with everything that landed on her desk while still maintaining "a congenial attitude." They appreciated that despite everything, she remembered the personal things like "notes, personally-chosen gifts, cheer at Christmas." Smith concluded: "You cope. With charm, and class, and poise.[41]

Plank's presidency, with its focus on transparency, brought credibility to the association in a time of need. Smith cited PRSA's financial situation as evidence of the attitude change Plank had managed to produce. "Despite the fact that 1973 was the Society's largest deficit year, everyone discussed it in matter-of-fact terms without the emotionally charged language one might have expected." Smith's comment is particularly striking when compared with Dr. Robert O. Carlson's statements about PRSA just six months earlier. Carlson, a former Standard Oil of New Jersey executive, had been hired as the Society's first full-time president to oversee its daily operations. After just eighteen months on the job, Carlson resigned, telling the *New York Times* that he thought he could change the organization but became frustrated when he realized he could not. He found it difficult dealing with the "various specialized interests in public relations—financial, corporate, government, foundation, and the rest," especially given that PRSA was operating with a $30,000 deficit. He said he "couldn't promise prospective members that they would get much for their dues." Plank, on the other hand, was able to do just that apparently.[42]

Smith told Plank that the phrase she heard most often was "Betsy's making things happen." Optimism about PRSA's future came with the increased activity and an "atmosphere of expectation" among the members.[43]

Smith was especially proud that Plank, as the first woman chair of PRSA, had handled herself so well. In fact, "this 'woman thing' got lost in the shuffle," she wrote. The members were genuinely grateful for Plank's contributions to public relations and PRSA during her tenure as chair.[44]

BECOMING A "HAS BEEN"

It is true that Plank wanted to be thought of as the twenty-fifth chair of the Society, rather than as the first woman to hold the position in its twenty-five-year history. And as Smith noted, Plank was successful in that endeavor. But there was no way around the fact that she was a woman, and that put the men who served in the presidency before her in a bit of a quandary.

The past presidents, or the "Has Beens" as they called themselves, had been getting together at the PRSA conventions for "an exclusive, unofficial, self-financed cocktail-dinner party" every year since 1959. What started out as a meeting of a couple of past presidents in the conference hotel bar evolved over the next twenty years into an exclusive, black-tie affair restricted to past presidents and their spouses.[45] It had also developed a format that was far from genteel. As the current president wound down his term and became a past president, he was subjected to a rowdy and often bawdy roast by his fellow alums. The problem for the past presidents in 1973 was that the immediate past president at the convention would be, for the first time, a woman. How should the past presidents handle that little detail?

Most of them did not know Plank well enough to know how she would react to a roasting. After careful consideration, they decided to play it safe and avoid the situation completely by putting her husband on "trial" instead. The venue was an authentic Japanese restaurant in Hawaii, the site of that year's national conference. Rosenfield's "test" was to face off in a strip tease competition against a Geisha in "several layers of native costume." Rosenfield, clearly at a disadvantage, kept losing, "shedding watch and wallet, handkerchief and hotel key, then black tie, dinner jacket, studs, cuff links, socks, cummerbund, shirt and undershirt. All to much urging, cheers and rowdy mirth of the assembled. On the cusp of a zipper, the Chairman called a merciful halt, declaring the initiation completed." The past presidents need not have worried about Plank's reaction; she loved every minute of it.[46] And that was one of Plank's strengths: the ability to fit in regardless of the situation.

A "SPECIAL CHARISMA"

Some of PRSA's members probably had doubts that a woman could lead the Society when Plank was nominated, but fortunately, the men in charge did not. They believed in Plank, and she did not disappoint them. Her focus on transparency and open communication combined with a logical approach to problem solving meant that the members felt respected and valued. The drama that sometimes surrounded the Society's actions did not arise in discussions about a fee increase or during the Pincus affair. Whether or not one agreed with Plank's decisions, one could at least understand how she arrived at them.

Plank had always been known as a hard worker, as someone who could get something done. But what she added to her leadership capabilities in her time as chair were transparency and accountability. She had served in enough organizations to know how it felt to be a member with little to no power over decisions. She understood the necessity of having a hierarchical structure in an organization, but she also recognized that, as with a democracy, those at the top served at the pleasure of those at the bottom. She worked for them and wanted them to know what the organization was doing to protect their interests and further their careers. And she was doing plenty. As one member put it, Plank was in there swinging for them. She was getting things done for the organization and fighting for the profession at the same time.

After completing her year of service as chair, Plank continued promoting public relations and PRSA. In 1976 alone, she made twelve speeches about the profession at universities and to associations throughout the Midwest. She also agreed to a major undertaking of which she was especially proud, serving as program chair of the International Public Relations Association's Seventh World Congress held in Boston that year in conjunction with PRSA, the first time the World Congress had been held in the United States in the organization's twenty-one-year history.[47]

Shortly thereafter, *PR News* asked Plank to write its annual New Year's message, offering her views on what practitioners could expect in 1977. Watergate's shadow still darkened the political climate, but "Americans are relearning the process of open, even reasoned, debate," she wrote, "and in that process may rediscover their original national genius for compromise and reciprocity. The catalyst in the process is communications—but effective only to the degree that it is credible, and credible only if there are manifest actions, integrity, and public accountability as witness to the words." Her message was well received. Bateman described it as "typically well organized, cogent and pertinent." Louis B. Raffel, executive vice president of the American Egg Board, wrote, "As always, you put more good sense on one page as most people do in a volume. Thanks for pointing the way." In response, Plank told him that she rarely read what she wrote after it was in print. "So it's nice to know that it made sense to someone whose judgment I respect so highly."[48]

The late 1970s were banner years for Plank. In 1978, she was named the *PR News*'s PR Professional of the Year, the first woman in the award's seventeen-year history. A year earlier, PRSA awarded her its Gold Anvil, the Society's highest individual honor, which is presented to a PRSA member who has made a major contribution to the profession. In his letter nominating her for the award, James F. Fox, the 1975 PRSA chair and former public relations vice president of Chase Manhattan Bank, described Plank as "a force for unity" within the Society. She had done more to bring the chapters and districts "alive" than any chair before her or since. She was proof "that a woman can compete all the way to the top in a 'man's world' in executive jobs without losing her femininity, without arousing male (or female) resentment." That alone made her deserving of the award. Despite a "forceful leadership" style, she had made few, if any, enemies along the way. Her ability to quickly garner acceptance within any group could be attributed to what Fox described as a "special charisma."[49]

CHAPTER 5

A Seasoned Leader

Our messages must be clear, open, and thorough—written
with a genuine concern and understanding for the men and
women for whom they are intended."

—Betsy Ann Plank

PLANK'S "SPECIAL CHARISMA" and leadership abilities did not go unnoticed
in public relations circles. AT&T certainly recognized her talents, recruiting
her to the corporate sector. But after briefly testing the public relations
waters in New York at the company's headquarters, she soon found herself
back in the comforting and comfortable surroundings of Chicago.

TACKLING NEW CHALLENGES

It was while Plank was dealing with the fallout from the Pincus affair that
Paul Lund, the vice president of public relations and employee communications at AT&T, approached her about joining the company. The two
met several times in Chicago and at AT&T's headquarters in New York
to discuss the possibility of her moving from the agency to the corporate
side. Only a special corporation would cause Plank to even consider such
a switch, and AT&T was just that. It was a well-established, highly stable
company. Although a monopoly in the telephone business, it had long been
known for keeping customer service front and center, thanks in part to the
influence of Arthur W. Page, the first vice president of corporate communications in the United States. Page believed that AT&T's success as a company depended on public approval, and the way to achieve that approval was
to earn it. The opportunity to work for a company that believed in a "Spirit
of Service" and valued public relations so strongly was appealing to Plank.[1]

On September 23, 1973, in conjunction with Edelman, Inc., AT&T
issued a news release announcing the hiring of Plank as assistant director
of planning effective October 15. Plank received many calls and letters

of congratulations on her move, and at least one person wrote to John deButts, chairman of the AT&T Board, to congratulate the company on acquiring Plank's services. Tilden Cummings, president of Continental Illinois National Bank and Trust Company, had gotten to know Plank when the two of them served together on Chicago's 1972 Crusade of Mercy campaign. "I thought I would tell you that you have acquired a very able gal," Cummings told deButts.[2]

AT&T was happy to have Plank on board and treated her accordingly. In addition to her $55,000 annual salary, the company agreed to reimburse her for living expenses in New York and twice-monthly trips home to Chicago until she and Rosenfield could set up residence in the city.[3] AT&T also made concessions for her speaking commitments as her PRSA presidential term wound down. She would use the opportunity to meet with her counterparts at the local Bell companies in the cities she visited for PRSA. For her part, Plank was thrilled to be joining AT&T but still felt some trepidation.

The decision to leave Edelman was by no means an easy one. She had spent thirteen years with the agency, the longest she had worked at one place in her life. Besides leaving the firm for which she had great affection, joining AT&T meant leaving Chicago and, for the time being, Rosenfield and their cat, Cinderella. Although Plank was not one to shy away from a challenge, in making the leap to AT&T and New York City, she felt as though she had been "blindfolded and told to jump confidently into the World's Largest Ocean and swim." Still, she had faith in Lund and the others at AT&T and so, she told them, "I Do Believe [sic] and [am] jumping. God willing, the water will be warm, and I'll soon swim to your satisfaction."[4]

Plank was right to feel some trepidation. The move from the agency to the corporate side was harder than she had anticipated it would be. She thought she knew how things worked in the corporate sector because for more than fifteen years she had served corporate clients. She had "done their marketing, suffered their annual reports, their meetings with media and shareowners, handled their crisis communications, [and] counseled their executives." She considered herself "an experienced, pretty smart cookie on corporate life" as a result. But it turned out she was naïve about exactly how decisions were made in a big company. "I just thought the president walked out of his office and issued orders and everybody ran off to carry them out," she once said, clearly exaggerating. The reality, of course, was far different. Power did not always follow the corporate hierarchical structure. Decisions were not even necessarily made at the top. They were often made "way down there" on the front lines where the public and the organization interacted. Plank soon realized that by the time she learned of an issue, it was often too late to influence the solution. Finding the individuals working on a problem before it could be put "in a form where it can escalate" was crucial.[5]

Another difference, and a more troublesome one for Plank, was that AT&T was highly bureaucratic. Shortly after starting, Plank was asked to report to the Personnel Office for an orientation. Finding the office in AT&T's huge headquarters near Wall Street was the first challenge. The second was being faced with a sea of forms, papers, guidelines, and policy manuals. "When I escaped that office, I had experienced a total immersion baptism in bureaucracy," she said later. Public relations agencies certainly had policies and forms, but they were much more freewheeling than AT&T was.[6]

The Personnel Office remained a frustration for her throughout her time in the Bell System. In the agency world, an employee was hired or fired based mostly on performance and the needs of clients. At Bell, however, Plank soon discovered it took "a paper-trail years long" to terminate anyone. She understood the rationale for the constraints, but at the same time, she felt that the personnel practices and procedures seemed to "grow like bunions, impeding pace and progress."[7]

The Personnel Office was not the only thing weighing down the company. The fear of failure also contributed. As a regulated monopoly, AT&T did not have to rush to market. It could take its time and be sure that any new products or services were customer ready before launch. While a luxury most companies did not have, that extra time had resulted in a risk-averse mindset that permeated AT&T. Extensive research was always done before any action, but "the company was so compulsive about being absolutely right that it felt compelled to research its research, second-guessing everything," she said. That was a far cry from the agency world where "you came up with ideas and you ran with them."[8]

In part because of the inertia that had set in, the AT&T Plank joined in the fall of 1973 was a company in transition. Many saw it as bloated and old. Ma Bell was no longer about quality service, critics argued, but just about maintaining her monopoly status. Her size, age, and domination in telephony had led her to become anti-capitalistic and to a certain extent antidemocratic. The public relations activities taken on her behalf appeared to be designed to keep competitors at bay and customers quiet. Beyond that, consumer groups were threatening to sue and unions to strike. Phone systems in big cities were overburdened and failing; morale among the one million employees was at an all-time low.[9]

This was the situation that John D. deButts, a lifelong AT&T employee, inherited when he became CEO and chairman of the board the year before Plank joined. "With a winning Southern drawl and a firm handshake," deButts set out to resurrect the company's image. He toured the country reaching out to the Bell employees on the front line, helping them install telephones and repair cable, all while encouraging them to recommit to AT&T's "Spirit of Service." He preached "plain old telephone service" or POTS over short-term profits. It worked. By the time, he retired seven years later, profits had risen nearly sixty-five percent, earnings had steadily increased, and service had reached its highest efficiency ever.[10]

In Plank's role as assistant director of planning, she regularly came into contact with deButts. Visually, the two made for an odd couple. He was a commanding presence at 6'4" and 220 pounds. Plank was more than a foot shorter and at least one hundred pounds lighter, but no less commanding. In describing his management style, deButts once said, "First, I am not a brooder. I like to make decisions. Second, I delegate easily because I work with the best in the world at what they do. Third, I like my work." And as a leader, he approached issues by studying, reading everything he could, and talking to different people before making a decision. It was a leadership style of which Plank approved.[11]

Her division—planning—was within AT&T's public relations department. Its mission was to plan and develop comprehensive information programs to address the company's public relations needs; to act as an information resource for the rest of the department; to provide creative services when needed to support business policies; and to inform senior management "continuously and in timely fashion" of external factors impacting the business. Those external factors included developments in ideas as well as trends in public attitudes and opinions.[12]

While conducting research, developing strategic information programs, and counseling senior leadership were within Plank's skill set, the heavy emphasis on those skills and the nature of the focus were not. Plank had spent her agency days helping clients market their products and services to consumers by setting them apart from their competitors. For twenty-five years, her job had been primarily media relations, writing countless news releases, and earning media coverage in furtherance of her clients' promotional efforts. But marketing public relations as she had practiced it at Edelman would not work in the Bell System because it was not a matter of bringing in new customers to increase market share. In fact, AT&T did not even have a marketing department until 1973. It did not need to convince customers to use its service and products; it needed to maintain legitimacy in the eyes of those customers. But that legitimacy was being threatened by competitors who were slowly and steadily creeping into the telephony space.[13]

"LET THE PUBLIC DECIDE"

As a result, one of her first assignments at AT&T was to develop a program to make the public aware of the threat that competition posed to their phone service. She was reluctant to accept the task at first and suggested to Lund that it might be better to have someone more familiar with the Bell System do it. But he said no, that she was ideal for the job precisely because she was an outsider. "Insiders are too close to the problem to see it. Outsiders take us for granted," he said. And it was true. Americans viewed owning a telephone as a basic right. It was part of the "unwritten social contract" between the Bell System and its customers. Bell would provide affordable residential service in return for its monopoly status. It was a pricing system that was subsidized by long distance and business service. But since the 1950s, the Federal Communications Commission (FCC) had been slowly eroding the breakwater that kept competitors at bay. AT&T's senior leadership saw it and recognized what it meant for the company moving forward, but few others within the System did.[14]

After a "few Moses-like protests of 'Why me, oh Lord?'" Plank took the six big binders she had been handed, all stuffed with releases, decisions, and backgrounders on the threat to the Bell System, and set to work with "the red balloon enthusiasm of a true believer." Her assignment? To develop a comprehensive public education campaign in simple language that would alert the public to what competition would mean to their service. In other words, her job was to find a way to convince people that the continuation of AT&T's monopoly was in their best interests. Her first stop was her fellow AT&T communicators. She wanted their suggestions for how to approach the campaign. It didn't go well. "I was very intense," she admitted. "But my peers didn't share this convert's convictions about the gravity of the situation. They laughed at my passion." To them, the Bell System was like the Rock of Gibraltar. It was not going anywhere.[15]

Left to her own devices, Plank developed a national public relations strategy for countering "the knee jerk reaction of most of the public." The public assumed that competition was always better, that it automatically meant lower prices and better service. It would not be easy to combat such "deeply held beliefs about the American way-of-life." To do so called for "the intelligent exploitation of every avenue of communication available to us, the careful targeting of specific points in unique approaches and all part of an over-all and systematic development of our case before the public." At the same time, Plank warned that implementing the plan also carried the risk that the public would come to perceive the Bell System as being incapable of competing in a market that demanded technological innovation.[16]

Plank titled her plan, "Let the Public Decide," in keeping with her belief in democratic rule. But, of course, the plan was not meant as an argument to convince the FCC and courts to "let the public decide" whether AT&T should remain a monopoly. The plan's purpose was to persuade the public that a monopoly was in their best interest regardless of what they or the FCC thought. Plank was quite proud of what she came up with and confidently took it into Lund's office for his review.

He thought it was "a good, strong program"; he could tell that she had drawn on her agency experience because it was highly marketing oriented. But when he got to the action plan, he paused. "Sit back, Betsy, I want to tell you something." She cringed. What came next was her "greatest professional embarrassment." He began gently. All that she had recommended about reaching the public with the information was fine. But, she recalled him saying, "stop and think. We have almost a million employees in the Bell System. Our first job is to play catch-up with this group. And if we can first just do a convincing information job with these one million people, half the job with the public will already be done." Plank had completely forgotten one of AT&T's most important publics, which she chalked up to "stupidity and ignorance." But it was understandable given that her experience until then had been with agencies focused on external publics. It was a mistake she would not make again.[17]

When her revised plan, which AT&T's Corporate Planning department renamed IMPACT (Improving Public Awareness of Concepts of
Telecommunications), was finally presented to deButts, he was impressed.
In a note to Plank, he wrote, that her report was "testimony that you are a
great professional—and we need all of that help we can get these days."[18]

LEAVING THE MOTHER SHIP

Although she was finding her sea legs at work, her personal life was suffering. In October, Plank's beloved father took ill and was hospitalized. While
flying back to New York from a weekend in Chicago, Plank reflected on her
insecurities and her worry about her father, whom she once described as a
native public relations person. She had reason to be concerned; on October
25, he died. He was not only her biggest fan, but also the one to whom
she turned for advice. Plank attributed much of her success to her father's
encouragement and support. As with many fathers of successful women in
business at the time, he was the one who helped her "dare to set high goals"
and pushed her to achieve those goals "in spite of the subtle, if not overt,
social stigma associated with career-oriented women." He expected her to
aspire to and prepare for a career and passed on to her his own view of a
career as an integral part of a person's life.[19]

Whether it was her father's death or a combination of that and being
away from Rosenfield, the move to New York weighed heavily on her. At
the beginning of the New Year, after just three months on the job, and with
much of that spent traveling for PRSA, Plank told Lund she needed to
resign. In her letter to him, she explained that when she took the position,
the plan was for her husband to join her in New York mid-year. With that
end in mind, they had even sold their just-purchased condominium in
Chicago. But over the Christmas holidays, Rosenfield's work circumstances
had changed; he would not be able to make the move after all. At least that
was the explanation she gave Lund for her change of heart.

Plank knew what her resignation might mean for her future in public
relations. "I realize that this unavoidable decision risks destroying a career
for which I've worked hard for many years," she wrote. "I am . . . mentally
prepared that it will probably be damaged irrevocably." Regardless, "Sherm
and our life together come first above all else and all other obligations.
And if my work-location does not include him in any foreseeable future,
then the answer for me must be unequivocal."[20] Plank hated disappointing

people, especially people like Lund who believed in her and knew what she was capable of, but she wanted, and more importantly needed, to be with Rosenfield. He was her rock, much as her father had been.

The prospect of having to look for work frightened Plank a little. She had not had to apply for a job since she interviewed with Mitchell McKeown for her first public relations job at the age of twenty-three. Looking for a new position at fifty was a completely different matter. But Plank need not have worried. Instead of letting her go, Lund arranged for a transfer to one of AT&T's operating companies, and on May 15, 1974, she became an assistant vice president of corporate communications, heading consumer and community relations for Illinois Bell.[21]

As she had when she left Chicago for New York seven months earlier, Plank received letters of congratulations on her return to the city and on her new position. Harold Bergen, president of the public relations agency Ruder & Finn, told her that "You've added so much lustre [sic] to the profession over the last several years that I for one am glad that you are again a part of the public relations community here in Chicago." Her old boss, Dan Edelman, wrote that "so many of us figured you and New York just weren't right for each other and we're delighted that you made the decision to return to where you belong." Edelman was right, Plank did belong in Chicago. But he wasn't right about New York, at least as far as deButts was concerned. After Plank's departure, he wrote, "I miss you already! I can't remember another time when anyone proved so invaluable to me in so short a period of time. I just wanted you to know how much I appreciate it."[22]

JOINING ILLINOIS BELL

Like its parent company, Illinois Bell had a mixed record of service in the 1960s and early 1970s. The company regularly faced opposition to its rate hike requests, especially since it was making huge profits. It was accused of harassing small rivals to keep them out of the telephony space and of discriminatory hiring practices. A strike in 1968 that lasted for 137 days was marked by violence and a disruption of phone operations and radio and TV coverage of the Democratic National Committee's convention held in Chicago that year. At the same time, by 1974, when Plank joined the company, it had been recycling its old directories for more than thirty years; had pledged the largest employee contribution to the city's United Way campaign for the third consecutive year; and had improved its hiring practices to the point that it was now leading Chicago utilities in minority hiring. Thirty percent of its 14,538 employees in the city were minorities. Of the 207 employees in the top three of its five levels of management, five were women, including one African American, which reflected the gender diversity of the Bell System overall.[23]

Plank was a beneficiary of the more inclusive hiring, becoming the first woman to head a department at Illinois Bell, "which shook them up a little," she acknowledged. Her first week on the job included a chance meeting in the ladies' room with another woman, a bookkeeper for the company. After introducing themselves, the woman said, "Gee, you know, I never thought I'd ever be in the same bathroom with a department head!" A bigger shock for the employees though was that she was new to the Bell System after a successful career elsewhere. For most of them, Bell had been their first and only employer. AT&T's policy of development and promotion from within ensured its employees stayed in the System.[24]

Plank's office in Illinois Bell's headquarters on Randolph Street was "traditional and highly functional." A large, orange sofa and two masculine, brown-leather chairs were "strong but non-obtrusive." An impressionist painting, chosen for its colors from the company's original art collection, hung on the walls along with a photo of Chicago and the river, which reminded her of the view from her old office at Edelman. On her desk was a personal telephone book with a quote from Emerson on its cover, "Write it on your heart that every day is the best day in the year." Plank described the saying as "not cute, but wise." And on one side of a pen set was a Goethe quote: "Treat people as if they were what they ought to be and you help them become what they are capable of being." The other side of the set said, "There is no limit to what can be accomplished if it doesn't matter who gets the credit." Also, on the desk was a dish of hard candy for visitors and an ashtray. Plank thought it looked like the "working desk of someone in the communications business; it looks busy. It probably also looks disorganized. I don't especially like that impression, but it doesn't worry me much." The prettiest thing about the office, according to Plank, was its thirtieth-floor view of Lake Michigan to the east and Chicago to the north.[25]

After Plank had been on the job six months, a retirement within the corporate communications team led to what would be the first of many department reorganizations she would experience at Illinois Bell. Plank was still an assistant vice president but was now over program development and

Fig. 12: Plank in her office at Illinois Bell on the 30th floor of the company's Chicago headquarters in 1978. Courtesy of the Plank Papers

put in charge of a department of 104 people, responsible for the research, planning, and development of Illinois Bell's public relations activities, as well as the "formulation and development of policy statements." Reporting to Plank were nine managers, all male, but to their credit, "they were gentlemen all the way."[26]

Plank adapted quickly to her new team, and they to her. Appraising Plank's performance as a supervisor, one female employee wrote, "I've been blessed with supervision in the past two years that has pressed for my best and accepted nothing less than that. I've been given great latitude of judgment, and I've never felt that I couldn't get a hearing for a new idea no matter how unconventional or risky."[27]

Handling her staff turned out to be the easy part of the job. Early in Plank's tenure with Illinois Bell, she realized just how much she had to learn about the company when she climbed down a manhole at the intersection of 81st and Halsted Streets in Chicago to inspect how underground copper wire cable was installed to provide telephone service.[28] That was her real initiation into the company and its business, and for as long as she was with Illinois Bell, she kept a lineman's hard hat in her office as a constant reminder of how much of the company's business one did not see. It also served as a reminder that practicing public relations in a company was different from being in an agency. Agency life revolved around public relations; it was the center of one's universe. But in a corporation, public relations was just one department among many all working together to achieve a common business objective.

For many companies in the 1970s, achieving a business objective through public relations meant convincing the public of the "truth" via "large doses of facts." That approach was not unlike "a fanatic who is convinced that the Good Lord would be on his side if only He understood the facts." Instead, Plank believed that companies had to begin where the public was. It was like teaching. If you wanted someone to learn something, "you must relate to *his* experience, not force him to leap to yours." Thus, her team developed a program called Customer Dialogue, in which officers of Illinois Bell met face-to-face with customers to listen to their concerns and answer their questions. Through such encounters, she hoped to "avoid the myth of manipulating opinion, engineering consent," because after all, "the public, too, has a mind and will of its own—and the power to exercise it."[29]

FOCUSING ON EMPLOYEES

Plank's client work at Edelman focused primarily on product publicity. Thus, she had not given much thought to employee communications. Like many public relations practitioners at the time, she thought it simply involved editing a company newsletter, full of company news and corporate policies. It was top-down, one-way communication. But her experience with Lund and the IMPACT plan at AT&T gave her new respect for the employee public. "So much so, that from time to time [she] made vigorous, born again speeches about it from several platforms." The upshot of her new-found dedication was that when Corporate Communications was reorganized again in early 1980, Plank found herself leading Employee Information and Communications.[30]

Plank brought with her a conviction that employees were vitally important to the continued success of Illinois Bell. It was simple arithmetic, as she explained to her new team. Active and retired employees added up to approximately fifty-five thousand people in their primary market. If, she said, they each had 2.5 immediate family members plus five other relatives, that would be a total of 1,017,500 people or one-third of the 1970 census of Chicago. And that didn't include "what the church and club and cocktail party periphery might be."[31]

As corporate communicators, she told them, they had a responsibility not only for the information, but "for the environment of that information—its openness, its clarity and credibility, its receptivity to two-way traffic." Employees wanted to know all aspects of an issue, not just the company line, and they were more willing to express dissent than they used to be. A paycheck did not command loyalty anymore, she reminded them. Employees had lives outside of work that impacted their perceptions and reactions to company information. "And," she continued, "we ignore at our peril the fact that many employees are highly influential—not only with their immediate friends and family, but in the community."[32]

Part of the problem was that the company was in transition. The Bell System had been a steady and constant feature in employees' lives. But now consumers, regulators, and legislators were all demanding changes. The System was restructuring and reorganizing in response. "All that impacts on their jobs, on them as individuals, on them and how they identify with an organization that is constantly moving, shaking, adapting," she said. For the first time, they were having to live with ambiguity—"that discomfort of not knowing what's coming next, and who—if anyone—is in charge or if we're all captive to some mysterious hands of control."[33]

From their research, her team knew that the department scored well on open communication, but she urged them to provide even more. At the same time, the research told them that they were not winning the persuasive battle on priority issues such as the company's need for higher earnings, that legislation was required, or that competition would have a serious effect on the cost and quality of service. For Plank, the answer was to do more and do it better. "Our messages must be clear, open, and thorough—written with a genuine concern and understanding for the men and women for whom they are intended." The most important thing her team needed to remember was that they were "the seminal source of encouraging, shepherding, and supporting two-way, face-to-face communications programs within departments."[34]

One of those departments was Personnel, once the bane of her existence. A staff study had shown that Personnel had an image problem. After a discussion with her counterpart in that department, Plank arranged for her team to conduct more research to define the extent and nature of the issue.

They found that Personnel was viewed as a "hindrance to the rest of the crew," rather than a positive help. Departmental Personnel Representatives were confused about what they were supposed to be communicating to the employees in their divisions, sensing a lack of overall coordination within Personnel. They had trouble getting answers from the department. "And shades of déjà vu, we found them talking and sounding like—would you believe—customers!" she told the Personnel staff. One answer was to have a coordinated plan, addressing the selling to and persuading of employees about various programs, including their timing and introduction. Other answers included more face-to-face communication; greater access to training; brief, comprehensive guides for managers; closer identification of Benefits and Training & Development with Personnel. These, among other ideas, were all tactics to help position Personnel as a welcome support system.[35]

Plank's recommendations to Personnel reflected her maturing understanding of employee relations and its importance to the company. Although she did not use the analogy, what she describes as the relationship between leaders and employees in a large corporation like the Bell System was in many ways analogous to a democracy. Employees were akin to voters who deserved and increasingly demanded information about the policies impacting them. "The bottom line for me is that the employee audience today must be viewed as more of an external public for us." She had come to believe that viewing employees in that way would serve them, and Illinois Bell, far better "than the traditional one of considering it solely internal, with all the paternalistic myths, assumptions, and sand-traps into which that can tempt us. . . ." Employees could no longer be taken for granted; they were owed respect and a listening ear.[36]

Plank encouraged her team to take advantage of all available means of distributing messages to employees. Video was quickly replacing print at Illinois Bell. In fact, the company had had its own studio and TV system, IBTV, since 1966. Its programming included specific skills training, as well as informational programs and shows. The benefits of in-house, closed-circuit TV was seen by management as an opportunity "to provide lower-level employees 'first-hand' access to 'straight *talk*' and 'authentic' information direct from the top brass." AT&T, which had incorporated CCTV into its annual shareholder meetings in the early 1950s, promoted the use of video because "there is something very effective psychologically about television . . . a closeness, an intimacy, a personal something about the television experience." According to Ed Block, AT&T's senior vice president of public relations, the company's "nationwide video network" provided "a means by which we can promptly develop common understanding on important matters and a common response to them."[37] It was a top-down approach reflecting the traditional paternalistic view of internal relations, one that Plank had moved beyond.

At Illinois Bell, Corporate Communications produced a monthly newsmagazine about the company for employees; a monthly fifteen-minute program on major issues for managers; and a bimonthly program in which the president met with six employees to discuss a subject of concern to all employees. As home video recorders became more prevalent, the department branched out, allowing managers to check out video tapes. That way they could watch at home "with [their] feet up and a bottle of beer." Not only did that mean less time wasted at work, but it also meant the company could reach and educate the wives and husbands of those managers at the same time.[38]

"PHIL DONAHUE, MEET THE BELL SYSTEM"

Video was also used to address anti-Bell sentiment on at least one occasion. On an episode of the Phil Donahue syndicated television talk show in early 1981, two consumer activists, audience members, and Donahue himself had "hurled stinging criticism" at the Bell System for its "alleged excessive profiteering." The Bell System was not represented on the show because apparently the producers had moved up the date of the taping on short notice, and the scheduled AT&T spokesperson was not able to make it to Chicago from New York in time. Of course, on air, the audience was simply told the Bell System declined to appear.[39]

Watching the show from Illinois Bell headquarters, Plank and her Employee Information team realized the extent of the inaccuracies that were being promulgated on the episode. They responded quickly. Within minutes of the conclusion of the telecast, work began on an employee bulletin countering the inaccuracies point by point. It was distributed to Illinois Bell's thirty-eight thousand employees within twenty-four hours and reprinted in employee publications of other Bell companies. A videotaped rebuttal was also produced and distributed widely throughout the Bell System.[40]

Illinois Bell was not the first corporation to use video to rebut a televised attack. Illinois Power distributed twenty-five hundred copies of a point-counterpoint video in response to a "60 Minutes" broadcast in 1979. According to the *Wall Street Journal*, the video was "effective in reaching a significant 'thinking' audience."[41] In Illinois Bell's case, the video was used to reach employees to ensure they knew the company's position and could advocate on their employer's behalf with people in their spheres of influence.

But the Corporate Communications department still needed to counter the inaccuracies publicly. Strategizing the message and its distribution to the public, they considered "print ads, a public rebuttal videotape and other options." The goal was to address the allegations contained in the show, while at the same time, not publicizing them to an even broader audience. They decided to use the Donahue show itself to correct the misinformation.[42]

At the end of the original show, Donahue had offered to have the company come on a future show to respond, an offer the Corporate Communications team now accepted. The show's producers agreed that Illinois Bell President Charles Marshall and AT&T's Vice President and Treasurer Virginia Dwyer could appear on a subsequent episode. With Donahue's audience primarily women, having Dwyer was a bonus, especially given the lack of female representation at the senior levels of AT&T. Although Marshall and Dwyer were experienced spokespersons, Plank and the others recreated the show in their corporate television studio using Corporate Communications employees playing Donahue and the studio audience asking tough questions.[43]

Marshall and Dwyer performed well according to a post-show survey, with eighty-two percent of respondents agreeing that they did an excellent or good job in presenting their side of the story. Employees, who had been hurt by the original broadcast, reported being gratified that the company took "strong courageous action to set the record straight." Donahue himself drew the audience's attention to the speed with which the company rebutted the allegations in its employee bulletin and called Dwyer "one of the most highly placed women in American business." Pleased with the success of the response, Plank had the video, along with a written case study showing how the company was able to "set the record straight," sent to the faculty advisors of the various Public Relations Student Society of America chapters for use in their public relations courses.[44]

Plank believed in giving public relations students exposure to "real world" situations. The video case study provided students and their professors an opportunity they would not otherwise have: the ability to examine a company's messaging in response to criticism in almost real time. As was typical of most corporate public relations campaigns at the time, this one was a presentation of the facts. The heated emotion of the activists was met with the "calm presentation of numbers and statistics" by the company. Rational appeals fit well with Plank's belief in democracy and the ability of individuals to self-govern. But a survey of undergraduate students who were shown the video after the fact revealed that the success of those appeals was mixed. On some criteria, the students thought more highly of AT&T after viewing the video, but on others, they thought less of the company, suggesting a potential backlash.[45]

MANAGING CHANGE

Plank's focus on transparency and openness served her well in her role as head of employee information at an important time for Illinois Bell and AT&T. The FCC had ordered AT&T to create a separate subsidiary to sell its equipment on the open market, paving the way for even more competition from companies such as IBM and Xerox. As the FCC deadline for the reorganization closed in, the level of anxiety among Illinois Bell employees about the changes escalated. At the same time, Plank recognized that there was also anticipation and excitement as employees sensed this would be a dramatic moment in Bell System history. Unfortunately, because the company had little control over the factors impacting it, there was a "vacuum of very explicit, specific information" she could share with the employees.[46]

Plank admitted it was as frustrating for her as it was for the employees. She wanted to be able to fill the void, to remove the ambiguity, but the best she could do was to tell the employees that Bell's senior leadership was singularly focused on planning for all the contingencies. As employees of an operating company, their job was to concentrate on service and earnings. But her favorite message was that a competitive future was going to be exciting, an opportunity for all of them, because that is how she saw it.[47]

Despite her efforts, rumors still ran rampant. She admitted that some of them "probably are fairly good-educated guesses, but a great many of them are really wild and out of sight." Personally, Plank had little tolerance for rumors. She felt they were counterproductive and a waste of energy. Change was coming regardless of what happened with the FCC—change to meet the problems of technology; change to meet the problems of competition. To a group of managers, she said, "I think that we shouldn't spend our time trying to read into every move some kind of special nuance or special portent for the future." She did reassure the managers though that "as soon as we know in the information department, managers will know, all employees will know, because we're working days and nights and weekends to turn around on a dime to get as much information out there as possible."[48]

Everyone associated with Ma Bell knew a wave of change was coming, but most had no way of knowing that it would be a tsunami. On January 8, 1982, almost eight years into Plank's tenure at Illinois Bell, the Justice Department and AT&T announced they had arrived at a consent agreement to "dismember the Bell System."[49] Back in 1974, the Department of Justice had filed a civil antitrust lawsuit against AT&T, claiming it was monopolizing the long-distance telephone market through its control of local telephone companies. Plank remembered well the day the suit was filed. She was riding in a car with Lund when he received a call on the car's mobile phone. He turned ashen as he listened to the voice on the other end. "It was the bombshell AT&T executives had been expecting and fearing," she said. But because the suit had dragged on in court for almost a decade, the initial trepidation Bell employees felt at the outset of it had given way to complacency and indifference as the years passed.

Thus, when the announcement of a settlement was finally made on that icy cold January morning, it seemed to come out of the blue and "shook [their] world." Shocking everyone, not just its employees. AT&T had agreed to divest its twenty-two local Bell companies, including Illinois Bell, into seven regional operating companies. Under the agreement, which would take effect in two years on January 1, 1984, the Baby Bells, as the regional companies became known, would provide local telephone service to customers, while AT&T would continue to handle the long-distance business and maintain ownership of Western Electric, the company's manufacturing unit, and Bell Laboratories, AT&T's research and innovation arm.[50]

While the rank-and-file employees may have been blindsided by the agreement, the AT&T leadership had been restructuring and reorganizing since at least 1978 in preparation for just such a potentiality and the open competition they knew was coming. As an "unabashed monopolist," deButts had worked hard to prevent a breakup. Plank's IMPACT program was one of his attempts at heading it off. But reading the writing on the wall, he took early retirement to allow for Charles Brown to take over as

CEO and chairman in 1979, marking a generational shift in leadership. As a *Washington Post* reporter wrote, "Brown was the first chairman to ever entertain the question of 'Why are we holding onto the local phone companies?'" For Brown, the future was not in telephones, but in computers. To position the company for that future, Brown knew he would have to sacrifice the local operating companies. It was a strategy that did not sit well with long-time Bell employees.[51]

A tongue-in-cheek "obituary" at the time noted that Ma Bell "was 107 years old. . . . She had no disease; there were no failures in any of her systems. She was remarkably healthy for her age." Yet, the country was preparing for her death, at which time, her eight living "children" would share her $152 billion in assets."[52]

The government may have thought the public wanted competition, but that was not necessarily the case. Many decried the breakup as evidenced by a column in the *Chicago Tribune* quoting letters the newspaper had received: "Why didn't the government ask us whether we minded the way the Bell System worked?" "I suppose it's too late to complain to the jerks who are responsible for this," and "We had a wonderful phone system—but government interference has once again worked against the public good."[53]

At the time of the breakup, AT&T was a "company with $150 billion in assets—more than General Motors, General Electric, U.S. Steel, Eastman Kodak, and Xerox combined—the country's second largest employer with over a million employees, (bigger than the U.S. Army), and the nation's most widely held security with over three million shareholders." The *Economist* predicted ominously that the divestiture would "affect, sooner rather than later, almost every household in the *world*."[54]

Although they would now be on their own, the local companies would not be left destitute. Even the smallest of the seven regional entities would rank twenty-third on the Fortune 100. Yet the success or failure of the new companies created by the agreement depended in large part on the ability of public relations practitioners to communicate the changed structure to employees and customers and get their buy-in. The goal was to divest AT&T of the operating companies, keeping their identities and culture, while at the same time, thinking and acting "as a single, spanking-new corporation." That was easy for AT&T headquarters to say, but not so easy for employees at the local level to accept. The break-up of the entire Bell System brought great angst—"'What's going to happen to me—my job—in all this?'"—and "genuine mourning for the family of Ma Bell."[55] In the intense atmosphere, "the only thing certain was uncertainty." Plank described the situation as "severe for Bell people. My ragged fingernails testify to that. Round-the-clock work, no vacations, pressures and strains."[56]

The announcement of the divestiture in 1982 was definitely a stressful time for all employees and greatly disrupted the way they worked. In one year, Illinois Bell downsized from twenty-six thousand employees to just over fourteen thousand. No one knew what was going on or what was going to happen. "Company goals, strategies, job descriptions, and supervisory personnel" changed monthly. While many employees suffered "significant performance, leadership, and health deficits" because of the tremendous stress they faced, others, including Plank, actually thrived during the time.[57]

In their longitudinal study of Illinois Bell supervisors and managers, researchers Salvatore R. Maddi and Deborah M. Khoshaba found that what they called "hardiness" determined how well their participants coped, and even thrived, during the divestiture. Hardy individuals sought to be involved in the changes, rather than feeling isolated; they tried to influence outcomes, rather than being passive; and they viewed the stressful changes the company was undergoing as opportunities for growth and learning. Plank did each of these, while doing her best to reassure others everything would work out.[58]

The majority of the employees had joined the Bell System right out of high school, fully committing themselves to the company and its values. They were proud to be Bell employees. Tearing apart the company, meant tearing apart the Bell family. The strength of the belief in the System and its culture put great pressure on AT&T's public relations department, as well as on each of the Baby Bells, including Ameritech, to which Illinois Bell would now belong. Ed Block, AT&T's senior vice president of public relations, was tasked with creating the public relations campaign to handle the breakup. It was an unenviable job. He had to make the historic divestiture in which "the company was losing [two-thirds] of its operating revenues and five-sixths of its assets," into a positive. It worked initially. The *Wall Street Journal's* reaction was typical of the coverage. "Now the phone company can apply its considerable marketing expertise and its technological skills where market opportunities arise."[59]

But the framing took an unexpected turn after it was reported that Illinois Bell President William Weiss and other Baby Bell executives suggested the divestiture would lead to rapid increases in local rates. In fact, they believed the rates would double in half the time predicted by AT&T. AT&T chairman, Charles Brown, rebuffed Weiss' statements, claiming that the divestiture would have "no effect" on the already existing upward trend of rates. The AT&T public relations team looked to its counterparts at the Baby Bells for help in stanching the bleeding. In a memo to them, Block addressed what he perceived as the potentially "nettlesome public relations problem" for AT&T of the news stories about rates and implored them to "promptly take whatever measures may be effective in correcting this misunderstanding."[60]

But things had changed. Illinois Bell no longer had to jump when AT&T demanded something; it had its own concerns. As Plank described the situation,

> Our immediate job in communications was to support confidence in the logic of the Consent Decree and in the management, which inherited the incredible job of reorganizing to make it work. As in personal mourning, our employees had to 'let it all out'—and we encouraged that for a time. But we also—and soon—wanted it to be replaced with an attitude of accepting the inevitable and welcoming a new challenge—like—'let's get the job done. The future of the company is new, exciting and independent and I can help shape it.'[61]

Affecting such change was difficult slogging at first; Illinois Bell's employees were reluctant to let go of the past. But then, according to Plank, "something wonderful happened." Congressman Timothy Wirth (D-Col.), Chair of the House Communications Subcommittee, introduced amendments to a bill that would put even more severe restrictions on the Bell System even though the Consent Decree would not take effect for two more years. Although Wirth's goal was to open the telecommunications industry to free market competition, his actions ignited a competitive fire of a different kind. Bell System employees had a common cause again.

> It instantly rekindled a great family spirit. Employees had rallies with speeches and balloons and signs. They wrote letters and made calls. They cared—and they shouted about it. That effort—that enthusiastic rally by employees' calls and letters to Congress—a 'first' for the Bell System—dispelled some of the earlier mourning about divestiture. When House Bill 5158 was laid to rest—employees felt they had a victory and they needed it.[62]

Capturing that spirit and turning it inward, Illinois Bell's public relations team was able to channel the energy toward doing a great job for the company's customers.

Acceptance of the change came down to communication. Management team meetings were set up, a bimonthly video program with the company president was created to give employees at all levels a chance to talk candidly with him, and information was sent out in monthly newsletters to existing and retired employees. Management also enlisted the help of the authors of the book, *Corporate Culture: The Rites and Rituals of Corporate Life*, in planning the transition. The authors recommended establishing some rites of passage to create closure as well as a new beginning. Plank loved celebrations and threw herself into organizing the special events with great enthusiasm. Thus, when the divestiture finally took effect in January 1984, Illinois Bell held a headquarters rally and parties throughout its seven hundred units. Employees signed a book of charter members to commemorate the New Illinois Bell, and in a classic Plank move, spouses were honored and thanked for their service.[63] Plank understood the importance of spouses to an employee's ability to do the job well because she knew that Rosenfield's support and patience were what allowed her to spend twelve-hour days at work.

The celebrations belied the real hardships the divestiture caused some employees. Plank and her team had wanted the changeover on January 1 to be as transparent as possible, but it ended up being "about as transparent as a whirling propeller blade." Some employees remained where they were but with new responsibilities; others suddenly found themselves following their jobs to "other offices, companies, or cities." Employees who had once worked together now found themselves competing against each other for customers. They even had t-shirts printed with the words, "Breaking Up is Hard to Do," the title of a Neil Sedaka song.[64]

Of course, customers also needed to know what was happening. Understandably, they had questions too: Is my phone number going to change? Will I still be able to call long distance? Will I have to get a new phone? What does this all mean for me? Tactics employed to reach customers included information folders and a "Let's Talk" hotline. In one year, the Illinois Bell Corporate Communications department made "502 speeches in the community; 232 in schools. Held nine share information meetings for 9,500 share owners and six consumer group conferences. Worked extensively with media, produced advertising—held press conferences, did countless interviews."[65]

Still, confusion reigned. Confused customers flooded into Illinois Bell phone centers trying to figure out what to do with their old phones and service plans in advance of the transition date. Others missed the whole thing. Shortly after the divestiture, Plank recalled being at a cocktail party with several University of Chicago faculty and administrators. Much to her surprise, after two years of non-stop communication, many of them were unaware of the breakup or what it meant. "As a communicator, it was a very enlightening and humbling experience!" she said.[66]

Where once a single company handled everything from installation to repairs to phones to local and long-distance calls, obtaining that same service required at least three companies. Customers were unhappy and employees frustrated. Immediately after the divestiture, Illinois Bell sent its senior managers on the road for face-to-face meetings with employees. Plank was assigned to the Rockford Installation and Repair Garage. She was heartbroken by what she heard. "Employees . . . didn't want to say no to customers." They were used to solving all the customers' service problems, but they no longer were allowed to. That reduced many of them to tears or anger.[67]

Regardless of the confusion, it had been a massive undertaking. Jack Koten, Illinois Bell's vice president of corporate communications and Plank's boss, appreciated her efforts. In a note to her, Koten wrote, "Through the critical time of divestiture, you kept our internal world calm (at least as calm as possible) . . . . I have enjoyed working with you and appreciated your support and the way you've handled many difficult situations."[68]

THE NEW NORMAL

With the divestiture behind them, Plank was named Assistant Vice President of Community Affairs, or "the keeper of our corporate reputation in Illinois," as Koten put it. It was the position Plank had originally held at Illinois Bell, but this time was different. The company was working to es-tablish its brand in a competitive space. Yet, so far, the company continued to invest heavily in her department, which was responsible for "community relations, consumer affairs, educational relations, economic development and urban affairs." She told her team that the investment was a vote of corporate confidence and "deserves not only the daily best that we already give, but some new, imaginative perspectives, too."[69]

Privately, Plank worried that community relations might eventually be penalized by the company's leadership now that revenue generation and cost-cutting measures were the priorities. When AT&T was a monopoly, community relations was important to the business's continued social legitimacy. But in a competitive environment, it could be difficult to justify a community partnership without a direct link to a pragmatic payoff for the company. She decided that the answer was to put emphasis "on visibility and interpretation, both within the company and outside." Internally, employees needed to be reminded that Illinois Bell was a good corporate citizen and active in the community, that it continued to be a company for which they could be proud to work. Similarly, the community needed to understand all that the company was doing to invest in the neighborhoods it served.[70]

Plank's department and the goodwill it sought to create in the community was put to the test in 1988 when a fire swept through an electronic switching center in the suburb of Hinsdale on Mother's Day. The Hinsdale office was an important fiber optics hub in the Chicago area, serving as the connecting point for long distance service and housing more than thirteen thousand special circuits for businesses. On average, the office handled more than 3.5 million calls per day. The fire caused severe damage to cables and switching equipment, meaning that no calls could begin, end, or travel through the center. To make matters worse, smoke and water damage caused corrosion to what remained. In all, thirty-five thousand customers lost service in six communities.[71]

The Community Relations division of Plank's department responded immediately, implementing an emergency communications service plan. Fire, police, hospitals, ambulances all needed access to temporary phone lines. Trailers with coin-operated phones for public use were brought in, and foreign exchange lines were hooked up for nursing homes and schools. In the days and weeks that followed, Plank directed the many community-oriented actions the company took. As always with her, the credibility of the messaging was imperative. Because the cause of the fire was unknown, "careful attention was given not to promote confusion or any speculation regarding the fire's origin." Special editions of the employee communication publications kept employees informed of the latest news on the fire and restoration efforts, and human-interest stories celebrated the efforts of the 950 employees working to restore the Hinsdale office.[72]

Within days, the company realized that the switching equipment needed to be completely replaced. Normally, a project of that size and complexity would take fifty weeks, but they were determined to accomplish it in two. The threat of lawsuits from businesses that were suddenly without phone service contributed to their haste. Photographers and video cameramen tracked the restoration progress daily to document the "incredible undertaking." The photos and videos were used to communicate the company's efforts to employees and the public alike.[73]

Because the Hinsdale center was in a residential area, Plank's team worked "with the neighbors, answering questions, solving problems, and even delivering a special thank you note and complimentary fruit basket to residents in appreciation for their patience and understanding throughout the restoration process." Tens of thousands of informational fliers were produced with details about the status of the disruption, communities affected, and the location of temporary call centers, and distributed in neighborhoods and at train and bus stations. Four weeks after the fire, all customers had regained telephone service, and the crisis was over.[74]

As was Plank's way, the "Hinsdale crew" who worked around the clock to restore service were thanked with an Appreciation Breakfast and were sent a letter from the company president thanking them personally for their service. A special commemorative photographic booklet, "The 28-Day Year," was also produced. Media quotes and customer comments were used to "narrate" the photos, which told a story of teamwork in a time of crisis. In addition, the grounds around the building that had burned were refurbished. Visits were made to local officials to thank them for their cooperation, grants were given to local community governments to help with expenses associated with the fire, and newspaper ads taken out to thank the public for their support. The purpose of it all, of course, was to show that Illinois Bell was "a concerned and socially responsible corporate citizen" that appreciated its customers.[75]

A SEASONED LEADER

Illinois Bell gave Plank the opportunity to practice public relations as she thought it should be. For Plank and the Bell System, public relations was about ensuring the company was accountable to the public interest. It was about maintaining legitimacy by meeting society's expectations. Transparency and credibility were vital. Public relations was not about selling the public on an idea, product, or service; it was about persuading and advocating for those things via logical appeals. The public was to be treated with respect and dignity always.

The company also gave her the chance to fully develop as a public relations leader. She had had a variety of experiences in her twenty-five years in the field prior to joining the Bell System, but she had not dealt with an internal public. Many in public relations in the 1970s and early 1980s held the traditional view of employees as simply workers who did what they were told. Internal communication was top-down, telling employees what management believed they needed to know. But early in her tenure with the Bell System, Plank came to appreciate the importance of employee relations. Employees were autonomous individuals who deserved accurate and credible knowledge about the company they worked for. Of course, she also recognized their influence over others outside of the company. Keeping employees informed and happy went a long way in gaining and maintaining legitimacy with external publics as well.

Her earlier experiences combined with her new emphasis on employees and research meant a servant leadership style that enabled the members of her team to be creative and feel supported. She listened to a variety of sources, conducted research into her publics, whether internal or external, and found solutions that worked. But she took no credit. She worked alongside her team and found ways to ensure they received what they needed to be successful. What comes through in her time with Illinois Bell is her profound respect for others and her belief in the dignity of all. She persuaded via facts, not by playing on emotions. And yet, she was fully aware of the importance of emotional connection with others.

Whether sending fruit baskets to customers or delivering thoughtful "surprises" at corporate meetings, Plank kept the feelings of others front and center for which people were appreciative. "What a lovely surprise! Thank you for your thoughtfulness," wrote one woman. Another said, "I just love my book. Many thanks for your kindness in thinking of me, although I must say, you shouldn't have done it!" When Plank was able to combine her thoughtfulness with an event, it was even better. Thanking Plank for the marvelous events she arranged for his retirement, an Illinois Bell colleague wrote, "each function had that creative Plank touch—a real touch of class."[76]

CHAPTER 6

Shaping the Future

Agreement isn't necessarily the objective. But
understanding is.

—Betsy Ann Plank

WHILE PLANK WAS working to help solve the myriad problems and opportunities facing Illinois Bell, she was also considering how to do the same
for her profession. She was concerned that public relations practitioners
were not cognizant of the changing landscape in front of them. Business
expectations, technological innovations, public relations education, and
women in the field were just some of the issues she saw on the horizon.
Each had opportunities for the field if its practitioners took advantage of
them, but she was afraid they were not ready to, or worse, perhaps not
capable of taking them on. For that, she turned her focus to students.
They would be the saviors of the profession.

CHANGING BUSINESS EXPECTATIONS

As PRSA chair, Plank had recruited others to join her in addressing
the negative view of public relations caused by the Watergate scandal.
Together they were able to get some positive media coverage, but they
accomplished only so much. The profession was still being maligned. Yet,
she persevered. She wrote a letter to the 1984 Democratic presidential
nominee, Walter Mondale, after he called Senator Gary Hart, his compet-
itor in the primaries, a candidate of "tinsel and public relations." Reading
Mondale's comments as inferring that public relations was "in some way
artificial and dishonorable," she told him that he had disappointed her,
and that by casting aspersions on public relations, he was actually deni-
grating his own staff members. She reminded him that public relations
requires "a sensitivity to public needs and desires, which is not too afar
[sic] from being a responsible politician."[1] Of course, she was just one

woman going after one man. She would need to do better if she wanted to effect any lasting change.

The problem was not those outside of public relations. The problem, she decided, was within the profession itself. And she came to that realization via a quote from Peter Drucker, known as the father of modern business management. He wrote at the end of the 1960s that the United States was in an age of discontinuity and that "the new demand is for business to make social values and beliefs, create freedom for the individuals, and produce the good society." Meeting that demand, he argued, would take creative thinking and new action on the part of managers. "It cannot," he went on, "be handled in the traditional manner. It cannot be handled by public relations." And there it was. An indictment of public relations from a man of whom she considered herself a disciple.[2]

Writing in a *Public Relations Quarterly* article, Plank asked rhetorically, "Are public relations executives equipped to meet future needs of management?" The honest answer, she concluded, was "a reluctant No or just an optimistic maybe." Practitioners were not ready for the changing expectations of business leaders. Other disciplines such as law were moving in, co-opting public relations and meeting the demands of management. With everything top management was now facing and would continue to face in the future, the game of corporate hardball would be even more fierce. Future public relations executives will need to know how to navigate, communicate, and negotiate in the legal, legislative, and regulatory arenas because of their increasing importance to business, she told her readers. They will also need to understand and use research. No longer will practitioners be able to rely on instinct and intuition, the public relations currency for so long. Along with research comes measurement. "The familiar defenses that public relations performance can't be measured will find increasing mother-deafness in future corporate hierarchies." Every other division within a business must measure its productivity. If public relations practitioners continued to insist that public relations is immune from measurement, "its executives can expect diminishing credibility and influence among peers."[3]

In the future, Plank argued, public relations executives would be more managers than tacticians. They would have to discern and manage the appropriate corporate response to issues, balancing short- and long-term welfare of the business and its publics. In concluding, Plank returned to the themes of her inaugural address as PRSA Chair. If the profession rose to the challenge, the risk would be greater visibility and vulnerability for practitioners, but "the prize is to become a more powerful contender in shaping corporate and social history. Prepare not to be less loved, but more respected."[4]

Two years later speaking to an Illinois Bell managers' conference on measurement, Plank repeated her assertions about the changing demands of business, especially about the importance of measurement in public relations. It was not a position she was quick to accept. In fact, she philosophically resisted research and measurement because like many of her fellow practitioners, she still considered public relations an art, a creative business, not a science, and hence not about numbers. But after she moved to the corporate side of the practice, she came to change her mind. She recognized that, like it or not, "the managers of American business today . . . do require accountability in all aspects of their business." They were used to numbers and increasingly wanted to see them before committing money to achieve a business objective. No longer could public relations be practiced "by guess and by gosh."[5]

It was, she admitted, easy to tell practitioners that they needed to develop a more sophisticated take on research and measurement but another thing to do something about it. She felt fortunate that Illinois Bell was one of the few companies in the late 1970s willing to devote resources and staff to measuring its communication efforts. The push came from AT&T's senior management after realizing that regulatory commissions were increasingly disallowing the company's public relations and advertising expenses because of a lack of performance indicators. In 1976, Edward Block, AT&T's vice president of public relations and employee information, established a PR Measurement Committee to develop measurement criteria for the Bell System's public relations functions. That criteria became the template for Illinois Bell's measurement efforts.[6]

For example, Plank's Community Relations department, which was divided into seventy-five teams representing the seventy-five communities served by the company, undertook to research those communities every two years. The survey asked questions such as: Do you like the service Illinois Bell is delivering? Do you feel its employees are well trained? Do you feel they are courteous and efficient? Do you feel the company is contributing toward the quality of life in this community? The responses to those questions became the benchmark for her teams, their "special kinds of report cards," to guide future public relations programming. She hoped the results would make them "more confident and more disciplined and more accountable in our work." Although these "pioneering" measurement efforts were still in the early stages, she noted that they were beginning to see evidence of real progress. People inside and outside the Bell System were "sitting up and taking notice."[7]

TECHNOLOGICAL INNOVATIONS

One area that practitioners could lay claim to was technology and its potential impacts on society. Plank recognized the benefits of the new communications technologies for public relations early on. Of course, she had an advantage in that area. Working for a large communications company, she had at her disposal technological innovations before many other practitioners did. In addition to having its own CCTV studio and video capabilities to reach employees throughout the state, Illinois Bell's Corporate Communications department had more than thirty word processors in those pre-personal-computer days. Those word processors were connected to the studio so that changes could be made to scripts instantly. They were also wired to data banks like Nexis for research. They even had the hardware for email, but as of 1983, the idea of email had "not yet experienced the warm embrace with which [the communicators] welcomed word processors."[8]

Working daily with these new technologies, Plank recognized their potential for public relations. Unlike Plank, most practitioners "were slow to appreciate the benefits of technical advances in communication and held doggedly to print-based models." Trade and association publications contained articles on what was then called the "Information Age," but the majority discussed the new technologies without connecting them specifically with public relations. They saw them as ways to improve and make easier a practitioner's work output rather than as a means of message dissemination. In Plank's eyes, the public relations profession was "uniquely qualified to be a catalyst, a steward, an architect in . . . improving the value and quality of life as the Information Age impacts on society."[9] Public relations practitioners, she believed, would embrace these new technologies and adopt them as their own because they would help improve the profession's effectiveness and influence.

Invited to present at a 1983 seminar in Washington, D.C., on "The Next Revolution in Public Relations: New Uses of Electronic Communications,"

Plank spoke about how practitioners needed to develop strategies for their clients to harness the new technology to best serve their needs. She reminded her audience that one of the most important roles of a public relations practitioner was to be an agent of change and help clients manage their entry into "the Information Age."[10]

At the same time, however, Plank urged practitioners to remember that technology was simply a tool, albeit an important one, to reach publics and not a replacement for personal communication. "The content and integrity of the information we deliver are still our overriding priorities," but "to that professional commitment we must now add the responsibility to use the new telecommunications technology wisely and well," she said. In another speech a year earlier, she expressed presciently her concerns with the Information Age and about "the potential for instant feedback which may threaten time to nurture the American genius for compromise and consensus"; about privacy "in an environment where machines are corruptible"; and about the impact of computer literacy on "language and writing skills." She also worried about what would happen when "opportunities for human encounter—in the marketplace, in the workplace—[were] diminished or altered" as more people began working from home. "Will we need new institutions to provide human contact and avoid isolation?" she asked. Would it all result in a caste system of information poor/information rich? "If information is the most valued commodity of the future, will a concentration of that power dangerously rupture our national stability?"

She assured her audience that her concerns did not amount to a "doomsday prophecy"; they were simply "a caring apprehension."[11] Always at the forefront of Plank's thinking was her belief that human communication is "a most precious—ever sacred—commodity." A framed poem, extolling the limitless abilities of humans, hung in her office as a testament to that belief.[12]

EDUCATING FOR THE FUTURE

Given Plank's interest in and emphasis on improving the reputation of, and professionalizing, public relations, it is perhaps not surprising she became passionate about public relations students and their education after Dr. Albert Walker of Northern Illinois University asked her to speak to his class. One of the features of a profession is specialized knowledge acquired through education.[13] A standardized educational program also helps acculturate students into the profession and inculcate them with appropriate standards of practice. Thus, for Plank, education became the key to shaping the future of the field.

Plank was the Chicago chapter's delegate to the PRSA Assembly in 1967 when the Public Relations Student Society of America was created. PRSA had first considered forming a student organization in 1950, just three years after the national association itself was established. But the idea quickly lost steam in part because the timing was not right. PRSA was still in its infancy with more pressing concerns than chartering a student group. Developing students was not a high priority for a membership that had acquired public relations skills on the job. Only a handful of practitioners in 1950 would have taken a course in public relations; even fewer would have had a degree in it. Most practitioners would have come from the ranks of journalism, the military, or, if they had a college degree, liberal arts. Public relations, these practitioners believed, was not something that could be taught. One acquired the necessary skills on the job.[14]

The topic of a student group was not broached again until 1965, when the chair of PRSA's Education Committee proposed that the Society formally affiliate with the handful of student clubs that had formed on campuses where public relations courses were being taught. To test the waters, Ovid Davis, PRSA's president that year, invited six outstanding students—one from each of the programs at Boston University, Ohio State University, San Jose State University, the University of Texas, Utica College (N.Y.), and the University of Wisconsin—to attend that year's PRSA national conference in Denver as the Society's guests. That first mingling of professionals and students was so successful the students were invited back the following year.[15]

As the number of schools with public relations courses and programs increased in the 1960s, so did the number of independent student groups. By the summer of 1967, six universities had public relations student organizations of various types. One was a fraternal organization; four belonged to one of two honors societies that required a certain grade point average for membership; and the sixth was a general organization of public relations majors. Professor Walter Seifert of Ohio State University encouraged PRSA to "actively foster consolidation of the present public relations campus honorary societies into one unified, national collegiate group with many chapters," a position endorsed by the Public Relations Division of the Association for Education in Journalism. PRSA's Long Range Planning Committee considered the impact these groups, which lacked central guidance and common purpose, might have on the future of public relations and concluded: "Let public relations grow wild, without the benefit of academic preparation, and a half century from now it will be as forgotten as phrenology."[16]

As momentum for a student organization grew, J. Carroll Bateman, the 1967 PRSA President, appointed an advisory committee to prepare a position paper on the topic. The committee's report, complete with a proposed constitution and set of bylaws for a student organization, was presented to the PRSA Assembly at the 1968 national conference in Philadelphia. Plank, as Chicago's Assembly delegate that year, voted in favor of the new student organization. She described that vote as "an act of faith and . . . the beginning of a lifetime love affair with students."[17]

Her interest in public relations education led to her appointment as chair of PRSA's newly created Education and Research Council in 1971. The time had come for PRSA to carefully study public relations education. In the news release announcing the creation of the council, PRSA President Jon Riffel said that it would "take a look at our cradle to grave requirements, including the student society, the accreditation of college courses, and our own internal professional program." Joining Plank on the Council were eleven leaders in the field, all men.[18]

It is not surprising then that Plank referenced public relations students in her 1972 chair-elect acceptance speech, acknowledging their importance to the future of the profession. PRSA members had a vested interest, she suggested, in the kind of students entering the field and the education to which they were exposed. For her part, Plank indicated she intended to strengthen PRSA's relationship with students and educators. In fact, she announced she would be adding PRSSA students as ex officio members to several of the Society's national committees.[19]

Plank's emphasis on education was not lost on PRSSA's leadership. In an interview in the 1973 spring edition of *PRSSA Forum*, Plank was asked whether she thought PRSSA should have its own national leadership now that its membership was at more than twelve hundred. At the time, PRSSA was controlled by PRSA's Committee on Student Organization, which consisted of PRSA members and just two "token" PRSSA members. Plank, despite her focus on public relations education, said she did not believe PRSSA should be self-governing because it would take too much of the students' time when they should be focused on their studies. She also

saw geography as a barrier. It would be difficult for student leaders to find
the money and the time to travel to meetings. Nor did Plank believe that
PRSSA should hold its national convention separate from that of PRSA, for
the same reason she did not "like orphanages or homes for the aged. The
less alienation, the better."[20] She was concerned that a separate convention
would cause PRSSA to lose visibility at a time when not all PRSA members
were "converts" to education.

Just six months later, however, Plank presided over the PRSA Board of
Directors and Assembly that approved a resolution creating the PRSSA
National Committee, allowing the student organization to be self-governing
for the first time. While Plank could be adamant if she thought she were
right about something, she was also magnanimous when someone was able
to convince her otherwise. Clearly, Plank was impressed with and satisfied by the argument presented in the resolution put forward on behalf of
PRSSA by the student group's president, Joan-Patricia O'Connor, a graduate student at the University of Southern California. Finances may also have
played a role in Plank's change of heart. PRSA took a hard look at its expenses in 1973 because of the economic downturn the country was facing.
The growth in PRSSA was costing PRSA $50,000 annually, with half the
airfare and complimentary registration to PRSSA Assembly Delegates for
the PRSA annual conference accounting for an estimated $10,000 of that
alone.[21] Thus, an independent, dues-collecting student organization made a
great deal of sense financially at the time. Regardless of why Plank changed
her mind about the value of a self-governing PRSSA, she was proud the
approval of it came on her watch.

Plank continued supporting PRSSA, serving as its professional national
advisor from 1981 to 1983. At her first meeting with the PRSSA leadership
as their advisor, she mentioned the names of some PRSA members who
had been supporters of the student organization in the sixties and seventies.
Immediately, the eyes of the young student leaders "glazed over." Suddenly,
she realized that most of the students were not aware of the many professionals who had over the years championed PRSSA and were continuing
to do so. Part of the problem was the constant turnover in the student
ranks. They were PRSSA members for only a couple of years before graduating and moving on. That left little time to develop relationships with
PRSA members, which in turn impacted the number of PRSSA members
who subsequently joined PRSA. "So Lo! Overnight a bright idea dawned"

on her. The next morning Plank called fellow PRSA Past President Jon Riffel and proposed that they form their own group called the Friends of PRSSA to help build strong relationships between the professionals and the students.[22]

Within two weeks of gaining permission from the PRSA National Committee to move forward with their plan, Plank and Riffel had reached out to two hundred public relations professionals who had a special commitment to students, asking them to become Friends of PRSSA, a volunteer group of advocates serving as a liaison between PRSA and PRSSA. Minimal dues from its members funded the "Friends." During the first few years of its existence, the Friends published a brief history of PRSSA, held an annual reception during the PRSA/PRSSA conference for PRSSA members, and funded Chapter awards, among other activities. And when the PRSA Foundation ceased funding annual PRSSA scholarships in 1989, Plank immediately initiated a Friends Scholarship Program to fill the void.[23]

STANDARDIZING PR EDUCATION

Nineteen eighty-nine proved to be a pivotal year for public relations education as PRSA also established its Certification in Education for Public Relations (CEPR) that year. The CEPR came about thanks in part to Plank's involvement with the Commission on Public Relations Education (CPRE). The Public Relations Division of the Association for Education in Journalism (AEJ) formed the Commission after Bateman and Dr. Scott Cutlip of the University of Georgia presented a paper at AEJ's annual conference in the summer of 1973 on the "unsatisfactory and disparate state of public relations education" in the United States. The Commission's goals were to examine the requirements for the professional practice of public relations and issue recommendations for the improvement of public relations education. The latter recommendations were not only meant to meet the demands of the profession, but "also to effect ultimate improvement in the professional practice itself."[24] Subsequently, PRSA joined with AEJ in the sponsorship of the Commission.

As was typical of Plank's professional experiences, she was the only woman on that first Commission, joining co-chairs, Bateman and Cutlip, as well as Milton Fairman, Public Relations Consultant; Dr. James Grunig, University of Maryland; Dr. Otto Lerbinger, Boston University; and Dr. Alan Scott, University of Texas. The group met over the course of the next two years at conferences and in airport hotel rooms to hammer out recommendations. Their report, finally issued in 1975, proposed that the public relations curricula should include four courses in public relations, doubling PRSA's two-course requirement to qualify for a PRSSA chapter.[25]

While the Commission's report was an important document, certainly the first of its kind in public relations, and offered a way forward for the field, it produced few tangible results. The Commission had buy-in from only two organizations, PRSA and the PR Division of AEJ, and lacked enforcement capabilities. Still, the professionals and educators concerned with the future of public relations were undeterred. Ten years later, a second Commission on Public Relations Education was convened with Plank and Dr. William Ehling of Syracuse University as the co-chairs. This time, the organizations represented around the table had grown to twenty-five. The importance of education to the future of the industry was being recognized.

The second report, based on extensive research, focused on course content—such as principles of public relations, research, planning, ethics, implementation, and evaluation—rather than course names and semester hours.[26] But without the power of enforcement, either its own or through an accrediting body, the Commission's report again had little impact.

The call for PRSA to accredit public relations programs first came in 1966 from the Society's then president, Robert Wolcott, Jr. But educators quickly informed him that the Accrediting Council on Education in Journalism, an organization with established credibility among educators, was already accrediting public relations programs housed in journalism schools or departments. Cutlip, for example, saw no need for PRSA to get involved in assessing educational programs. "PRSA must face up to this fact," he advised Wolcott. "Public relations . . . logically belongs in journalism education. Journalism educators are coming to accept this fact. Public relations men will, too, in time . . . ."[27]

Robert Miller of American University saw things differently. He opted to have PRSA do its own accrediting, especially since it had already established an accrediting procedure for individual practitioners. Why would the Society accredit practitioners but give some other organization the power to accredit the courses incoming practitioners needed? To him, it made no sense. It seemed "that the Society is accrediting the finished product without really having any control over the courses and curriculums (sic) that are training the people who will become the practitioners," he argued.[28]

It was a valid argument. PRSA was not a member organization of ACEJ and had no input into the standards that the Counsel applied to programs. Nor was PRSA represented on the site teams that visited the schools and wrote the reports. Thus, none of the ten public relations programs accredited by ACEJ between 1957 and 1967 had been reviewed by a public relations practitioner or educator. To remedy that situation, Seifert and Ehling suggested that PRSA join ACEJ so that PRSA would at least have a voice in accrediting decisions. But there remained the question of what to do with those programs not housed in journalism departments and therefore not subject to ACEJ review.[29]

When Bateman assumed the PRSA presidency in 1967, he commissioned a study of the issue, naming John F. Moynihan, a prominent New York City public relations counselor, chair. The Moynihan Report was presented to the PRSA Board of Directors in November 1967. It recommended, among other things, that PRSA join ACEJ; develop a body of knowledge on which accreditation would be based; and work to develop accrediting procedures for those programs in other disciplines, with the goal of having its own accrediting program eventually.[30]

Despite those recommendations, the idea of PRSA establishing its own accrediting procedures lost momentum in the years following the report in part because joining ACEJ appeared to resolve the issue. Over the next eleven years, twenty public relations programs were accredited; an additional four were denied accreditation because they did not meet the standards of at least two core public relations courses, plus a practicum or internship, and more than one faculty member teaching those courses.[31]

Although a 1980 survey of public relations educators revealed that almost sixty percent believed ACEJ was the best accrediting body for their programs, debate continued among PRSA members. Much of the criticism centered on ACEJ's obvious journalistic bent. The majority of its nineteen member organizations were journalism- or broadcast-related, and its leadership was made up entirely of journalists and broadcasters. Also, PRSA's affiliation with ACEJ still did nothing to remedy the issue of programs housed in other disciplinary departments.

The first Commission on Public Relations Education Report in 1975 had not tackled the issue of accreditation head on. Instead, it said that the Commission's recommendations should "conform in a general way to the accreditation requirements" of ACEJ, even though the Commission recommended four public relations courses, not two.[32] By the time the second report was issued in 1987, ACEJ had changed its procedure. Instead of accrediting each individual program within a school or department as it had done in the past, ACEJ now accredited the academic unit, regardless of the strengths or weaknesses of individual programs.

For Plank, this was unacceptable. She was particularly concerned that weak public relations programs could claim to be accredited when they were not in fact meeting the ACEJ standards, never mind the Commission's recommendations. She appears, though, not to have been aware at the time that not all public relations programs were housed in departments or schools of journalism, even though it had been a topic of debate in PRSA circles since the late sixties, which suggests her focus was not on education until the early 1970s.[33] Regardless, she was soon advised by educators that some were in communication studies departments and even in business schools, which meant they were not being reviewed by ACEJ at all.

To ensure that public relations programs wherever housed and however accredited maintained certain standards of excellence, Plank worked through the PRSA Educational Affairs Committee to establish the Certification for Education in Public Relations (CEPR) in 1989. Plank's idea was that PRSA would independently assess public relations programs and certify them according to the standards set out by the Commission on Public Relations Education. The CEPR would provide the enforcement capability the Commission lacked. Creating an independent certification process meant that public relations programs would be rigorously reviewed by public relations practitioners and educators, regardless of where the program was housed administratively.[34]

"WANTED: 100 GIRLS"

As the number of public relations programs grew, the percentage of women majoring in public relations increased from approximately 25 percent of the students in 1970 to 67 percent by 1980. The ratio of female-to-male students was about eight to one by the end of the decade. Correspondingly, women represented just 27 percent of public relations practitioners in 1970, but 56.6 percent by 1987. Close to 75 percent of women in the field, however, were in the lower echelons. According to *PR Reporter*, only 30 percent of vice presidents and 34 percent of presidents of public relations firms were women as of 1989. And the women generally still faced salary discrimination. Plank's consciousness about gender discrimination had been raised in the 1970s, but she still did not embrace feminism. She did not believe that salary discrepancies warranted concern, for example, because salaries would, she argued, come into balance eventually. "The important thing was to fight inequities in your own organization," she said.[35]

But Plank was not always prepared to do that within Illinois Bell. In a standard executive speech from 1980 about women in the company that was in her files, it was argued that Illinois Bell had always been a major employer of women. The evidence? An ad that ran in the Help Wanted column of the *Chicago Tribune* in November 1926. Illinois Bell was seeking one hundred girls to become long-distance telephone operators. The "girls" had to be single and living at home. Some sixty-six years later, the speech read, there were no men's jobs or women's jobs at the company, only telephone jobs. Of course, Illinois Bell did not become more welcoming to women employees because it suddenly found enlightenment. The company was forced into it in 1973 when AT&T signed a consent decree with the federal Equal Employment Opportunity Commission to rectify its history of sex discrimination.[36]

Yet, in the speech, shock was expressed that the Bell System had been accused of discrimination against women. "I was shocked because I knew the Bell System employed more women than any other industry in the nation." But it was acknowledged that women were rare in management at Illinois Bell. And most of the "management women were stuck at the lowest levels." Still, women could be proud of the progress the company had made, although not enough for Plank to necessarily identify with the other women in management.[37]

Plank finally became a member of the Bell Management Women in 1984 after the group had been around for several years, perhaps because she had been asked to speak to the group. She knew they existed because a few of them had come to her years before and said they wanted to establish a group for women managers. She thought it was a worthy endeavor but clearly did not see herself benefiting from such a group at the time. If they asked her to speak because they expected her to praise them and give them words of wisdom in accord with "all the popular folklore on the subject" of women in management, they were sorely mistaken. Instead, she offered three criticisms of current thinking regarding women in business.

First, she did not believe one should go "after mentors in a conscious, deliberate way" as self-help books suggested. Mentors, she believed, find you. At the same time, one can, and should, be a mentor, role model, and sponsor to others. Second, she had a problem with entry-level and middle management women being singularly focused on their jobs. It was short-sighted not to seek out and take on additional responsibility because that is how one grows in one's career. The third problem was the failure of women managers to be concerned about their visibility. "If you don't make an effort to be visible, you can get paranoid wondering why nobody knows 'I'm the most wonderful person in the world,'" she said. To be visible, women must write and speak well and be involved in the community. "Too many women overlook these opportunities. They don't understand the importance of that kind of involvement, that showcasing of talent." So, her advice, based on her own life success, was to: "take on responsibility, get involved in the community, get involved in the profession, become a mentor yourself."[38]

Nothing in her advice to the Bell Management Women suggested forming a sisterhood for support. Except for Duffy Schwartz in the 1950s, Plank's mentors and sponsors had been men, although she said she had never heard the word "mentor" until she joined the Bell System. But within that bureaucracy, mentorship, formal or otherwise, was important to one's upward mobility. Paul Lund had brought her into AT&T and had arranged for her transfer to Illinois Bell. But he died suddenly in 1975, just a year after she moved back to Chicago. A few months after his death, Plank was having lunch with a retired vice president of Illinois Bell when he asked her, "Well, Betsy, what are you going to do now that your mentor died?" She said she "froze in mid-fork-lift." She put her fork down carefully and said, 'What do you mean?' And he said, 'Well, Paul was the one that brought you into the business. He's not here to look after you now. So now what are you going to do?" She recognized immediately what he was getting at. As she put it, "He was telegraphing to me that I had no history with the company; I had not earned my way up. I had come in at a top level and therefore I was resented by some. I had no champion. So there I was, lonely and paddling my own canoe. It also made me realize that I had never consciously looked for champions in my long work career."[39]

No champions, and certainly no women champions, other than Schwartz. So, it was not surprising that in 1979, when Plank received a call from an acquaintance asking her if she were interested in joining the Chicago Network, a new group that was being formed by women executives in the Chicago area, her initial response was no. "I don't belong to any women's groups," she told the acquaintance. "If you're a professional, you just belong

to whatever the professional group is, and it includes he's, she's, and it's."
But because she respected the woman, she agreed to attend the initial meeting, and probably surprising herself, Plank ended up deciding to join after
all, becoming a co-founder. She found that the group opened doors into
business but also into friendships. "Once we got together and trusted each
other, we began taking our colleagues everywhere on boards," she said. "It
was such a wonderful thing to walk in and not feel like a stranger."[40]

Although she had never complained about being the only woman, she
now found a kinship she had not experienced before. "You spent all your
life being the first woman this and the first woman that. Which is kind of
nice, but every time you opened your mouth, it was as if: 'Aha! You're representing the entire women's voice. . . .' The Network provided that confidence quotient. There are others there."[41] As was her way, Plank chaired the
Chicago Network the following year and in 1989 was awarded the group's
First Decade Award.

RETIRING FOR LOVE

By the end of the 1980s, Plank was deeply entrenched in professionalizing
the field through education. She recognized that students were the future of
public relations. The better prepared those students were for the practice, the
stronger the profession would be. She was not an educator herself, although
she often spoke to classes, so she worked with other forward-thinking professionals and educators on the Commission on Public Relations Education
to create a curriculum that would ensure students gained the knowledge
and acquired the skills that would be needed in the future. And then, she
helped establish the Certification in Public Relations Education to certify
that programs were indeed offering the appropriate courses. She did not
just steer the boat, she set its course with a steady hand. She was the visionary who sought to shape the future of the field.

At the same time, Plank was happy with her work at Illinois Bell even
though she was stuck at the assistant vice president level. The vice presidency of corporate communication had come open three times over the
years she had been with the company. Each time it was filled by a man.
Numerous factors were probably at play in her not being promoted to vice
president. The first was the company's glass ceiling. Women simply were
not considered for senior leadership positions at the time. In fact, as of
1989, only three women within AT&T had risen to the position of vice

president of a department. Despite the moniker "Ma Bell," the System had always been a patriarchy. As much as Plank thought of herself as a "good ole boy," she clearly was not, especially since her mentor and sponsor, Paul Lund, was no longer alive to advocate on her behalf.

Another important factor was that Plank did not join Illinois Bell until she was fifty years old. As such, she was an outsider. AT&T was "built on the family structure: fathers and sons, mothers and daughters, husbands and wives, brothers and sisters. All dedicated to service. All working for Bell." She felt a part of the Bell family, but it was like she was an in-law by marriage, not by blood. The men who rose to vice president had worked for the Bell System for decades. For example, Jack Koten, who became vice president of corporate communication in 1977, originally joined Illinois Bell in 1955, and that was typical of senior leadership in the Bell System.[42]

Age was also a factor. Plank was sixty when the divestiture took place, which had effectively slowed the upward mobility of employees. Her only option after 1984 would have been to move up to Ameritech, but she would have been older than the individuals in more senior positions, such as Koten who was five years her junior. Marilyn Laurie who was the first woman to join AT&T's executive board started with the company in 1971 at the age of thirty-two and was forty-eight when she became an officer. Plank was fifteen years older.[43]

Still, she had no real thoughts of retiring until her husband became ill in the late 1980s. Rosenfield's diagnosis of cancer and subsequent hospitalization in 1988 forced her to reconsider how she wanted to spend the rest of her life. She was only sixty-four and still vibrant but being with Rosenfield trumped everything else. Thus, in March 1990, Plank retired from Illinois Bell after sixteen years. That Illinois Bell was seeking to reduce its management force by one thousand through a salary buyout plan probably contributed to her decision to leave at that time. Rosenfield's cancer was in remission, and the two spent a perfect summer together at their cottage on Lake Michigan.[44]

Plank and Rosenfield purchased the A-frame cottage in South Haven, Michigan, in 1967, and named it Zanahoria, which is Spanish for carrot. With its approximately one hundred feet of Lake Michigan frontage, wrap-around deck, and rough-sawn timber interior, Zanahoria was the metaphorical carrot at the end of the stick, the perfect escape for the couple. As an invitation to their friends to visit them, Plank prepared a "brochure" in

Fig. 13: Plank and
Rosenfield loved to
entertain, which often
involved costumes.
Here they are
celebrating the 4th of
July. Courtesy of the
Plank Papers

the style of a campground promotional piece. It was a place where "fun is in
season 365 days a year!" she wrote. "Zanahoria is comfortably nestled atop
a gently wooded dune providing a breathtaking panoramic view. Down and
out, across the glistening sand, over the ever-changing blue of majestic Lake
Michigan, on toward the endless horizon. This is living. It's part of the good
life. A million miles away from it all (though metropolitan Chicago is only
140 miles down the road.)"[45]

It was to Zanahoria that Plank and Rosenfield retreated that summer.
And for a few months, it must have felt a million miles away from the
heartache and worry of Rosenfield's illness. She concluded her "brochure"
by telling everyone that Zanahoria was "not the world as you know it. It's
the world as you'd like it."[46] Unfortunately, their idyllic life together was
fleeting. Rosenfield died that November.

CHAPTER 7

Leaving a Legacy

**Tunnel under, go over, walk around, walk away . . . do
whatever you have to do to move on.**

—Betsy Ann Plank

PLANK WAS DEVASTATED by the loss of her husband. She turned to God for
support, praying for an open door to show her a path forward. A door did
eventually open, one that led back to The University of Alabama and to
what would become her legacy, The Plank Center for Leadership in Public
Relations.

"A DEEP EXCORIATING BURN"

Sent into a tailspin by Rosenfield's death in November 1990, Plank struggled to right herself. At first, it seemed the life had been sucked out of
her. She did not think she could even summon the energy to speak at his
memorial service, but she did manage to and thanked their special friends
who came to celebrate the life of "this magnificent man" with her.[1] Plank
and Rosenfield always celebrated their wedding anniversary on the tenth
of every month, and while their friends teased them about it, they enjoyed
438 "anniversaries." It sounded like more than a lifetime's worth, but it was
still not enough. As she often did, Plank described Rosenfield as a saint for
putting up with her, while describing herself as a "royal nag" and a pushy
broad who was never satisfied.

It was true that Plank did not suffer fools gladly. Front-line employees
who did not deliver the excellent customer service she was expecting were
especially prone to receiving her wrath. When they traveled, Rosenfield was
inevitably sent back to the hotel lobby after they checked in to request a
room change because Plank always found fault with the first one. But as
saints are wont to do, Rosenfield took it all in stride, loving her uncondi-
tionally. She reminisced to the assembled guests how, "We still held hands

Fig. 14: Plank and
Rosenfield attending
a formal dinner in
1989, a year before
Rosenfield's death.
Courtesy of the Plank
Papers

when we walked together—and never a single day went by that we didn't hear out loud from one another, 'I love you.'" In despair after the service, Plank wrote herself a to-do list that included: "Learn to drive, Decide what to do with Sherm's ashes, Decide what to do with rest of life."[2]

On Plank's list, it was the last item that gave her the most pause. She had never imagined life without Rosenfield, and yet, here she was—without him and retired. Bereft of her two life anchors—her husband and her work—she was adrift. She prayed to God and Rosenfield to help her stop crying. "Help me. Help me. Help me find the right way. Oh Shermy, in all your wonderful travels, travel back to me," she wrote a day after what would have been their 443rd monthly anniversary.[3]

Somehow, Plank managed to get through that first year following Rosenfield's death but at the cost of relationships with some of their dearest friends and family. She pondered the reasons for her actions:

Maybe because I'm angry at them . . . for not helping enough, or caring enough or not knowing how to care and help. Or for being happy, in control, and managing. Who knows? For feeling sorry for me? Such a sin. For feeling duty? Whatever. I've cut them off and, in effect, said, 'I can do without you.' Of course, the big question is, 'Can I!' If I could, do I really want to? And the answer could well be 'Maybe so.'

Distancing herself from that which caused her pain failed to ease her grief. Of course, it could also be, she thought, that they were part of her old life, a life that included Rosenfield. "The reality is," she wrote, ". . . the old doesn't fit, won't work, drags me down, back, while I'm struggling to put one foot in front of another." She also recognized that grief can get tiresome for those not experiencing it. She refused to be cut loose by her friends because they found her no longer fun to be around. She preferred to jettison them first.[4]

Plank struggled to do her best to get on with life. She accepted every invitation she received to speak, to visit, to travel, anything to keep busy. At times, she even felt the old adrenaline rush, such as the day the pastry shop forgot to give her the $2.40 pastry she had ordered, and she let them have it, just like her old self would have. Pleased, she thought "the bitch is back."[5] It was not growing old that bothered her; retirement did. Retirement was supposed to be her time to "be happy loving" Rosenfield. She wondered whether there was an "after work" for her now that "be happy loving" Rosenfield was out of the question. She kept looking to God for an answer:

Surely somewhere, God, there is an opening door.
Oh Amazing Grace, wherefore art Thou?
Oh God. You promised. I watch. And search. And wait.
What's grief for one so deeply loved?
So all-in-all. So everything in one's life?
So much a part of the incarnate tapestry?
So sainted, kind and loving and forgiving?
It is a deep, excoriating burn.[6]

The smoldering burn was tamped down over time, but never fully extinguished. While Plank waited for a door to open, she busied herself and kept putting one foot in front of the other.

As she had since 1975, Plank continued to serve as a member of the advisory board of *Illinois Issues*, a magazine devoted to the analysis of public policy issues in Illinois and published by the University of Illinois at Springfield. She also remained chair of the Citizenship Council of Metropolitan Chicago, a role she had first assumed in the spring of 1990. And in 1992, she received the Volunteer of the Year Award from Chicago's YWCA. They were worthy pursuits she was proud of, but none rekindled her passion for life.

DEFENDING HER PROFESSION

But then Dr. Clarke Caywood of Northwestern University asked Plank to serve on an Integrated Communication Task Force.[7] The advertising and public relations divisions of the Association for Education in Journalism and Mass Communication established the task force in 1991 to explore the changing communications landscape and to determine the appropriate academic response. Its original three members were Caywood, an integrated marketing communication (IMC) and advertising professor; Tom Duncan, an IMC professor from the University of Colorado at Boulder; and Douglas Ann Newsom, a professor of journalism and public relations at Texas Christian University.[8]

Although Caywood told Plank that her "role in advertising, sales promotion, public relations and direct response marketing" would provide leadership on the task force, his choice of Plank as a member was no doubt more strategic and understandably so. Plank's presence would lend instant credibility and respectability to the task force among public relations practitioners and educators. But for Plank's part, the decision to join was an odd one given her definition of public relations, which she saw in its purest and broadest sense. The primary mission of public relations, she once said, "is to forge responsible relationships of understanding, trust and respect among groups and individuals—even when they disagree." In Plank's eyes, integrated marketing communication was simply one aspect of the full profession. Under normal circumstances, she would never have agreed to serve on a task force that was seeking to reduce public relations to a fraction of its totality, but the invitation to participate came at a time when she was still grieving and saying yes to everything. She also may not have fully understood the task force's purpose. In the background materials provided to her initially, it was described as exploring changes in communications broadly; it was only later she learned that by "communications," they meant "marketing communications."[9]

The first meeting of the task force was via conference call and involved a preliminary discussion of three major issues: first, to what extent is marketing communications changing; second, should students be trained as communication specialists or generalists; and third, should a student of integrated marketing communications be separated from the study of total communications programs. On the call, Plank questioned the task force's focus on marketing communications. Not surprisingly, she thought it too narrow. Marketing communications was, as she noted, just "a sliver, albeit an important sliver," of the practice of public relations.[10] But others on the call attempted to assure her that although they had started with a narrow focus, as the idea had evolved, they had broadened it to include public relations.

Unconvinced, Plank continued to express views that clashed with those of the others. For instance, she believed that public relations students should be trained as generalists, not specialists, and that students of integrated marketing communications should be taught the total communications package. As she explained, to do otherwise was to view customers myopically. "A customer is a voter, a customer may be an environmentalist, a customer may have all kinds of different concerns that ultimately perhaps affect buying habits," she said. Not all of those would be taken into consideration in an IMC program.[11]

Six months later, as Plank prepared to attend another meeting of the group, she mentioned the task force to David Ferguson, a PRSA Past President and former co-chair of PRSA's Educational Affairs Committee. Ferguson did not know anything about it even though the task force purportedly involved public relations education, and he was well known in PRSA circles for his dedication to improving the field's educational requirements. That piqued her interest. Why had he not been invited to serve on the task force, or at least, why had he not been informed about it? Suddenly, Plank's spirit awakened. What exactly was going on here, she thought. What was the real agenda?

At the October 1992 meeting, Plank learned that the task force now consisted of twenty-two people, only one-third of whom were public relations practitioners or educators. Plank wrote to Ferguson and a few others who were fellow travelers in public relations education immediately following the meeting to apprise them of the situation. Piecing it together, she surmised that "advertising programs in academe [were] 'in trouble' and [needed] a new approach to save themselves for the sagging industry. . . ."[12] The result was a push to bring advertising and public relations programs together under "a Marketing-driven umbrella." The advertising division of AEJMC floated the idea and later the leadership of the PR division joined in. Although some public relations educators challenged the notion at the time, the task force was given approval.

Plank went on to describe her take on that first face-to-face meeting of the task force. Dr. Lauri Grunig of the University of Maryland was, Plank wrote, "God bless—eloquent and substantive" in carrying the public relations flag. Plank described herself, on the other hand, as "obstreperous." She "got tired of advertising and direct mail people talking about PR in 'publicity' terms and did a passionate number about the broader practice, which IMC ignores." Later, she "erupted again, questioning their assumption that public relations would buy into being co-opted under the marketing rubric." As Plank recalled it, that prompted a "bloody reaction." IMC was the future and if public relations were not on board, it would be run over by the speeding IMC train.[13]

Plank decided that the task force saw marketing as the salvation for advertising and wanted public relations along for credibility. She advised her co-conspirators that they would have "to seize the initiative and take a position" on it. Otherwise, the task force would "soon be asserting out loud that we're marching to this drummer in lock step." If they decided to develop a position regarding the task force and its pending recommendations, it should first be "1) conveyed to the Task Force Co-Chairs (and perhaps copied to all Task Force members) and to the Chair of the [Public Relations Division] of AEJMC; 2) ready for press response when the White Paper is introduced. If the White Paper is circulated for review by Task Force members, perhaps those/some of us representing public relations will wish to provide a Minority Report."[14]

The group mobilized immediately. Pat Jackson, who had also been asked to join the task force, wrote to the group two days later. The task force, he indicated, was honest in admitting that "since their one-way, propagandistic disciplines are less and less effective, they now want to move in on the relationship arena. Is this a chance for public relations to demonstrate that it is the umbrella, and these other pieces are tactical implementations?" he asked. Jackson apparently answered his own question in the negative and dropped out of the task force. Another member of the group and a PRSA past president, Jerry Dalton, also opted out because he strongly disagreed with the Task Force's "assumption that marketing is driving the future of public relations."[15]

So why did Plank stay when others such as Jackson and Dalton, whom Plank regarded highly, chose to step aside? Initially, she too wanted to quit, but having said yes originally to Caywood when he asked her, she hated to step down part way through the process, at least not without having her say. Despite their philosophical differences, Plank respected Caywood. But there were two other, more important, reasons for remaining on the task force. First, Plank realized that her voice from within would have some legitimacy, and she had been promised that a minority position would be respected.[16] And second, like a mole in an intelligence organization, she knew she could accomplish more if she had an inside track on exactly what the IMC task force was proposing. She used that information to tip off the others. In July 1993, she wrote to Ferguson and Judy VanSlyke Turk, the co-chairs of PRSA's Educational Affairs Committee, to inform them about a revised version of the Integrated Communications Report. The revision was "fair game" for the EAC's discussion at its August meeting. Plank warned Ferguson and Turk in the letter that a practitioner who was a member of the PRSA board was a "believer in IMC." Plank suggested they "might wish to get to [that practitioner] to bring her up to speed on EAC reservations, especially since she sits on the PRSA board and could do damage."[17]

Plank went on to say that she had heard from "a very knowledgeable colleague outside of public relations" that the "whole business of subsuming public relations under marketing and as an adjunct to advertising" was part of a much larger strategy. The task force's agenda was one of "total integration of advertising and public relations under marketing's umbrella—not only in education but also in practice." Alerting professionals who had a stake in both camps to the public relations concerns would be smart, she suggested, because they would have credibility on both sides. Another concern was that Ray Gaulke, the chief operating officer of PRSA, was primarily from an advertising and marketing background, making him at risk of being "captured" by the IMC interests. "However," Plank advised, "Ray is currently in the mode of 'proving himself' to the public relations community and thus could be persuaded to join the right side of this issue if he's 'gotten to' early on."[18]

The EAC's eventual position statement in response to the Task Force report outlined the philosophical differences between the two camps. The EAC saw advertising, marketing, and public relations fulfilling different purposes within organizations and using different strategies and tactics to accomplish their respective goals. Because public relations was the broadest of the three functions in terms of purpose, focus, and audiences, it required a broader education, one based in both communications and the social sciences.[19]

In Plank's own response to the Task Force report, she wrote, "[Unfortunately] the report continues to convey the attitude that there is Only One True Gospel, Only One Way to Salvation, and Eternal Damnation for any alternate view of a universe revolving around Planet Marketing." The Task Force's initial purpose of "exploring" soon translated into an agenda of support for total integration of advertising and public relations. Many on the task force, in Plank's eyes, viewed public relations solely in terms of marketing, a view which was "patently self-serving, outdated and ludicrous." Their attempt to take over education of the field was not only misguided, but "potentially self-defeating for both advertising and public relations, their students and future professionals."[20]

The Task Force's report made little headway in public relations programs around the country. How much of that had to do with Plank's ability to rally the troops for a spirited defense of public relations education cannot be known, but regardless, the situation gave Plank a focus and stirred within her a passion she had not felt since before Rosenfield's death. She had been a strong advocate for public relations education before, but it was now her purpose.

PROFESSIONALIZING PUBLIC RELATIONS

Plank worked tirelessly to promote the Public Relations Student Society of America to students, educators, and practitioners. PRSSA members became "her children," children she carefully nurtured and mentored. Over the next sixteen years, she spoke to numerous student chapters and faithfully attended the PRSSA national conference annually, which was held in conjunction with the PRSA conference albeit at a different hotel. Plank always stayed in the student hotel to be close to her "children" (that she could still get a smoking room in that hotel was an added bonus).

At the 1991 PRSSA conference, Plank met Mary Beth West, a 19-year-old student attending her first such event. West's experiences with Plank are typical of countless others. West remembered Plank standing in the front of a packed room addressing the attendees. She was "small in stature but towering both in presence and in command of her subject matter. Most of all though, I could immediately tell she really cared about every single young person in that room. It was palpable," West recalled.

West sought out Plank after the session was over to ask advice on how she should go about getting local PRSA professionals involved in a new mentoring program her PRSSA chapter was instituting. As a sophomore, West had no existing relationship with the professionals. Plank immediately took her aside and started asking "truly engaged" questions. What was West trying to accomplish? What were her concerns and challenges in setting up the mentoring program? In hindsight, West realized that through Plank's questions, she was sizing up the younger woman in terms of her level of inexperience to determine how much counsel was needed. As one educator noted, young people who needed more self-confidence got it after speaking with Plank. But those who needed a little less brashness also got that after talking with her. "And both came away liking her." For her part, West said she came away from that conversation "feeling a sense of excitement, fresh energy, empowerment (I'd never quite felt *that* before!)." Suddenly, she "knew what to do, and how to do it—it just clicked—and all it had taken was speaking with this incredible woman." At the following year's convention, West reintroduced herself to Plank, who remembered her.[21]

Students, like West, and public relations education in general were major components of Plank's vision for the future of the field. For her, public relations was a profession much like law, but she knew many on the outside failed to recognize it as such. Professions operate in the public interest, have a body of knowledge that can be obtained only through specialized education, and are licensed, among other criteria. In Plank's eyes, public relations easily met the first requirement because it was essential to a democracy, providing a voice to organizations and allowing them to seek public consent. She took to heart the description of public relations that said its function is to identify "the policies and procedures of an organization with the public interest, and [plan] and [execute] a program of action to earn public understanding and acceptance."[22] It was the other professional criteria that were more problematic for the field.

Licensing was an especially tricky issue that produced sharp disagreement among practitioners. Edward Bernays, the self-proclaimed father of public relations, was a long-time advocate for the licensing of practitioners, which he argued was the key to professionalization. He and other senior public relations practitioners formed a national committee in 1986 to promote the idea of licensing. They believed licensing would define public relations, encourage uniform curricula in colleges and universities, help set uniform ethical standards for the practice, allow for decertification of ethics violators, and overall, raise the credibility of the field. Others disagreed, arguing that licensing would restrain trade, encourage government intervention, and limit the mobility of practitioners, much as licensing had for attorneys.[23]

About a decade earlier, a survey of Public Relations Division members of the Association of Education in Journalism had revealed similar results. Almost seventy percent of public relations educators were opposed to licensing, with government control and the creative and complex nature of public relations among the reasons for rejecting it. One educator was adamantly against licensing because "PR is neither a profession (law, medicine) nor a trade (plumbers, barbers)."[24] Plank would have vehemently disagreed with the first part of that statement. She often compared public relations to law in terms of professionalism and believed it was only a matter of time before public relations would take its rightful place beside the legal profession as a necessity in society. But at the same time, she would have agreed vehemently with the second part. Public relations was not a trade in her eyes. She was convinced licensing would reduce the stature of the field, not elevate it, and she refused to have the plumber/barber connotation connected with public relations.

In her role as PRSA chair, Plank had asked J. Handly Wright, a former vice president of the Association of American Railroads and past president of PRSA, to prepare a memorandum for her on the licensing issue. In his report, Wright concluded that although the Society appeared to be polarizing around licensing, "relatively few of the society's 7,000 members have been heard from on the subject."[25] Probably because of the unsettled attitudes and Plank's own opposition to the idea, she did not pursue the issue. Instead, PRSA put its focus on the accreditation of practitioners, an alternative option often proposed by those against licensing.

The Accredited in Public Relations, or APR, credential was developed in 1963 and implemented two years later by PRSA after it opened its membership to those new to the profession. Initially, to become a PRSA member, one had to have five years of full-time public relations experience and be sponsored by a member in good standing. Plank, herself, did not join PRSA until 1959, twelve years after she first began practicing. The Chicago chapter at the time required a potential member to have a proven track record of performance. Successful practitioners would then be invited to apply for membership. But in the early 1960s, PRSA removed the five-year requirement and the sponsorship, opening its ranks to anyone working full-time in the profession. The fall out was that some of its newer members lacked experience and expertise in the field. Most practitioners at the time had studied journalism or the liberal arts, not public relations. The accrediting process was an attempt by PRSA to establish norms of practice and to ensure that practitioners were qualified and possessed the necessary knowledge, skills, and abilities to provide strategic communications advice to their clients.[26] Viewed cynically, it can be interpreted as a means to head off governmental regulation.

Getting internal and external support for the APR, however, proved more difficult than anticipated. Clients, not knowing what the credential represented, paid little attention to it. As a result, practitioners had no meaningful incentive to obtain their APR, which was a demanding process, requiring about a year of study and the successful completion of an oral exam at the end. By December 1973, eight years after the first practitioners were accredited, just forty percent of eligible PRSA members had their APR. Making little to no headway in convincing clients and employers to require the designation, PRSA shifted its focus to its membership. Perhaps by requiring the APR for leadership roles within the Society, PRSA could pressure practitioners to obtain it. Thus, PRSA began requiring chapter delegates to the association's assembly to be accredited. Similarly, membership in the organization's College of Fellows, an honorary organization established in 1989, required a minimum of twenty-years of public relations experience plus the APR, among other criteria.[27]

Plank, who was grandfathered in and granted her APR in 1965 without having to take the exam, supported PRSA's efforts to encourage the growth and further development of accreditation by requiring the designation for chapter delegates to the PRSA assembly.[28] But in itself that created the problem of disadvantaging some of the smaller chapters that were lacking members with the APR. With no one to send as a delegate to the PRSA assembly, those chapters were essentially disenfranchised.

It was the College of Fellows requirement, however, with which Plank really took issue. In 1997 Ed Block, AT&T's senior vice president of public relations, was nominated for the Gold Anvil, PRSA's highest individual honor. The Gold Anvil winner was supposed to be automatically inducted into the College of Fellows, but Block did not have his APR and could not, therefore, become a Fellow. Plank, who had great admiration for Block, believed in accreditation but also recognized that requiring the APR for membership in the College of Fellows had its limitations. It was, she noted, an "absurd necessity for a legend" like Block.[29] Thus, she ensured that Block's nomination letters for the Gold Anvil were so strong that the College of Fellows could not deny him entry. PRSA was essentially forced to back track and waive the APR requirement in certain situations such as to prevent the disenfranchisement of some chapters and the preclusion of "legends" from its College of Fellows.

STANDARDIZING EDUCATION

Undeterred by the unintended consequences of the APR requirement, Plank turned her attention to the idea of a standardized education, the third criteria for a profession. Plank had never taken a public relations course and had to learn everything, as she said, "by the seat of her pants," as did most practitioners of her age and time. While that clearly worked for those like Plank who entered the field in the late 1940s and early 1950s, the practice of public relations had changed considerably since then. It had gone from "one slim reed of the practice—publicity—to a forest of functions and [was] still growing."[30] It had also gone from an art based on intuition to a science. Now it required specialized education and training and knowledge of behavioral science research into "how and why people react, emotional barriers to listening and persuasion, cultural conditioning."[31]

In an attempt to ensure future practitioners were prepared for the practice, Plank put emphasis on the Certification for Education in Public Relations (CEPR), which she helped establish in 1989. The CEPR applied the curricular recommendations of the 1987 Commission on Public Relations Education (CPRE) to public relations programs in universities around the country to ensure that those programs had, and maintained, the proper level of expertise for the field.[32]

But as was the case with the APR, gaining exposure and credibility for the certification took some time. In the beginning, schools had no incentive to spend the time and money to apply for something that did not appear to have value in the profession and thus would not benefit their students.

Recognizing that was an issue, PRSA's Educational Affairs Committee, which managed the CEPR, asked Plank and Pat Jackson to co-chair a task force to promote the program. The goal was to get an additional eight to ten reviews scheduled over the next year with a target of six new certifications. Jackson had suggested to Plank when they first began talking about certification that the two might have to lean on schools where they had personal contacts and convince them that it was important for their programs to apply. "That point has now come, my prescient friend!" Plank wrote to Jackson, providing him with a list of schools for the two to contact.[33]

One of Plank's tactics to heighten the visibility of the CEPR was to convince PRSA to recognize the newly certified schools at its annual conference during the individual awards luncheon. "This recognition has special value," she wrote, "in encouraging other schools . . . and in improving visibility for Certification among our conferees."[34] She wanted professionals to recognize that certified schools had met the educational standards for the practice of public relations. Acknowledging those schools at the PRSA conference would draw attention to their commitment and efforts in preparing qualified future public relations practitioners.

As it happened, the PRSA conference that year was to be held in conjunction with the International Public Relations Association's World Congress. That meant a full agenda. The only concession PRSA could make was to invite the schools to the Assembly luncheon and have them recognized there. At first, she was disappointed, "to put it mildly." But she soon realized that having the schools acknowledged at the Assembly would put them before an audience with a more "vested interest" in education and the future of the profession. Plank offered to not only notify the schools herself about the Assembly luncheon, but also to prepare a draft of the presentation comments, and have the certificates printed and framed if that would make it easier on the PRSA staff. And if representatives from the schools could not be PRSA guests for the luncheon, she would buy tickets for them, thereby removing any financial obstacle to their attendance.[35]

Her mission to move public relations toward greater professionalization required constant adjustments and a focused effort. She became concerned in the nineties that PRSA once again was in danger of becoming a trade association, playing to the lowest common denominator. One sign of the move was that the new PRSA president had reconstituted the Educational Affairs Committee, removing from it her and others with institutional history.[36] Although Plank no longer had an official voice in furthering public relations education, she continued to work behind the scenes to avoid the possibility of the profession becoming diluted, drawing on her personal contacts to influence education and students.

One of Plank's concerns was that public relations programs were most often housed in journalism departments and did not receive their fair share of funding despite being responsible for most of the departmental growth. In 1991, Plank and Dr. James Grunig, a University of Maryland public relations professor, headed a task force to determine the kind and amount of administrative support public relations programs received from their universities; whether the department within which those programs were housed affected funding; and what could be done to improve funding levels.[37] The result of that look at philanthropy was discouraging. The profession was clearly not investing in the future of the field, despite the great need for such investment. As Plank put it, public relations education was in dire need of more "angels."

Even more discouraging for Plank was a proposed bylaw amendment urged on PRSA by PRSSA to allow student-at-large affiliate memberships. Affiliate members of PRSSA would be those who attended colleges or universities that either did not have a public relations program or failed to meet the requirements for a PRSSA chapter, which at the time required five public relations courses—introduction to public relations, public relations writing, strategy and implementation, research, and an internship.[38]

Plank argued against allowing affiliate membership because she believed it would reduce the professionalism of the field, a position contrary to the one she had taken earlier with respect to practitioners who had no previous public relations experience. In 1973, as the PRSA president, she sought to encourage such practitioners to join PRSA to have them acculturated into the profession. She knew it was highly unlikely that these individuals would return to school to master the material necessary to become a true public relations professional. PRSA membership was the only option to ensure consistency of professional values and ethical standards. But the students who would become affiliate members were already in school. They could have attended a college or university that taught public relations but for whatever reason did not.

By creating an affiliate membership for students at schools that did not qualify for a PRSSA chapter, PRSA would be sending the wrong message in

Plank's eyes. It would devalue the strict course requirements for a chapter and dilute the profession by allowing, as she saw it, unprepared students to enter the field under the PRSSA banner. Plank was seeking to establish, as much as possible given the amorphous nature of public relations, a standardized educational background for all students to provide them with the necessary specialized knowledge for the field moving forward. The idea of affiliate membership seemed to work against her goal of professionalization.

As she had with the task force on integrated communication, Plank cobbled together a "Loyal Opposition," some fifty educators and practitioners, who signed a letter to the PRSA Assembly protesting the proposed bylaw. They put forward instead a two-pronged solution: 1) the responsibility of student outreach to potential affiliates would be placed with PRSSA; and 2) affiliate membership would be restricted to students in accredited four-year universities that did not have a PRSSA chapter, but that did have at least one full-time faculty member who was also a PRSA member. The group believed that this proposal would achieve PRSA's objective of reaching more students without compromising the integrity of the Society's educational mission. To the group's satisfaction, the PRSA Board withdrew the proposed amendment and appointed a Task Force to examine the issue. Plank and her Loyal Opposition only succeeded in delaying the measure, however. PRSSA eventually created an affiliate program open to any student at a school without a PRSSA chapter.[39]

AN OPENING DOOR

While focused on PRSSA during the summer of 1999, Plank received an unexpected call from the dean of the College of Communication and Information Sciences at The University of Alabama. Although Plank had been born in Tuscaloosa and had graduated from UA, she had had little contact with the university since her graduation. After her grandmother Annie died in 1944, she had no reason to visit. It was not until Dean Cully Clark reached out to her that she became aware of UA's public relations program, whose faculty and students had not been active in either PRSA or PRSSA for some time. Intrigued by the call, she agreed to meet with Clark and the College's development officer, Bonnie LaBresh, to hear what they had to say. She did not realize it immediately, but God was opening a door for her. It was a door that would bring her full circle, back to The University of Alabama and Tuscaloosa.

That first meeting led to more and to an invitation to visit UA in January 2000.[40] As was her custom, Plank did her homework before setting foot on her alma mater's campus again. She reviewed the public relations program's history, courses taught, and the faculty. She was pleased to find the curriculum and faculty strong. But no one outside of the program knew about it. That had to change.

In a letter to Clark following her visit, Plank set out her marching orders for him. First, the PRSSA chapter had to be brought into compliance because her colleagues took "commitment to PRSSA very seriously." The faculty advisor had to be a PRSA member, and that, she noted, was already in the process of being corrected. But a professional advisor for the chapter was also required. She had already put that one into motion, indicating she had taken the liberty of speaking with a colleague in the Birmingham PRSA chapter to put pressure on the chapter's membership, challenging them to step up to the plate. In addition, the PR faculty in general would do well to join the PRSA Educators Academy, one of the Society's interest sections specifically devoted to the teaching of public relations and conducting industry research. "We need," she wrote, "representation at PRSA as well as at PRSSA national conferences." Once all was in order, the program would be ready to apply for PRSA certification, she counseled Clark.[41]

In closing, Plank wrote, "Enough for now. (But fair warning about more in the future— . . . .) In this corner, I began some proselytizing last week to a few key educator and practitioner leaders and with PRSA's Director of Education, who also oversees PRSSA. And more within earshot or the receiving end of my fax machine will not be spared." She realized that perhaps all of this was more than Clark had bargained for or even wanted when he invited her to campus in the first place, but if so, "for the record, I send apologies, . . . not regrets." A month later, no doubt at Plank's urging, Dr. Melvin Sharpe of Ball State University wrote to the chair of UA's advertising and public relations department, telling him that on Plank's recent visit she had been so pleased to learn about the quality of the PR program in Tuscaloosa. As a former chair of the Educators Academy, Sharpe stated that he hoped to see an Alabama presence again at PRSA.[42]

Having rekindled a connection with The University of Alabama, Plank discussed leaving her estate to UA for the benefit of the public relations program. Then one night in March 2004, Plank came up with an idea. Instead of waiting until her death, she would go ahead and deed to UA property in Michigan, which she and Rosenfield had purchased on impulse thirty years prior. The proceeds from the sale could then be used to fund a public relations chair in the department of advertising and public relations. As she was contemplating that thought, a proposal came from Dean Clark. What if the College established a center dedicated to public relations in her name? It was the perfect proposal at the perfect time. Plank had once lamented that she had nothing tangible to show for her life. She had no children; she had never published a book; she had created no works of art. And now, here was Clark offering her a very tangible legacy. God had indeed opened a door. In a letter to her attorney, Plank wrote that she had procrastinated putting into writing her intention of leaving her estate to UA. "As it turns out, that procrastination may have been destined, given this new Institute proposal. Doesn't God always have something in mind? Amazing!"[43]

While pondering Clark's suggestion, she sought the advice of John "Jack" Koten, her boss for a few years at Illinois Bell. He was a trusted friend and colleague, and she valued his advice. After a luncheon at which Koten met Clark for the first time, Koten wrote to Plank about the proposed center at Alabama: "Your inspiration makes it possible for the University of Alabama to become a national, if not world, leader in promoting not only ethics, but the value of public relations as minders of corporate and individual conscience. It's a tall order, but the time is at hand to make an impact and I don't see why Tuscaloosa isn't a good place to start."[44]

But the center almost did not come to fruition. The proceeds from the sale of the Michigan property were to initially fund it but gifting the land to the University involved a steep "learning curve" for Plank. The university's Vice President of Advancement had explained to Plank the real estate gift process, but it would take more time and effort than Plank wanted to expend on it, including going with the university's representative to view the land. It was all too much at the time for the eighty-year-old Plank, and she wrote to LaBresh about her desire to back out of the deal. She would always be grateful for the College's center idea, but they could establish it after her death if they so wished. Clark immediately sought to ease her mind. She did not have to be bothered with the details; the university could deal with her attorney if she gave them permission to do so. But more importantly, he wanted her to know that "our planning of the Plank Center will go forward under any circumstance. . . . I had begun noodling the Plank Center . . . last fall, long before I knew a deed of land might be possible. All the land has done is to give us (perhaps) an earlier trigger."[45]

The sale of the land did go through as planned, and the proceeds were used to fund the Betsy Plank Center for Public Relations Studies, as it was first called, much to Plank's displeasure. She thought it sounded too pretentious. But that was the least of her worries. More challenging was assembling a board of advisors and deciding on the Center's mission, which was, according to Plank, like "herding cats." A couple of individuals came immediately to mind as potential board members: Koten and another long-time friend from PRSA, John "Jack" Felton. But after Koten and Felton, the decisions became more difficult. The trick was figuring out how to narrow the list of highly worthy potential candidates. Eventually, five others were selected to join Koten, Felton, and Plank on the inaugural board; some, like Ron Culp of Ketchum (Chicago) and Professor Maria Russell of Syracuse University, were chosen because of their close relationship with Plank. Others were asked to join because they were alumni of the university. In total ten professionals and educators formed the inaugural board of advisors.[46]

The first formal meeting of the Center's board took place on January 23, 2006, in Tuscaloosa. It was, as the minutes state, an historic occasion.[47] That first board would forge the mission and create a vision for The Plank Center. At that meeting, Plank, as chair, spoke about the future of the Center and emphasized the importance of ethics to its focus. But it was Dr. Bruce Berger, in his role as Center director, who gave shape and direction to the Center's future. He suggested the emphasis be "on helping develop leadership skills and talents, and especially ethics, among public relations students." Initiatives supporting leadership in public relations might include, he offered, funding to support research into public relations leadership, a collection of leadership materials and documents at the Center, a national public relations student leadership conference, the production of a student magazine focused on leadership, and perhaps other leadership workshops for educators and practitioners.[48]

Spirited discussion followed about the concept of "leadership." Should it, for example, be limited to "ethical leadership" or was "leadership" alone sufficient? Did the latter encompass the former? And to what extent should the Center be student-oriented? A real concern for Plank was the gap between practitioners and educators. Little interaction occurred between the two resulting in a lack of mutual understanding on both sides for which public relations students suffered. Plank wanted to see the Center work to close that gap and bring the groups together.

Despite the differences of and variations in opinion among its members, the Board reached consensus on some matters in that first meeting. The members agreed to issue a national call for research proposals to investigate various aspects of public relations leadership; to follow through with the PRSA Student Ethics Advocacy Competition that Plank had already begun work on; and to develop a proposal to create a leadership magazine targeted to public relations students and educators around the country. In adjourning, they scheduled a second meeting for August in Chicago.

Between the two board meetings, it was decided that the Betsy Plank Center for Public Relations Studies be renamed The Plank Center for Leadership in Public Relations. From the beginning, Plank had been adamant that her first name not be used. But more than that, the new name more accurately reflected the now settled direction and focus of the Center. It also ensured differentiation from The Arthur W. Page Center for Integrity in Public Communications, which had been established at Penn State University a year before The Plank Center. The Page Center was "dedicated to the study and advancement of ethics and responsibility in corporate communication."[49] Thus, the focus on leadership for The Plank Center was strategically important in that it carved out a niche distinct from, while complementary to, the Page Center, but it also was befitting of Plank. Ethics was important to her, but she was most known for her leadership in the field.

The Plank Center gave Plank a renewed sense of purpose and a formal role once again influencing the professionalization of the field. She continued to pour everything she had into public relations education, but she now added "trying to identify what it takes for genuine leadership in the profession. It's a passion which keeps me alive!"[50] And indeed, she kept up a grueling schedule, speaking at PRSA and PRSSA chapters around the country, serving on committees, attending the PRSA/PRSSA annual conferences, and chairing The Plank Center's Board of Advisors.

But privately, she was still lonely. "I've learned to live alone—or perhaps that's what I began learning long ago. One comes alone into this world and leaves alone. But along the way is the opportunity to collect angels," she wrote in a planner. Her New Year resolutions for 2008 were practical—"Learn the computer, Get files down to size, Grow the center"—but also melancholy—"Be kind, like my father said; Be with the Yearling [her boat] and Zan [the Michigan cottage]; Organize my will and trust; Remember that every day is the best day of the year—and that life is an adventure."

Fig. 15: Plank at the harbor with her boat, the Yearling, which she and Rosenfield bought for their first anniversary. Plank used water and boating metaphors often in her speeches and letters. Courtesy of the Plank Papers

She also listed forty-six deceased family members and friends, along with the names of five pets.[51]

At the same time, she had been experiencing hip pain for a while. By 2009, the pain had become so extreme that it began to interfere with her ability to travel. Silicone shots helped ease the symptoms for short periods, but relief was fleeting. Plank was told the only remedy for the pain was a hip replacement, which she was reluctant to have. Recovery from such an operation would require a significant convalescence, and she hated to impose and depend on others. When her doctor refused to give her any more silicone shots, Plank finally agreed to have her hip replaced. But just days before the scheduled operation, she was rushed to the hospital with severe abdominal pain. The next day she underwent emergency surgery for intestinal issues. She died nine months later at home on May 23, 2010, of complications from that surgery.

Obituaries told the story of her many "firsts" and accolades, but they did not capture the essence of the woman. The response of the people she named in her will to attend the scattering of her ashes and those of

Rosenfield and their cat, Cinderella, on Lake Michigan did. On the boat for her "burial at sea," were "four old sea captains . . . . Four members of her club of Chicago businesswomen (the Pushy Broads). Four neighbors from her vacation house in Michigan. Four staff members from her Chicago condo. And four PR people." Plus, a close friend's widow.[52] Each of the twenty-one individuals who attended thought they knew Plank best, that they were the closest to her. She made each of them feel as though they were the chosen one. And that was her essence—the ability to make chief communications officers and sophomore public relations students alike feel as though they were the only ones who really mattered.

Plank did not go "gentle into that good night." Her eternal optimism, coupled with her toughness and competitive fire, would not let her give up. In the end, her body succumbed, but her spirit did not. It lives on in the work of The Plank Center for Leadership in Public Relations, the scholarships in her name, the awards she helped establish, the practitioners she mentored, the students she guided, and all those who were fortunate to work with and to know her, and who still feel her presence and her guiding influence.

CONCLUSION

I cannot believe that the purpose of life is to be 'happy.' I think the purpose of life is to be useful, to be responsible, to be compassionate. It is, above all, to matter: to count, to stand for something, to have made some difference that you lived at all.

—Leo Rosten

IN 1978, BETSY ANN PLANK was named Public Relations Professional of the Year by *PR News*, the first woman to be given that honor. In her acceptance speech, she described public relations as "a profession still in the process of becoming, still being shaped by each of us in our daily practice, still being challenged to grow and change." Professionalism, she said, "is a product of individual knowledge and expertise, individual standards and performance, personal character and courage."[1] Plank not only believed that, but she also lived it.

Plank may have died in 2010, but her legacy—her belief in the professionalization of public relations and the importance of public relations education to that process—lives on through organizations and programs she helped establish and lead such as the Commission on Public Relations Education (CPRE), PRSA's Certification in Public Relations Education, the Champions for PRSSA (formerly Friends of PRSSA), and of course, The Plank Center for Leadership in Public Relations, as well as through the practitioners, educators, and students she mentored and influenced over the years.

A TIME OF CHANGE

Plank came of age as a leader in the tumultuous 1960s and early 1970s when society seemed to be fraying at the edges and trust in institutions and businesses plummeted in the aftermath of the Watergate scandal. Keeping

175

her faith in public relations, Plank challenged her fellow practitioners "to become professional in fact as well as in title."[2] But that was easier to say than to accomplish. Most practitioners at the time came from journalism or had an educational background in liberal arts. They, including Plank, had learned on the job, relying on common sense and practical experience. But the practice was no longer just about publicity. Practitioners were being called on to build relationships and communicate with consumers, employees, investors, and activists, among others. They were being asked to anticipate trends and to measure the results of their campaigns. The answers to the issues of the day could not be "sucked out of their thumbs" anymore, as Plank used to say. Specialized training was needed now and would be even more so in the future.

The number of public relations programs in universities and colleges had been accelerating through the sixties and seventies. By the time Plank took office as chair of PRSA in 1973, eighty-eight colleges and universities had a program in public relations; an additional 303 institutions offered at least courses in it. But quantity did not equate to quality. Through Plank's work with the Commission on Public Relations Education, she came to see that the lack of standards in these programs would do nothing to improve the practice even as she recognized that education held the key to the professionalization of public relations.[3]

Persuading practitioners that a strong public relations education was needed would not be easy, but it was a fight Plank was willing to take on. Justice Ruth Bader Ginsburg once told a group of young women: "Fight for the things you care about but do it in a way that will lead others to join." Plank did just that, and others did join her because her optimism about public relations and its place in society was infectious. She fought to encourage others to work toward a common vision, a vision that would lift everyone's boat. In fact, although competitive, she recognized, especially as she grew older, that "there is no limit to what can be accomplished if it doesn't matter who gets the credit."[4]

SERVANT LEADERSHIP

Plank certainly exhibited the dimensions of excellent public relations leadership: vision and self-reflection, team collaboration, ethical orientation, relationship building, strategic decision-making capability, and communication knowledge management. But what separates her from other public relations leaders is that she was a servant leader. Based on the teachings of her church, Plank believed that "every person owes his or her best in time and talents to the human community and paying that debt adds unique value to one's life."[5] Although compelled to serve, she did not go looking for leadership opportunities necessarily. They found her because of her willingness to fight for the things that mattered to her and to the organizations to which she belonged. Thus, she rose from the ranks into leadership positions, a characteristic of servant leaders.[6] In one two-year period in the late sixties, she was president of four different professional and community organizations.

One of her greatest strengths as a leader was her ability to put the well-being of others first. Plank "clearly derived great joy from giving to others," and in helping them develop as individuals and practitioners, one mentee noted. Another said, "she encouraged, prodded, challenged and celebrated so many growth points in my own life and dozens more." She sent countless notes of encouragement and congratulations to friends, colleagues, and acquaintances alike over the years. On her own eightieth birthday, she took a friend to dinner. After that, the friend received two birthday cards from Plank—one on her birthday, and one on Plank's—every year until Plank's death in 2010. The note on both was always the same, "You're my best birthday present."[7]

Plank was successful as a leader and a public relations practitioner in part because she was a quick study and a hard worker, which allowed her to overcome deficiencies, such as being naïve when she first went to AT&T about how corporations worked. It is unclear why she had a blind spot when it came to understanding the role of CEOs. She may well have been exaggerating for effect. But it is true that she had only worked in agencies before joining AT&T. Since her father was the vice president of a utility, she may have gained her perspective on corporations from him. He may have talked about following his CEO's orders, which made her think that was how all corporations worked. Even while working with McKeown, she dealt with executives who would have had close contact with their CEOs.

Her strong work ethic meant she did not ask others to do anything she was not willing to do herself. As Dan Edelman once said of her, "she doesn't shirk unpleasant tasks or unpopular decisions." That made her popular with those above and below her in the corporate and agency hierarchies. She was not perfect, of course. "She has occasional lapses of temper, she sometimes procrastinates and make mistakes." But, Edelman said, "I would like to be more like her—professionally and personally."[8]

Another factor in her success was her Presbyterian upbringing. It was instrumental in several ways, most notably in her desire to serve, but also in her strong moral code and belief that every individual deserves respect. Robert Greenleaf, who is credited with first describing servant leadership in 1970 drew on the Christian values outlined in the New Testament, especially depictions of Jesus, for his conceptualization of the style. And Margot Opdycke Lamme has written from a historical perspective on the connection between religion and public relations, arguing that evangelicalism influenced the development of public relations in the United States. Some of the themes that emerged from Lamme's study included truth, democracy ("faith in the ability of the individual and the public to discern the truth") and professionalization, all themes that are echoed in Plank's life.[9]

POLITICAL IDEOLOGY

Perhaps because of her faith and her education in political science, she tended to favor the liberalism of the late nineteenth and early twentieth centuries. Plank believed that individuals were rational and capable of self-governance. The role of public relations in a democracy, in Plank's eyes, was to ensure individuals had the full spectrum of views to consider on a subject. Treating individuals with dignity and respect meant being open and transparent and always doing the right thing. Edward Bernays, the so-called father of public relations and nephew of Sigmund Freud, on the other hand, operated on "the demonstrable theory that men in a democracy are sheep waiting to be led to slaughter." He rejected the liberalism of the nineteenth century and embraced "the 20th-century 'necessity' of uniting liberalism with social control."[10]

I am not suggesting that Plank can be compared with Bernays in terms of historical significance, but a comparison of the two does illustrate how one's ethical beliefs and political philosophy can influence how one practices public relations. In 1928, Bernays declared that "intelligent men must realize that propaganda is the modern instrument by which they can fight for productive ends and help to bring order out of chaos." For Bernays, public relations practitioners were adept at "manipulating public opinion" and "manufacturing consent." He was an elitist and held, as historian Marvin Olasky described it, a "vision of authoritarian liberalism."[11]

For her part, Plank found the chaos simply a sign of a strong democratic society. She had faith in individuals and their ability to make decisions that would ultimately lead to order. She too sought to motivate people through advocacy and persuasion, but she was concerned with the means to the ends. Being transparent was important to her because it was the right thing to do and because it acknowledged that those receiving the message deserved to be treated with dignity. Bernays, on the other hand, took the position that the ends justified the means. Inaccuracies were unfortunate in Bernays's eyes, because if discovered, they would lead to mistrust of the persuasion.

Not surprisingly, given their ideological differences, Plank held Bernays in little regard. Public relations for her involved "a sensitivity to public attitudes." It was about transparency, openness, and doing the right thing, not manipulating people. Not everyone agreed with her, of course. In 1974, while Plank was wrapping up her term as the PRSA president, Philip Lesly, a prominent Chicago practitioner and author of many public relations books, was writing about "the consequences of the extremism of 'democracy'—never foreseen by the most visionary of the founders of our democratic society—that seeks to give a voice and power to everyone on every issue and in the running of every institution, regardless of his merit in serving society or ability." Lesly, like Bernays, was an elitist. In, *The People Factor*, he wrote about managing the human climate. Organizations, he wrote, should put emphasis on "leading the target—on establishing the climate of attitudes in the future." He also argued that "reasoning together" was not always possible. Familiarity did not necessarily lead to "mutual respect and understanding."[12]

Plank's way of thinking was closer to that of John Hill, another public relations icon and founder of the Hill & Knowlton agency. In his 1963 book, *The Making of a Public Relations Man*, Hill wrote that "public opinion, confused, obscure, and unpredictable as it may often seem, is the ultimate ruling force in the free world." The role of public relations was to gain the "understanding, goodwill, and support" of the public to the extent that the organization deserved it. Both Hill and Plank held strongly to a belief in democracy and in the public's ability to make rational decisions.[13]

What separates Plank from these three men was her relentless focus on others. Bernays and Lesly considered themselves better than some and therefore believed they knew what was in the best interest of others. Hill spoke the language of respect but did not always live up to his own words.[14] Plank did.

Many would consider Plank's optimism about individuals and the role of public relations naïve and perhaps even quaint. Yet the rapid nature of the changes today, thanks to the explosion of new technologies, and the challenges those changes bring with them in terms of the amount of information and disinformation, the speed with which it accosts practitioners, the pressure on ethical behaviors, the sharp decline in trust of institutions and leaders, and the corresponding growth in distrust and division, has increased the demand for leadership. Plank would argue, as she did in the 1970s, that today "those skilled in public relations can make a strong contribution to better understanding of diverse or misunderstood viewpoints. Agreement isn't necessarily the objective. But understanding is."[15] Servant leaders like Plank with her strong moral compass, high standards, and positive vision for the future, are needed now more than ever.

In fact, a recent study into the kind of leadership needed for today's "perpetual, pervasive, and exponential" change found that a new model was needed, that of Sapient Leadership. "Sapient Leaders exhibit authenticity, humility, vulnerability, inspiring the necessary trust and psychological safety that drives shared learning and intelligence." The result is greater collaboration and better performance overall. Interestingly, those are the same characteristics that mark servant leadership. The authors went on to note that "the days of 'leader as hero'—the solo, individualistic leader who inspires certainty in a deterministic way—are over."[16]

Plank was never the hero leader. She built trust through openness with her formal teams and informal networks. That trust meant those who worked with her and for her felt psychologically safe to take risks and empowered to perform at their best. She was also able to articulate with conviction a purpose and values that others came to share. A shared purpose enhances team cohesion and resiliency. It "can also powerfully mobilize large numbers of people to solve complex problems together," which it would appear Plank was able to do with her legion of supporters. Purpose in this sense has been defined as an "intention to accomplish something that is both personally meaningful and serves the world larger than the self." Each of these aspects of Sapient Leadership can be associated with those found in the servant leader model.[17]

Some critics of servant leadership find the model involves an inherent paradox. The concept of servant is typically associated with subjugation and a needs-focused attitude. Serving, therefore, is a stereotypically feminine trait. The concept of leader, on the other hand, is associated with domination and a results orientation, which tend to be seen as masculine traits. Others, however, argue that the model involves gender integration, blending traditionally masculine and feminine characteristics.[18]

GENDER INTEGRATION

It is this gender integration that enabled Plank to lead in a male-dominated business world. She exhibited the more masculine dimensions of leadership such as "foresight, awareness, conceptualization, and persuasion." And she was decisive, assertive, and a risk taker. She thought stereotypical gender roles and society's strictures that perpetuated them were silly and a waste of time. Perhaps it was because of this attitude that she found no reason to openly challenge discrimination or demand change. Her intention was simply to work hard and get things accomplished to further the organization's or client's cause. In fact, one reason she was successful was because she did not identify solely with women's issues.[19]

At the same time, she brought the more feminine leadership characteristics of "caring, compassion, and community" to everything she did. And that was also part of her success. Her apparent selflessness and willingness to put the needs of others first endeared her to those she worked with. Men took her seriously but did not feel threatened by her. She was not about domination; she was about the empowerment of others. As her father said, she was not militant, an apparent compliment at a time when feminism was being viewed warily by corporate America. Plank was a smart, professional woman, and men seemed to respect her for that and, more importantly, like her despite it.[20]

Plank never wavered in her pursuit of professionalism in public relations. To that end, she was singularly focused on education, forever shaping its "direction, content, and delivery." As Laurie Wilson, an educator, put it, "Her efforts changed the substance and practice of public relations in ways we may never fully realize." Plank herself said she would like to be "remembered as someone who championed the next generation of our profession."[21]

At a memorial event in 2010 to celebrate Plank's life, Maria Russell, a professor at Syracuse University and a member of the initial Plank Center Board of Advisors, best summed up what Plank had meant, and still means, to public relations,

> She dreamed into the future. She knew that public relations would never evolve, never be a true profession, never reach its full potential in service to organizations and to society and to the democratic process *without* a collective commitment to education, to mentoring, to life-long learning, and to developing and supporting new leaders. She moved those dreams and beliefs into personal action, and she led the rest of us down those important pathways.[22]

And that was Plank's real power as a leader: her ability to reach minds, touch hearts, move souls, and inevitably change lives.[23]

NOTES

INTRODUCTION

Epigraph. Matshona Dhliwayo, "20 Qualities that Will Help You Stand Out as a Leader," *African Leadership Magazine*, May 7, 2017, https://www.africanleadership-magazine.co.uk/20-qualities-that-will-help-you-stand-out-as-a-leader/.

1. "1972 Conference Highlights," *Detroit Free Press*, Nov. 13, 1972, special edition. The chair of PRSA was previously known as the president; Betsy Plank, "Public Relations: Our Crisis of Identity," (speech at PRSA annual conference, Detroit, MI, Nov. 15, 1972), Betsy Ann Plank Papers, The Plank Center for Leadership in Public Relations, University of Alabama.

2. Plank, "Our Crisis of Identity," Nov. 15, 1972, Plank Papers. Alfred North Whitehead, *Modes of Thought* (New York: The Free Press, 1968), 16.

3. It would be another ten years before a woman would lead the organization again. PRSA Past Presidents/Chairs, https://apps.prsa.org/AboutPRSA/Leadership/PRSAPastPresidents/.

4. Plank Biography, Plank Papers; Trevor Jensen, "Betsy Plank, 1924–2010: Public Relations Leader," *Chicago Tribune*, May 25, 2010.

5. "Betsy Plank Obituary," *New York Times*, May 25, 2010; Jensen, "Betsy Plank, 1924–2010."

6. Historian Thomas Carlyle wrote in 1907 that "the history of the world is but the biography of great men." Thomas Carlyle, *On Heroes, Hero-worship, and the Heroic in History* (Boston: Houghton Mifflin, 1907), 18; Margaret B. Wilkerson, "Excavating Our History: The Importance of Biographies of Women of Color," *Black American Literature Forum* 24, no. 1 (Spring 1990): 84.

7. "Bylaws," *Public Relations Journal* 5 (Aug. 1949): 34; U.S. Census (1970). Detailed occupation of employed persons by race and sex for the United States: 1970, https://www2.census.gov/library/publications/decennial/1970/pc-s1-supplementary-reports/pc-s1-32.pdf. Karlene Lukovitz, "Women Practitioners: How Far, How Fast?" 15-34,; in 1973, PRSA membership was approximately seven thousand. U.S. Census (2019). Employed persons by detailed occupation, sex, race, and Hispanic or Latino ethnicity from the Current Population Survey, https://www.bls.gov/cps/cpsaat11.htm.

8. Although no definitive list of leadership traits exists, the following are most often cited: intelligence, self-confidence, determination, high energy level, emotional stability, integrity, a desire to influence others for pro-social ends, moderately high achievement orientation, and vision. Joe C. Magee and Carrie A. Langner, "How Personalized and Socialized Power Motivation Facilitate Antisocial and Prosocial Decision-making"

1547–1599; Gary A. Yukl, *Leadership in Organizations*. Emotional intelligence, which includes self-awareness, self-regulation, motivation, empathy, and social skill, is also often considered necessary for leadership. Daniel Goleman, *Emotional Intelligence: Why It Can Matter More Than IQ*.

9. James F. Fox, Gold Anvil Nomination letter, Aug. 12, 1977, Plank Papers; Ron Culp to Karla Gower, Aug. 9, 2020.

10. Bruce Berger to Karla K. Gower, Apr. 17, 2020.

11. Berger to Gower, Apr. 17, 2020.

12. Juan Meng and Bruce Berger, "An Integrated Model of Excellent Leadership in Public Relations: Dimensions, Measurement, and Validation," 143; Keith Burton to Karla Gower, Oct. 21, 2020.

13. Dirk van Dierendonck, "Servant Leadership: A Review and Synthesis," 1233, 1235; Kae Reynolds, "Servant-Leadership as Gender-Integrative Leadership: Paving a Path for More Gender-Integrative Organizations through Leadership Education," 164. The public relations literature on leadership does not mention the servant leadership style. It focuses instead on transformational leadership, which emphasizes the organization over the individual.

14. Ralph Waldo Emerson is credited with this particular expression of the "who gets the credit" sentiment, but similar statements have also been attributed to President Harry Truman; Blanton Collier, a one-time Cleveland Browns football coach; and famed UCLA basketball coach John Wooden. Variations of it can be found dating back to the late 1880s. Culp to Gower, Aug. 9, 2020; Robert C. Liden, Sandy J. Wayne, Hao Zhao, and David Henderson, "Servant Leadership: Development of a Multidimensional and Multi-level Assessment," 162.

15. Dierendonck, "Servant Leadership," 1231; Brien N. Smith, Ray V. Montagno, and Tatiana N. Kuzmenko, "Transformational and Servant Leadership: Content and Contextual Comparisons," 82.

16. "The Design for Undergraduate Public Relations Education," a report for the Commission on Public Relations Education, 1987. Betsy Plank, Speech to Rockford IABC (International Association of Business Communicators), Mar. 20, 1984, Plank Papers.

17. Gene Edward Veith, "The Protestant Work Ethic," *Tabletalk Magazine*, Sept. 1, 2006, https://www.ligonier.org/learn/articles/protestant-work-ethic/.

18. http://dictionary.reference.com/browse/protestant-ethic; Enrique Loza, Nomination, 1989 Paul M. Lund Public Service Award, June 30, 1989, Plank Papers, photocopy.

CHAPTER 1 / AN UNCOMMON HERITAGE

Epigraph. Betsy Ann Plank, "An Uncommon Heritage," *The University of Alabama Sesquicentennial, 1831–1981*, Vol. 10, Tuscaloosa, AL, no publisher, Plank Papers.

1. Birth Certificate of Betsy Ann Plank. According to her birth certificate, she was born at 12:30 p.m. on Apr. 3, 1924, and weighed 6 lbs., 15 oz.

2. Plank, "An Uncommon Heritage," Plank Papers. Her Grandmother Annie Hood lived at 2009 8th Street, less than a tenth of a mile from campus. "Wreck Victim," *Birmingham News*, Aug. 29, 1927, 4.

3. Kathleen Thompson. "Alabama's Man of Letters: Remembering Hudson Strode." *AL.com*, Dec. 25, 2011. Updated Jan. 14, 2019, https://www.al.com/entertainment/2011/

12/alabamas_man_of_letters_rememb.html. Thomas Henry Garner was the director of the University Chorus and the University Glee Club and was affectionately known as "Uncle Tom." "Tom Garner, Great Man." *Tuscaloosa News*, Dec. 14, 1944, 4, accessed Sept. 25, 2021, https://news.google.com/newspapers?id=FeY-AAAAIBAJ&sjid=E00M AAAAIBAJ&pg=6185%2C6957846. Agnes Ellen Harris joined The University of Alabama in 1927 as Dean of Women. At the time five hundred women attended the University. She increased that number to more than two thousand. "Julia Tutwiler opened the doors of the University to women, but it was Agnes Ellen Harris who brought the women into the University." E. Neige Todhunter, "Agnes Ellen Harris: A Tribute," May 2, 1953, http://www.ches.ua.edu/tribute-to-dean-harris.html.

4. Plank, "An Uncommon Heritage"; Betsy Plank, Untitled Personal Family Stories, Apr. 21, 1996, Plank Papers. For example, at the wedding of Annie's niece in 1910, Annie played the piano, accompanied by thirteen-year-old Adelyne on the violin. *Yorkville Enquirer*, S.C., June 28, 1910, 4, accessed Nov. 30, 2018, https://newscomwc.newspapers.com/image/339344985. "Local No. 10, Chicago, Ill," *The International Musician: Journal of the American Federation of Musicians of the United States*, 19 (Dec. 1920): 10, and 20 (May 1921): 8, https://hdl.handle.net/2027/uiug.30112014347857. There were no musical expectations for Bettye and Israel, although Bettye's seventh grade report card indicates she was a good student, receiving excellent or good on everything except drawing, which was passable.

5. Plank, Untitled Personal Family Stories, 1, 2, Plank Papers. Once, when Plank was six, she and her mother were riding the train to New York, and a woman, thinking they were sisters, told Bettye they were too young to be taking the train by themselves. News Clipping, n. d., no newspaper, Plank Papers; U.S. Passport of Bettye Ann Hood issued May 9, 1929; Hood Family Tree, Plank Papers.

6. Plank, "An Uncommon Heritage," Plank Papers. Of course, Plank would only have been three years old when Stacey was killed. Her recollection was of what she had been told, not what she remembered.

7. The student population on UA's campus in 1921 was 2,134. https://www.ua.edu/about/history. Plank, Untitled Personal Family Stories, 3–4, Plank Papers.

8. Bettye does not appear to have been a performer or part of the Pantheon Singers. In her letters home to Dick, she makes no reference to any official role she had with the group.

9. News clipping, *Tuscaloosa News*, Dec. 11, 1922, no page, Plank Papers.

10. News clipping, *Tuscaloosa News*, Dec. 11, 1922, Plank Papers.

11. Annie's husband Quit died at the age of sixty-five, a year after Plank's birth.

12. Of course, the family would have known the story of Helen Keller who was from Tuscumbia, about 120 miles north of Tuscaloosa. Why Bettye wanted to study sign language and why she wanted to do it in England rather than in the United States is not clear. It was the second time Adelyne had paid for a Bettye adventure. She had also funded Bettye's travels with the Pantheon Singers.

13. Annie to Billy, Bettye and Adelyne, May 17, 1929; Bettye to Annie, June 19, 1929, Plank Papers.

14. Annie to Bettye, Nov. 30, 1930, Plank Papers. Annie and Adelyne both used the Southern dialect of African Americans in letters when referring to statements made by Blacks.

15. Georgette Terrill to Plank, Apr. 14, 1998, Plank Papers.

16. The *Tuscaloosa News* was reporting on Plank's seventh birthday party that was held at Annie's home in the city. Sixty children attended the party. "Charming Birthday Party is Given by Miss Betty [sic] Plank," *Tuscaloosa News*, April 7, 1931, 3; "Profile: Betsy Plank," *Today's Chicago Woman*, May 1984, Plank Papers.

17. News Clipping, no date; Plank Diary, Nov. 1, 1933, Plank Papers; Toni Falbo, "Only Children: An Updated Review," 38.

18. "Rotary Held Ladies' Night," *Wellsboro Gazette*, May 31, 1933, 1, https://newscomwc.newspapers.com/image/37142441; "Present Play at High School," *Wellsboro Gazette*, Apr. 18, 1934, 1, https://newscomwc.newspapers.com/image/37149276.

19. Plank, "Footnotes to Personal History," undated, circa 1980s, Plank Papers; "Betsy Ann Plank, Mt. Lebanon High," *Pittsburgh Post-Gazette*, Feb. 13, 1940, 13, accessed June 18, 2016, https://archives.post-gazette.com/image/88914325.

20. Plank Diary, Apr. 1, 1937, Plank Papers.

21. Plank Diary, Apr. 7, 1937; May 14, 1937; June 4, 1937, Plank Papers. For a discussion of charismatic personality, see Jasmine Verguawe, et al., "The Double-Edged Sword of Leader Charisma: Understanding the Curvilinear Relationship Between Charismatic Personality and Leader Effectiveness," 110–130.

22. Plank Diary, May 5, 1937; Feb. 2, 1940; Jan. 15, 1940, Plank Papers.

23. Plank Diary, Jan. 22, 1940; "Indian Peer for House of Lords," *Straits Times*, Jan. 22, 1940, 14, accessed July 3, 2021, https://eresources.nlb.gov.sg/newspapers/BrowseNewspaper?nid=straitstimes.

24. Plank to Georgette Terrill, Apr. 14, 1998, Plank Papers.

25. The early precocity of only children often leads parents to have high expectations of academic success of their children. Falbo, "Only Children," 43. Plank Diary, Feb. 3, 1933; Plank to Terrill, Apr. 14, 1998, Plank Papers.

26. Plank, "Footnotes to Personal History," Plank Papers.

27. Marion K. Sanders, *Dorothy Thompson: A Legend in Her Time* (Boston: Houghton Mifflin Company, 1973; "Betsy Plank," PRSSA, https://prssa.prsa.org/about-prssa/history/betsy-plank/.

28. Kirstin Downey, *The Woman Behind the New Deal: The Life and Legacy of Frances Perkins—Social Security, Unemployment Insurance, and the Minimum Wage* (New York: Random House, 2009); Robin Finn, "Helen Wills Moody, Dominant Champion Who Won 8 Wimbledon Titles, Dies at 92," *New York Times*, Jan. 3, 1998.

29. Plank, "Uncommon Heritage," Plank Papers.

30. Plank, "Uncommon Heritage," Plank Papers.

31. Plank, "Uncommon Heritage," Plank Papers.

32. "In the late 1940s, only one-third of all American women, single as well as married, worked outside the home, and women constituted only 29 percent of the nation's labor force." Nancy L. Cohen, *Delirium: How the Sexual Counterrevolution Is Polarizing America*, 16.

33. The Disciples sought to restore Christian unity by returning to the New Testament's faith and practices. History of the Disciples, Christian Church (Disciples of Christ). http://disciples.org/our-identity/history-of-the-disciples/.

34. "About Bethany," Bethany College. https://www.bethanywv.edu/about-bethany/mission-goals/. Alexander Campbell was an early proponent of universal female education. Brent Carney, *Bethany College* [Kindle version], Location No. 142.

35. Jacqueline Foertsch, *American Culture in the 1940s*.

36. D. Duane Cummins, *Bethany College: A Liberal Arts Odyssey*, 193. According to the U.S. Census, 5.5 percent of men and 3.8 percent of women had completed four years of college in 1940. By 1947, those numbers had risen to 6.2 percent of men and 4.7 percent of women. Plank graduated in 1944. United States Census Bureau, "Percentage of the U.S. Population Who Have Completed Four Years of College or More From 1940 to 2020, by Gender," 2021, Historical Time Series Tables – Educational Attainment, Table A-2. https://www.census.gov/data/tables/time-series/demo/educational-attainment/cps-historical-time-series.html; United States Census Bureau, "1940–2010: How Has America Changed?" Mar. 14, 2012.

37. Plank to Bettye, n.d., ca. fall 1940, Plank Papers.

38. Plank to Bettye, n.d., ca. fall 1940, Plank Papers; Cummins, *Bethany College*, 198.

39. Zeta Tau Alpha was founded at Virginia in 1898. "Our Beliefs," accessed June 27, 2015, https://zetataualpha.org/about. The Bethany College chapter was founded just seven years later. "Chapter History," http://bethanywv.zetataualpha.org/chapter-history. Although Plank spent much of her free time socializing with the Zetas, she did not actually pledge until April. Plank to Bettye, Apr. 6, 1941, Plank Papers.

40. Cummins, *Bethany College*, 199. The Beta Theta Pi fraternity was founded in 1839 at Miami University (Ohio) and its purpose was to "develop men of principle for a principled life." "The Founding of Beta Theta Pi," https://beta.org/about/about-beta-theta-pi/. The Psi Chapter of Beta Theta Pi was founded at Bethany College on Dec. 8, 1860. It closed on Feb. 5, 2003. Carney, *Bethany College,* Location No. 377.

41. Cummins, *Bethany College*, 386, fn. 37. For a discussion of the literature on only children, see Falbo, "Only Children."

42. Plank to Bettye, May 20, 1941; Plank to Bettye, n.d., ca. May 1941, Plank Papers.

43. Rappaport to Plank, June 13, 1941, Plank Papers.

44. Plank's sophomore class had 112 students, down from 177 in her freshmen year. Her junior class in 1942 was just 65. Cummins, *Bethany College*, 386, fn. 37. Bethany had a strong pre-med program under the leadership of Dr. Bernard Weimar, the chair of the biology department. A 1949 study of liberal arts colleges ranked Bethany among the top 30 colleges in the nation in the education of scientists. Cummins, *Bethany College*, 195. Plank to Family, n.d., Plank Papers.

45. Donald K. Wright, "History and Development of Public Relations Education in North America: A Critical Analysis," 236–255. By 1953, Bethany College had four courses in public relations. Cummins, *Bethany College,* 195.

46. Plank to Bettye, May 28, 1941, Plank Papers. Hoagland attended Cornell University in the 1920s, received a master's in English from Columbia, and then her Ph.D. in 1936 from Cornell.

47. Plank to Bettye, Jan. 31, 1942, Plank Papers.

48. Plank to Bettye, Jan. 31, 1942, Plank Papers.

49. Plank to Bettye, Oct. 8, 1941; Plank to Bettye, Nov. 4, 1941, Plank Papers.

50. Plank to Bettye, Feb. 16, 1942; Handwritten note on February issue of *Bethanian* 1942; *Bethanian*, Feb. 1942, 4, Plank Papers.

51. *Bethanian*, Feb. 1942, 4, Plank Papers.

52. Plank to Bettye and Dick, Jan. 29, 1943, Plank Papers. Plank continued to be controlling until the end of her life. For example, when The Plank Center for Leadership in Public Relations set up an online magazine for public relations students by public relations students, Plank wanted to review all the copy before anything was uploaded. Interview with Dr. Bruce Berger, May 7, 2019.

53. Dick to Plank, n.d., 1943; Plank to Bettye, Feb. 1, 1943, Plank Papers.

54. According to Bethany College's 1940 catalog, tuition was $125 per semester for a total of $250 per year. Other annual costs included $210 for room and board at Phillips Hall; a $20 student activities fee; a $20 health and matriculation fee; and a $10 admissions fee. "Bethany College Bulletin, 1940–44," https://archive.org/stream/bethanycollegeb194044beth/bethanycollegeb194044beth_djvu.txt. See also, Cummins, *Bethany College*, 194. The College did give her $50 for serving as editor of two of the seven issues. Plank to Bettye, Oct. 1941. She tried for a job in the kitchen, although her parents were not sure the kitchen was the appropriate place for her to work. They need not have worried. She did not get the job. Plank to Bettye, Mar. 3, 1943, Plank Papers.

55. Bethany only accepted students who were in the upper half of their high school graduating class. Cummins, *Bethany College*, 198. "Mt. Lebanon Youth Rated as Most Able," *Pittsburgh Post-Gazette*, June 8, 1940, 4, accessed June 18, 2016, https://archives.post-gazette.com/image/89920879.

56. Plank to Bettye, Mar. 31, 1941; Oct. 8, 1941; Jan. 16, 1943, Plank Papers.

57. Plank to Bettye, Nov. 13, 1941, Plank Papers.

58. Rappaport to Plank, Dec. 7, 1941, Plank Papers. "The Year 1940 from The People History," accessed June 27, 2015, http://www.thepeoplehistory.com. In total, 100 Bethanians served in World War II, and 29 lost their lives. Cummins, *Bethany College*, 198.

59. For American attitudes regarding World War II before Pearl Harbor, see David Halberstam, *The Fifties* (New York: Ballantine Books, 1993). Plank to Bettye and Dick, Dec. 10, 1941; Plank to Family, n.d., ca. fall 1942; Plank to Rappaport, Aug. 24, 1942, Plank Papers.

60. Rappaport to Plank, Oct. 27, 1941, Plank Papers.

61. Plank to Rappaport, n.d., ca. Feb. 1943; Rappaport to Plank, Aug. 18, 1941; Rappaport to Plank, n.d., ca. 1941, Plank Papers.

62. Rappaport to Plank, n.d., ca. 1941, Plank Papers. The birth control pill was not approved for sale in the United States until 1960. As late as 1965, only 14 percent of married white women with no previous births were using the pill. N. B. Ryder and C. F. Westoff, *Reproduction in the United States 1965* (Princeton: Princeton University Press, 1971), 148. According to Cohen, in the mid-1950s, 40 percent of women had premarital sex. See *Delirium*, 11. Rappaport to Plank, n.d., Plank Papers. Rap was right in one regard. The number of illegitimate births among white girls aged 18 to 19 in 1940 was low, just 5 per 1,000. Unwed, sexually active teens in the 1940s relied primarily

on condoms for birth control. Charles E. Bowerman, *Unwed Motherhood: Personal and Social Consequences*, 409.

63. Plank to Rappaport, Feb. 22, 1942, Plank Papers.

64. Plank to Rappaport, Feb. 22, 1942, Plank Papers.

65. Rapport to Plank, Mar. 28, 1942, Plank Papers.

66. Plank to Bettye, May 26, 1942; June 2, 1942, Plank Papers. To her mother, Plank wrote that Mrs. Rappaport "takes the attitude that I'm Rap's guest and sometimes a whole boring evening at home will pass and no one will say a word. She makes me feel uncomfortable by constant references to 'someone taking Bub's (Rap's) mind off his work and on to excessive recreation.'"

67. Plank to Rappaport, June 6, 1942; June 10, 1942; June 12, 1942, Plank Papers. Despite the bad taste left in her mouth from the visit, Plank wrote thank you letters to both Rap's mother and sister as would be expected of her, given her upbringing and Southern heritage, although hints of sarcasm come through in the note to Rap's mother. Plank to Verna Rappaport, June 9, 1942; Plank to Dorothy Rappaport, June 9, 1942, Plank Papers. Bettye always made Plank write thank you letters, send birthday cards, etc. It became a habit that she carried with her for the rest of her life.

68. Plank to Rappaport, Aug. 11, 1942; Sept. 9, 1942, Plank Papers.

69. Plank to Rappaport, Feb. 1943, Plank Papers.

70. Rappaport to Plank, Feb. 26, 1943; Plank to Bettye, Mar. 3, 1943, Plank Papers.

71. Rappaport to Plank, Mar. 26, 1943, Plank Papers. Cummins, *Bethany College*, 192. Wilbur Cramblet, February 1936, quoted in Cummins, *Bethany College*, 198.

72. Rappaport to Plank, Mar. 26, 1943, Plank Papers.

73. Ruth Rutherford to Plank, Apr. 1, 1943, emphasis in original, Plank Papers.

74. Rutherford to Plank. Forty-two air cadets came to Bethany College in the summer of 1942 for naval officer training. Bethany College was one of 131 campuses selected for the V-12 Navy College Training Program. By the end of the program, 836 sailors had gone through Bethany College. Carney, *Bethany College,* Location No. 1059; Rutherford to Plank, April 3, 1943, Plank Papers.

75. Laurie Goodstein, "At Camps, Young U.S. Sikhs Cling to Heritage," *New York Times*, July 18, 1998; Plank to Bettye, July 2, 1943, Plank Papers.

76. Plank to Bettye, n.d., ca. July 1943, Plank Papers.

77. Plank to Bettye, July 12, 1943, Plank Papers.

78. Plank to Bettye, August 1, 1943, Plank Papers.

79. Plank to Bettye, Aug. 9, 1943, Plank Papers.

80. Plank to Bettye, Aug. 9, 1943; Aug. 17, 1943, Plank Papers.

81. Plank to Bettye, Aug. 17, 1943, Plank Papers.

82. Plank, "An Uncommon Heritage," Plank Papers.

83. "Education: Success Story," *Time*, July 30, 1945, accessed July 3, 2021, http://content.time.com/time/subscriber/article/0,33009,801694,00.html; Annie to Adelyne, Nov. 4, 1943, Plank Papers.

84. Rappaport to Rutherford, July 27, 1943; Rutherford to Plank, Sept. 4, 1943; Rappaport to Plank, Sept. 11, 1943, Plank Papers.

85. Rappaport to Plank, n.d.; Rappaport to Plank, May 26, 1944, Plank Papers.

86. Bethany ultimately awarded degrees to both Rap and Plank. Plank held no ill will toward the College and later would be active in her alumni chapter in Chicago. Thomas D. Pollard, "Ray Rappaport Chronology: Twenty-five Years of Seminal Articles on Cytokinesis in the *Journal of Experimental Zoology*," 9–14. Ray Rappaport died in Dec. 2010, seven months after Plank.

87. Betsy Plank, interview by Albert Walker, n.d., ca. Nov./Dec. 1978, transcript, Northern Illinois University, DeKalb, IL. For many in the United States, the war in Europe did not begin until U.S. forces landed on the continent in June 1944. Halberstam, *The Fifties*, 8.

CHAPTER 2 / FINDING HER PASSION

Epigraph. Plank, "An Uncommon Heritage," Plank Papers.

1. "Miss Adelyne Hood Now Lives in Pittsburgh," *The (South Carolina) Chester Reporter*, April 3, 1944, News clipping, Plank Papers.

2. KDKA began as 8XK, changing its name in 1920. Lynn Boyd Hinds, *Broadcasting the Local News: The Early Years of Pittsburgh's KDKA-TV* (State College: Penn State Press, 1995). Wikipedia, s.v. "KQV," last modified April 13, 2021, 15:36, https://en.wikipedia.org/wiki/KQV.

3. Several independent stations banded together to form the Mutual Broadcasting System in 1934 to share syndicated programming. It existed until 1999.

4. Plank, "Footnotes," Plank Papers.

5. Plank, "Footnotes," Plank Papers; Betsy Plank, interview by Gigi McNamara, June 26, 2006, transcript, The Arthur W. Page Center for Integrity in Public Communication, University Park, PA. www.bellisario.psu.edu/page-center/oral-histories/betsy-plank/; S. I. Steinhauser, "Station in Hollywood Starts Campaign to Save Youth from Jive," *Pittsburgh Press*, Mar. 31, 1946, 38, https://news.google.com/newspapers?id=fDEbAAAA-IBAJ&sjid=x0wEAAAAIBAJ&pg=1929%2C6802734; "Open House," *Pittsburgh Press*, March 31, 1946. See also, "Profile, Betsy Plank, Chicago's PR Pro," *Today's Chicago Woman*, May 1984; Plank to Annie McGrath, June 14, 1946, Plank Papers.

6. Plank Resume, ca. 1960s, Plank Papers. The geographical location of Pittsburgh meant that warm air was trapped. Joel A. Tarr and Bill C. Lamperes, "Changing Fuel-Use Behavior and Energy Transitions: The Pittsburgh Smoke Control Movement, 1940–1950," 563. In 1940, of the 175,163 dwellings in Pittsburgh, 141,788 burned coal. The remainder burned a cleaner fuel such as natural gas.

7. Tarr and Lamperes, "Changing Fuel-Use Behavior."

8. For a discussion of Pittsburgh's efforts to clean up its air, see, Tarr and Lamperes, "Changing Fuel-Use Behavior." For a history of the environmentalist movement that sparked a change in soft coal use, see, David Stradling, *Smokestacks and Progressives: Environmentalists, Engineers, and Air Quality, 1881–1951* (Baltimore: Johns Hopkins University Press, 1999); Edward K. Muller and John F. Bauman, *Before Renaissance: Planning in Pittsburgh, 1889–1943* (Pittsburgh: University of Pittsburgh Press, 2006); Plank Resume, ca. 1960s, Plank Papers.

9. Kirk joined KQV in Feb. 1945. Si Steinhauser, "'Plugless' Radio," *Pittsburgh Post-Gazette*, Feb. 19, 1945, 21, accessed June 23, 2016, https://archives.post-gazette.com/image/147718238. Before moving to Pittsburgh, Kirk had been with CBS radio in

Chicago. *Pittsburgh Post-Gazette*, Mar. 24, 1945, 12, accessed June 23, 2016, https://archives.post-gazette/image/88491606; *Pittsburgh Post-Gazette*, Feb. 21, 1945, 22, accessed June 25, 2016, https://archives.post-gazette.com/image/87624530. Plank to McGrath, June 14, 1946, Plank Papers.

10. Plank, "Footnotes." Kirk filed for divorce from his wife, Martha, in June 1946. "Divorce Suits Filed," *Pittsburgh Post-Gazette*, June 11, 1946, 24, accessed June 25, 2016, https://archives.post-gazette.com/image/149676097. Plank to McGrath, June 14, 1946, Plank Papers. The letters to McGrath describing this time in her life appear not to have been mailed, although Plank kept them. Mooseheart is a residential child-care facility that was started by the fraternal organization, the Loyal Order of Moose, in 1913. http://www.mooseheart.org.

11. Although the story sounds implausible, it may well have been true. Kirk's brother, Marine Sergeant Terry Kirk, had been held in a Japanese prison camp for four years. He was released in the fall of 1945 and spent that Christmas with his brother, which may well have been the first time Terry Kirk met his brother's wife. *Pittsburgh Post-Gazette*, Dec. 22, 1945, 14, accessed June 23, 2016, https://archives.post-gazette.com/image/88925989. See also, *Pittsburgh Post-Gazette*, Sept. 24, 1945, 22, accessed June 25, 2016, https://archives.post-gazette.com/image/87715340. Plank to McGrath, June 14, 1946. "Divorce Suits Filed," *Pittsburgh Post-Gazette*, June 11, 1946, 24, accessed June 25, 2016, https://archives.post-gazette.com/image/149676097; "Divorce Proceedings," *Pittsburgh Post-Gazette*, Oct. 8, 1946, 4, accessed June 25, 2016, https://archives.post-gazette.com/image/91057942.

12. "Mt. Lebanon Church Scene of Plank-Kirk Ceremony," news clipping; Patricia Pitt, "The Smart Set," *Pittsburgh Sun-Telegraph*, Apr. 16, 1947, 23, Plank Papers. Plank stood up with Adelyne two years earlier when Adelyne married A. J. Phipps, a successful food broker in Pittsburgh. News clipping, "Miss Hood is Bride of A. J. Phipps," *Tuscaloosa News*, July 1, 1945, news clipping, Plank Papers. It was the forty-eight-year-old Adelyne's first marriage. Although she did not graduate from college, her choice of not marrying young and not having children reflects the marriage data of women who graduated during the years 1908 to 1917. A full 50 percent of them "either never married or had no children by the time they reached the age of 45." Claudia Goldin, "The Meaning of College in the Lives of American Women: The Past One-Hundred Years," 10.

13. Plank to Annie McGrath, Oct. 26, 1947, Plank Papers. *Pittsburgh Post-Gazette*, Sept. 16, 1947, 35, accessed June 23, 2016, https://archives.post-gazette.com/image/1496717-09.

14. For a discussion of life in Chicago at the end of World War II, specifically for renters, see Laura McEnaney, "Nightmares on Elm Street: Demobilizing in Chicago, 1945–1953," 1265–1291. Plank to McGrath, Oct. 26, 1947, Plank Papers.

15. The Depression still took its toll, however. As an adult, Plank had habits that were the result of being a child of that era. She saved empty margarine tubs and took hotel soaps and shampoo bottles to use at home, for example.

16. Plank to Georgette Terrill, April 14, 1998, Plank Papers.

17. Georgia Sims Carson, "Lavinia Schulman Schwartz," *Vassar Quarterly* 73, no. 2, (Jan. 1977): 28; Irene Powers, "Ad Club Names Woman of the Year," *Chicago Tribune*, April 22, 1959, B2, Plank Papers.

18. Carson, "Schwartz."

19. Carson, "Schwartz"; Kenan Heise, "Ad Council's Lavinia 'Duffy' Schwartz, 93," *Chicago Tribune*, Dec. 7, 1991, accessed July 3, 2021, https://www.chicagotribune.com/news/ct-xpm-1991-12-07-9104200217-story.html.

20. Heise, "Ad Council's Lavinia 'Duffy' Schwartz, 93"; Powers, "Ad Club Names Woman of the Year." See also, Carson, "Schwartz."

21. Carson, "Schwartz," 29.

22. President Franklin D. Roosevelt created the OWI in 1942 to coordinate the federal government's propaganda efforts during the war. Allan M. Winkler, *The Politics of Propaganda: The Office of War Information, 1942–1945* (New Haven and London: Yale University Press, 1978); Tawnya J. Adkins Covert, *Manipulating Images: World War II Mobilization of Women through Magazine Advertising* (Lanham, MD: Lexington Books, 2011); Carson, "Schwartz," 29. See also, Powers, "Ad Club Names Woman of the Year," B2; "Stauffer Names Schwartz and McAlister OWI Deputies," *Billboard Magazine*, Aug. 7, 1943, 8, accessed July 3, 2021, https://worldradiohistory.com/Archive-All-Music/Billboard/40s/1943/Billboard%201943-08-07.pdf.

23. Covert, *Manipulating Images*; Frank Fox, *Madison Avenue Goes to War: The Strange Military Career of American Advertising, 1941–1945*, 40. For a discussion of the Advertising Council's early history, see J. A. R. Pimlott, "Public Service Advertising: The Advertising Council," 209–219.

24. Allan Jaklich, "Duffy and Ad Council Bow Out," *Chicago Tribune (1963–1996)*, July 8, 1969, C8, ProQuest Historical Newspapers.

25. Plank, Schwartz Eulogy, Dec. 9, 1991; Carson, "Schwartz," 28, Plank Papers.

26. Plank, interview by McNamara. See also, Plank, interview by Walker. Edward Bernays taught the first course actually called "Public Relations" in 1923 and 1924 at New York University. Wright, "History and Development of Public Relations Education in North America."

27. David W. Guth and Charles Marsh, *Public Relations: A Values-Driven Approach*, 72; Karen Miller Russell, "Public Relations, 1900–Present," in *The Media in America: A History*, eds. William David Sloan and James D. Startt, eds., 4th ed. (Northport, AL: Vision Press, 1999), 429.

28. Karla K. Gower, "Rediscovering Women in Public Relations: Women in the *Public Relations Journal*, 1945–1972," 15.

29. Gower, "Rediscovering Women." The number of women admitted in that period represented just 3.8 percent of the total members admitted.

30. Plank, interview by Walker.

31. Plank to Terrill, Apr. 14, 1998; Plank, "Schwartz Eulogy," Plank Papers

32. Scott Cutlip, *Fund Raising in the United States: Its Role in America's Philanthropy*, 161.

33. Cutlip, *Fund Raising*, 158–159. Carlton Ketchum later opened his own fundraising agency. George and Carlton together opened an advertising agency that eventually became the public relations agency still in existence today. While still with Ward & Hill, Tamblyn had hired Brown as publicity director for a campaign to raise money to rebuild churches in France destroyed during World War I.

34. John Crosby Brown, "Public Relations in the Philanthropic Field," 143.

35. John Crosby Brown in *Proceedings Marts & Lundy Fourth Annual Staff Conference*, 66, as quoted in Cutlip, *Fund Raising*, 165; Cutlip, *Fund Raising*, 165–166.

36. Tamblyn and Brown, *Raising Money*, 4. The partners tended to hire "publicity experts" who had held "responsible positions on leading newspapers and magazines."

37. "Executive Board Action," *A.L.A. Bulletin* 42, no. 13 (Dec. 1948): 611–613. Through the Red Cross, McKeown became a close personal friend of Martin H. Kennelly, who was the head of the organization during World War II and then served as Chicago's mayor from 1947 to 1955. Both men benefited from the relationship as they worked together on many community projects. *The American Catholic Who's Who*, Vol. 5, Vol. 7–9, Vol. 11–20, 294. McKeown would go on to serve as the director of many of Chicago charities' fundraising campaigns. For example, in 1934, he served as director of the Community Fund. "Talking Over Charity Game," *Chicago Daily Tribune (1923–1963)*, Sept. 28, 1934, 28, ProQuest Historical Newspapers. In 1940, the Community Fund exceeded its goal by a record $50,000 under his direction. "Chicago Fund Over Goal," *New York Times (1923–Current file)*, Dec. 30, 1940, 36, ProQuest Historical Newspapers. "Mitchell McKeown Reported in Line to Fill CTA Post," *Chicago Daily Tribune (1923–1963)*, Mar. 9, 1949, ProQuest Historical Newspapers.

38. Jimmy Stewart was the first major American movie actor to serve in World War II. He rose from private to colonel during his four years of service, making him an appropriate speaker at the kick-off event. Mark Eliot, *Jimmy Stewart: A Biography* (New York: Random House, 2006). Helen Hayes was also a well-known and well-liked stage and movie actor at the time. Eric Pace, "Helen Hayes, Flower of the Stage, Dies at 92," *New York Times*, March 18, 1993. Betsy Plank, "Oral History Clip 2," interview, PRSA, VHS recording, digitized in m4v format, 2:04, Plank Papers.

39. "President to Talk in Red Cross Drive," *New York Times (1923–Current file)*, Feb. 27, 1949, 32, ProQuest Historical Newspapers; George Eckel, "Eisenhower Backs Red Cross Appeal," *New York Times (1923–Current file)*, Mar. 1, 1949, 21, ProQuest Historical Newspapers; John H. Thompson, "Gen. Ike Opens U.S. Drive Here for Red Cross," *Chicago Daily Tribune (1923–1963)*, Mar. 1, 1949, 3, ProQuest Historical Newspapers.

40. Plank to Terrill, April 14, 1998, Plank Papers.

41. Plank, "Schwartz Eulogy," Plank Papers.

42. Plank, "Schwartz Eulogy," Plank Papers.

43. Plank, "Footnotes," 6, Plank Papers. Plank did not join the Public Relations Society of America until 1958. At the time, PRSA required five years of executive experience in public relations for regular membership. One could become an affiliate member with one year of experience.

44. PCC Bylaws, http://publicity.org/about-pcc/bylaws/. Membership in the PCC was restricted to those who were working as paid professionals in public relations, marketing or integrated communications. "Blurbs," Newsletter of Publicity Club of Chicago, Sept. 1961, Plank Papers.

45. Publicity Club, "Two Hundred and Six PC'ers Can't Be Wrong," lines 1–5, Plank Papers.

46. PRSA had its own official organ, *Public Relations Journal.* The *Journal* was established in 1945 by the American Council on Public Relations. When the ACPR merged

with the National Association of Public Relations Counsel in 1948, forming PRSA, the *Journal* continued under the auspices of PRSA.

47. Plank, interview by Walker.

48. Divorce Decree, Superior Court of Cook County, July 17, 1950.

49. "Profile," *Today's Chicago Woman*, May 1984; Plank, "Handwritten Notes," 2, Plank Papers.

50. "Profile," *Today's Chicago Woman*.

51. Plank, "A Professional Woman's View of the Business World" (speech to International Oxygen Manufacturer's Association Conference, Bermuda, Oct. 7, 1964), Plank Papers; "Profile," *Today's Chicago Woman*.

52. Margaret Hennig and Anne Jardim, *The Managerial Woman*, 120.

53. "Profile," *Today's Chicago Woman*.

54. Plank Resume, ca. 1960s, Plank Papers.

55. Plank, "Handwritten Notes," 3–5, Plank Papers.

56. "Sherman V. Rosenfield," *Chicago Tribune (1963–Current file)*, Nov. 6, 1990, D96, ProQuest Historical Newspapers; "Sherman V. Rosenfield," *Chicago Sun Times*, Nov. 7, 1990, https://chicagosuntimes.newsbank.com.

57. "Feast of the Mainland," *Milwaukee Journal*, July 23, 1959, news clipping, Plank Papers.

58. "Feast of the Mainland," *Milwaukee Journal*.

59. Death certificate of Bettye Hood. The Hoods did not have great longevity. Billy, the oldest son of Annie and the brother of Adelyne and Bettye, died in 1952 at the age of 52. Annie's youngest child, Israel (Ish) died in 1967 at 61 of a brain tumor.

60. The Chicago Council on Foreign Relations is now the Chicago Council on Global Affairs.

61. Plank Resume, Plank Papers.

62. Plank, "Footnotes," 8, Plank Papers. "Allied Arts," *Broadcasting Magazine*, Oct. 20, 1947, 58, accessed June 18, 2021, https://worldradiohistory.com/Archive-BC/BC-1947/1947-10-20-BC.pdf. "Ronald Goodman Named to PR Post Here," *Chicago Daily Tribune (1923–1963)*, May 28, 1952, Pt. 3, B8, ProQuest Historical Newspapers.

63. Laura Littel, "Case Study Project, Communication Research" (unpublished student paper, Dec. 6, 1991); "Woman Executive is Assistant to President," n.d., news clipping, Plank Papers.

64. Plank, "Footnote," 9, Plank Papers.

CHAPTER 3 / THE EMERGENCE OF A PUBLIC RELATIONS LEADER

Epigraph. Laura Littel, "Case Study Project, Communication Research," (unpublished student paper, Dec. 6, 1991), 11, Plank Papers.

1. Plank, "Footnote"; Letter from Anne Bedrosian to Dan J. Edelman, August 20, 1973, Plank Papers.

2. Franz Wisner, *Edelman*, 8-9.

3. Wisner, *Edelman*, 9-12. Even though it meant one could get a permanent at home, which was obviously cheaper, one still needed a second person to help apply the product. Hairdressers claimed that the person applying the product was acting as a hairdresser. See also, Sean D. Hamill, "Irving B. Harris, 1910–2004," *Chicago Tribune*, Sept. 27,

2004, accessed July 3, 2021, https://www.chicagotribune.com/news/ct-xpm-2004-09-27-0409270100-story.html.

4. Press agent Max Cooper started Max Cooper & Associates in Chicago in 1952. The firm would later become GolinHarris, now Golin. Kate Macarthur, "The Player: After 50 Years in Business, MCD's Vet Still Looks Ahead," *AdAge*, June 10, 2002, accessed July 3, 2021, https://adage.com/article/news/player-50-years-business-mcd-s-vet-ahead/51983. The statistic appears in a 1950 Occupational Trends in the United States. Burson-Marsteller opened in New York in 1953.

5. Wisner, *Edelman*, 23. Fortunately, the Toni Company, Edelman's first client, kept the agency afloat. Russell, "Public Relations, 1900–Present," 444; Guth and Marsh, *Public Relations*, 72.

6. Although medical schools did not have written quotas, the number of women and other minorities admitted suggested there were unwritten rules in place. Few hospitals accepted minorities as interns or residents. The same barriers existed in law schools. See "Women or Doctors," *Newsweek*, Nov. 12, 1945, 84; Daniel, *American Women in the 20th Century*, 112; Gower, "Rediscovering Women."

7. Wisner, *Edelman*, 36.

8. Wisner, *Edelman*, 36.

9. Daniel J. Edelman, "Managing the Public Relations Firm in the 21st Century," 4. Plank, speech to Publicity Club of Chicago, Mar. 1986, Plank Papers.

10. Plank Resume, Plank Papers; Richard L. Harmon, "Job Responsibilities in Public Relations," 22–24; Walter Carlson, "Advertising: Campaign for Family Planning," *New York Times*, Mar. 22, 1966, 61; Dan Edelman to All, Feb. 17, 1966, Plank Papers.

11. Plank Resume, Plank Papers. During Plank's tenure with Edelman, the agency opened offices in New York (1960), Los Angeles (1965), London (1967), and Washington, DC (1969). https://www.edelman.com/about-us/our-history. Edelman to All, Feb. 17, 1966, Plank Papers.

12. Plank, speech to Advertising Federation of East Central Indiana, Oct. 31, 1997, Plank Papers.

13. Thomas Heinrich and Bob Batchelor, *Kotex, Kleenex, Huggies: Kimberly-Clark and the Consumer Revolution in American Business*.

14. Heinrich and Batchelor, *Kotex, Kleenex, Huggies*, 89. Plank, speech to Advertising Federation, Plank Papers. Emphasis in original.

15. Plank, speech to Advertising Federation, Plank Papers.

16. Plank, speech to Advertising Federation; Draft of Dan Edelman's letter nominating Plank as Ad Woman of the Year, n.d., ca. 1968, Plank Papers; Lennon, "The Role of Industry in Consumer Health Education," 133. Getting parental support for the teaching of sex education in public schools was always problematic. Parents did not want schools usurping the parental role of teaching children about sex. At the same time, they believed that teaching them about sex would make students more open to premarital sexual experimentation. Valerie Huber, "A Historical Analysis of Public School Sex Education in America Since 1900," 34.

17. Harvard Business School Library, Lehman Brothers Collection. http://www.library.hbs.edu/hc/lehman/chrono.html?company=playskool_manufacturing_company. Playskool is now a subsidiary of Hasbro. "Playskool, Inc.," *International Directory of*

Company Histories (Detroit: St. James Press, 1999), 25. http://www.encyclopedia.com/doc/1G2-2842900112.html.

18. Official Entry Form, Publicity Club's Best Feature (Print Media) category, 1964, Plank Papers. President Lyndon B. Johnson created the Head Start program in 1965 to help meet "the emotional, social, health, nutritional, and psychological needs of preschool-aged children from low-income families" to ensure their readiness for kindergarten. David Hudson, "This Day in History: The Creation of Head Start," The White House, May 18, 2015. https://obamawhitehouse.archives.gov/blog/2015/05/18/day-history-creation-head-start.

19. Plank, interview by McNamara. Bruno Bettelheim was a child psychologist with the University of Chicago's Sonia Shankman Orthogenic School, a residential laboratory for emotionally disturbed children. Although well-respected when Plank would have consulted him, his reputation is now clouded over revelations that he did not have a doctorate from the University of Vienna and accusations that he abused and misdiagnosed children at the Orthogenic School. Plank would likely have known of the allegations and controversy because they were covered by the *Chicago Tribune*, and yet as late as 2006, she was referring to him in a positive way in an interview.

20. "Profile," *Today's Chicago Woman*.

21. Plank, interview by McNamara. Mary Daniels, *Morris: An Intimate Biography* (New York: William Morrow & Company, 1974).

22. Plank to Carol Kleiman, Apr. 30, 1965. Plank, speech to Advertising Federation, Plank Papers.

23. Commission on Public Relations Education, "The Design for Undergraduate Public Relations Education," 1967, Plank Papers. John R. Thomson, "Finicky Morris, 17, dies of old age," *Chicago Tribune (1963–current file)*, July 13, 1978, 4, accessed Aug. 16, 2015, ProQuest Historical Newspapers. The "obituary" also indicated that "The understudy is said to be nearly identical to Morris, and he will be given the same name."

24. "Blurbs," Publicity Club of Chicago, Sept. 1961, Plank Papers.

25. Plank to Cast of the Peak Production, Oct. 28, 1971, Plank Papers.

26. Plank credited Bain with her success; he had masterminded the whole thing according to her. Plank, interview by McNamara, 15. Plank served as president in 1963–64. "Past Presidents," Publicity Club. https://www.publicity.org/about/past-presidents/.

27. Publicity Club, "A Song For Betsy Ann," lines 1–18, Plank Papers.

28. Welfare Public Relations Forum (Chicago, Ill.) records, 1924–1965, Chicago History Museum. It is not known when Plank joined the organization, but given the group's focus on public welfare, it is likely she joined in the 1950s when she was still working in nonprofit public relations.

29. PRSA, "News Release," April 26, 1971, Plank Papers.

30. Ruth MacKay, "White Collar Girl," *Chicago Daily Tribune (1923–1963)*, July 26, 1961, A5, ProQuest Historical Newspapers. MacKay interviewed several secretaries at an institute for educational secretaries held at Northern Illinois University, noting that they were in favor of the coffee break because it was an opportunity "to get away from the stresses and frustrations of a job." Plank was the lone "secretary" who said, "Usually I find the morning too interesting to take a break." Edelman to Robert B. Thompson, Director of Marketing, Faultless Starch Co., Missouri, Mar. 4, 1966, copy, Plank Papers.

31. "The National Organization for Women's 1966 Statement of Purpose." https://now.org/about/history/statement-of-purpose/. Marney Keenan, "Forging Ahead: The Chicagoans Who Helped Change the Way Women Do Business," *Chicago Tribune (1963–Current file)*, Oct. 9, 1988, F1, ProQuest Historical Newspapers.

32. Plank, speech to National PR Council, Southeast Seminar, June 1, 1973, Plank Papers. Plank had originally written in the draft, "constant struggles with the president of our firm" to raise the salaries of women account executives but changed it to "constant struggles within our firm . . . ." Plank to Kleiman, Apr. 30, 1965, Plank Papers.

33. Plank to Kleiman, Apr. 30, 1965, Plank Papers. Plank argued that because public relations was a relatively young field, its first generation of practitioners had to borrow from newspapers, radio, marketing, etc. That forced the field to put a premium on competence and motivation, which gave women an opportunity.

34. Plank to Kleiman, Apr. 30, 1965, Plank Papers.

35. Marcille Gray Williams, *The New Executive Woman*, ix. Plank, speech to National PR Council, Plank Papers. For an example of how another woman in public relations felt about the changing times, see Pat Lawson de Leon, "Some of My Best Friends are Chauvinists," 25–26.

36. Institute on the Church in an Urban-Industrial Society records, in Chicago Federation of Settlements and Neighborhood Centers Collection MSCFSN82, United Christian Community Services 1967 to 1971, box 11, folder 69, Richard Daley Library Special Collections, University of Illinois Chicago. "Association House Elects 7 Officers," *Chicago Tribune (1963–Current file)*, Jul. 21, 1968, NW3, ProQuest Historical Newspapers.

37. Ken Pierce, "Weary Preacher Severs Ties with Chicago Gang," *The Washington Post*, May 1, 1971, E9, ProQuest Historical Newspapers.

38. John R. Fry, *Fire and Blackstone*, 4.

39. Fry, *Fire and Blackstone*, 5.

40. Fry, *Fire and Blackstone*, 5. According to Fry, the Rangers had agreed to turn over their guns to the Church. The guns were kept in a locked storage room at the Church.

41. Richard Philbrick, "Church Clears Rev. Fry of Improper Gang Work," *Chicago Tribune (1963–Current file)*, Sept. 17, 1969, 1, ProQuest Historical Newspapers. The Blackstone Rangers eventually changed their name to Black P. Stone Nation. Donald Mosby, "'You'd Better Watch Out,' Rev. Fry Warns McClellan," *Chicago Daily Defender*, July 1, 1969, 1, ProQuest Historical Newspapers: Black Newspapers. The Senate investigation resulted in the conviction of three Blackstone Rangers of conspiring to defraud the federal government. No charges were brought against Fry. Tom Brune and James Ylisela, Jr., "The Making of Jeff Fort," *Chicago Magazine*, Nov. 1, 1988. https://www.chicagomag.com/chicago-magazine/november-1988/the-making-of-jeff-fort/. For a detailed discussion of the Rangers and their connection with Fry, see Natalie Y. Moore and Lance Williams, *The Almighty Black P Stone Nation: The Rise, Fall and Resurgence of an American Gang* (Chicago: Lawrence Hill Books, 2011).

42. Dr. Martin Luther King, Jr., "Sermon," March 8, 1965, Selma, Alabama. Quoted in Frederick W. Mayer, *Narrative Politics: Stories and Collective Action* (Oxford: Oxford University Press, 2014), 133.

43. Florence Fisher Parry, "I Dare Say," *Pittsburgh Press*, Sept. 5, 1941, 2, news clipping, Plank Papers.

44. Plank, "What is Diversity Worth?" (presentation, PRSA Conference, Nov. 4, 1991), Plank Papers.

45. Plank, interview by McNamara.

46. Plank to Edelman, Aug. 21, 1973, Plank Papers.

47. Plank, interview by McNamara.

48. Plank, Itemized list on why she should leave DJE, n.d., Plank Papers.

49. Plank to Edelman, Aug. 21, 1973, Plank Papers.

50. Plank to Edelman, Aug. 21, 1973, Plank Papers.

51. Anne Bedrosian to Edelman, Aug. 20, 1973; Plank to Edelman, Aug. 23, 1973, Plank Papers.

52. Harris left Edelman in 1966 to become vice president of Needham, Harper & Steers. George Lazarus, "Harris Joins D.J.E.," *Chicago Tribune (1963–Current file)*, Feb. 12, 1973, ProQuest Historical Newspapers. The second time Harris left, it was to assume the presidency of Foote, Cone & Belding Public Relations, a position he held until 1978 when he and Al Golin formed GolinHarris. http://prabook.com/web/person-view.html?profileId=175279.

53. Plank to Edelman, Aug. 25, 1973, Plank Papers.

54. Plank to Edelman, Aug. 25, 1973, Plank Papers.

55. Harvey Posert and Paul Franson, *Spinning the Bottle,* 7.

56. Plank, "Public Relations in Marketing—Does PR Sell?" (presentation, PRSA National Conference, Chicago, 1968), Plank Papers.

57. Plank, "Does PR Sell?" Plank Papers.

58. Plank, "Does PR Sell?" Plank Papers.

59. Plank, "Does PR Sell?" Plank Papers.

60. Berger to Gower, Apr. 17, 2020.

61. Charmayne Kreuz to Edelman, Jan. 7, 1969, Plank Papers.

62. Edelman to Staff, Sept. 20, 1973, Plank Papers.

CHAPTER 4 / LEADING BY EXAMPLE

Epigraph. Plank, "Our Crisis of Identity," Plank Papers; "1972 Conference Highlights," *Public Relations Journal* (January 1973): 24–25.

1. Plank, Speech, Northern Illinois PRSSA Chapter, ca. 1992, Plank Papers. Upon Hammond's death in 2003, Plank described him as "a man of many distinguished 'firsts' in the profession he loved." "George T. Hammond," Dec. 4, 2003, https://www.currentobituary.com/obit/8468.

2. Helen Reddy recorded the song "I Am Woman" in 1971. She co-wrote the song with Ray Burton. Susan Hauser, "The Women's Movement in the '70s, Today: 'You've Come a Long Way,' But . . ." *Workforce,* May 15, 2012, https://www.workforce.com/news/the-womens-movement-in-the-70s-today-youve-come-a-long-way-but; and "The Role of Women in the Seventies," Exploring the Seventies, https://sites.google.com/site/exploringtheseventies/home/politics/the-role-of-women-in-the-70-s. Marion M. Woods, "What Does It Take for a Woman to Make It in Management?" 41. George Hammond would be that man. He had promoted Muriel Fox to Executive Vice President of the Carl Byoir Agency in the 1970s, the first woman in the agency to serve in that role. Fox co-founded the National Organization for Women (NOW) in 1966.

3. Dick Plank to Plank and Rosenfield, Nov. 15, 1972, Plank Papers.

4. Plank to William G. Werner, Sept. 24, 1972, Plank Papers. She sent the identical letter to all of the living past presidents.

5. Averell Broughton to Plank, Sept. 30, 1972, Plank Papers. Broughton was one of three members of the National Association of Public Relations Counsel (NAPRC) who formed a committee with three members of the American Council on Public Relations (ACPR), one of whom was Virgil Rankin, to merge the two organizations into PRSA in 1948. Julie K. Henderson, "Come Together: Rise and Fall of Public Relations Organizations in the 20th Century," in *Sage Handbook of Public Relations*, Vol. II, ed. Robert L. Heath (Thousand Oaks, CA: Sage Publications, 2005), 353. According to Henderson, "the officers named to serve until the first annual meeting [of PRSA] were Earle Ferris as chairman of the board, Virgil L. Rankin as president, and five vice presidents representing five districts." Broughton was the first elected president of the organization.

6. Dan Forrestal to Plank, Sept. 25, 1972, Plank Papers.

7. J. Carroll Bateman to Plank, Oct. 4, 1972; J. Carroll Bateman, "Book Review," *Public Relations Journal*, Nov. 1972, Plank Papers. Bateman had long been concerned about the professionalism of public relations. He addressed the topic in his inaugural address to PRSA as president-elect in 1966. J. Carroll Bateman, "An Aristocracy of Excellence" (speech, PRSA 19th Annual Conference, New York, Nov. 11, 1966).

8. Plank, "Public Relations Fore and Aft: Some Sightings Under Way" (draft of speech, 1997 Vernon C. Schranz Distinguished Lectureship in Public Relations, Ball State University, n.d.), Plank Papers.

9. Quoted in Joseph Nolan, "Protect Your Public Image with Performance," *Harvard Business Review* 53, no. 2 (Mar./Apr.1975): 140. Plank, "How Scientists Can More Effectively Communicate with the General Public" (presentation, International Conference on Energy Use Management, Tucson, AZ, Oct. 25, 1977), Plank Papers.

10. Plank, "Public Relations Fore and Aft," Plank Papers. John G. Mapes, "Public Relations as We Know It," *Vital Speeches of the Day* 31, no. 12 (1965): 362–365, EbscoHost.

11. Karla K. Gower, *Public Relations and the Press: The Troubled Embrace*, 97-98; William E. Porter, *Assault on the Media: The Nixon Years*, 31, 34. Edward Bernays described public relations as being "deflated" by "Nixon's henchmen, wrongly called public relations men." Edward L. Bernays, "Public Relations Council: A Response," 8.

12. Rea Smith to Plank, Dec. 25, 1973, Plank Papers; "1972 Conference Highlights," *Public Relations Journal* (January 1973): 20–25; Robert D. Fierro, "'You PR Men Are All Alike'—A Survey of PR People under the Age of 30," 11.

13. Howard Penn Hughes, "How Corporate Chief Executives View Public Relations. Another Shocker," 5.

14. Art Stevens, "PRQ Poll: PR Field Ranks Itself Low on Professional Totem Pole," 3, 26.

15. Plank, "Our Crisis of Identity," Plank Papers.

16. Plank, "Our Crisis of Identity," Plank Papers.

17. Plank, "Our Crisis of Identity," Plank Papers.

18. Plank, "Our Crisis of Identity," 24–25, Plank Papers. The *Public Relations Journal*, PRSA's membership publication, downplayed Plank's election. In its first issue post conference, the *Journal* simply noted that she was now the chair elect and also happened to be the first woman to assume the leadership of the association.

19. Jane Shaw, "'Watergate No Instant Disaster,'" *Pittsburgh Post-Gazette*, June 23, 1973, 5, accessed June 18, 2016, https://archives.post-gazette.com/image/90067826.

20. Shaw, "'Watergate No Instant Disaster,'" 5. See also, Patricia Ford, "Dem Bug, PR Tie Denied," *Pittsburgh Press*, June 22, 1973, 16, accessed June 18, 2016, https://archives.post-gazette.com/image/147946141; PRSA Member Newsletter, 1973, 3–6, Plank Papers; Plank, "Editorials," *Public Relations Journal*, 1973, 2, Plank Papers.

21. PRSA adopted its first ethical code in 1950. Kathy R. Fitzpatrick, "Evolving Standards in Public Relations: A Historical Examination of PRSA's Codes of Ethics," 98. Expulsion from the Society had no real practical implications. The expelled member could still practice public relations.

22. Rea Smith to Plank, Dec. 25, 1973, Plank Papers; Fitzpatrick, "Evolving Standards"; Philip H. Doughtery, "Shining PR's Image," *New York Times (1923–Current file)*, July 31, 1973, 47, ProQuest Historical Newspapers.

23. Theodore Pincus to Plank, July 24, 1973, Plank Papers. "Pincus Quits PRSA in Face of Charges," *Jack O'Dwyer's Newsletter*, 6, no. 31, Aug. 8, 1973. According to PRSA's bylaws, the Society would not investigate ethical matters that were the subject of legal action until a decision had been made. Fitzpatrick, "Evolving Standards," 96.

24. Pincus to Plank, July 24, 1973, Plank Papers.

25. Smith to Plank, July 27, 1973; PRSA Grievance Board vs. Pincus, Plank Papers. Jonathan R. Laing, "The Drum Beaters: Many Companies Hire Public Relations Men to Publicize Shares," *Wall Street Journal*, Mar. 13, 1970, 1, ProQuest Historical Newspapers: Wall Street Journal; "Stock-Kiting Scheme Involving Texas Firm Charged Against 4 Men," *Wall Street Journal*, Aug. 3, 1972, 15, ProQuest Historical Newspapers: Wall Street Journal; John H. Allen, "It's Getting Tougher to Lie: S.E.C. Widening Scope of Disclosure Orders," *New York Times (1923–Current file)*, Mar. 26, 1972, F1, ProQuest Historical Newspapers: New York Times.

26. Allen, "It's Getting Tougher to Lie."

27. Allen, "It's Getting Tougher to Lie." Smith to Plank, July 27, 1973; Grievance Board vs. Pincus, Plank Papers. According to Smith, the investigation into the first allegation took a year because Pincus failed to return the calls of the Grievance Board's investigators. The third case involved Control Metals Corp. The SEC filed a complaint against the company and the FRB among others for "violations of the registration and anti-fraud provisions of the securities laws in connection with the purchase and sale of securities" of the company in October 1970. "Complaint Names Control Metal Corp., Others," *Securities and Exchange Commission News Digest* (Oct. 16, 1970), 2.

28. Ethical investigations were confidential. Members of the Society only learned of violations if the Board of Directors "adopted a resolution of censure, suspension, or expulsion, all of which required notice to members." Fitzpatrick, "Evolving Standards," 96.

29. The draft was reviewed by several members of the Grievance Board and Judicial Board.

30. Plank to VIPs, July 28, 1973, Plank Papers.

31. Plank to PRSA Members, July 30, 1973, Plank Papers.

32. Eleanor Haas to Plank, Aug. 2, 1973; Edelman to Plank, Aug. 8, 1973; David Fletcher to Plank, Aug. 8, 1973; Montez Tjaden to Plank, Aug. 9, 1973, Plank Papers.

33. Sherwood Lee Wallace to Plank, Aug. 7, 1973; Allen Sommers to Plank, Aug. 15, 1973, Plank Papers.

34. William Ruder to Plank, Aug. 15, 1973; Charles C. Vance to Plank, Aug. 21, 1973, Plank Papers.

35. "Pincus Quits PRSA in Face of Charges," *Jack O'Dwyer's Newsletter* 6, no. 31, Aug. 8, 1973; *Public Relations News* 29, no. 32, Aug. 6, 1973, Plank Papers.

36. Pincus to PRSA members, Aug. 22, 1973; Fran Kafka to Pincus, Aug. 28, 1973; Vance to Plank, Aug. 15, 1973, Plank Papers.

37. Plank to Egoroff, Aug. 27, 1973, Plank Papers.

38. Plank to Egoroff, Aug. 27, 1973, Plank Papers.

39. Plank, "PRSA Past President Testimony," 1987; Smith to Plank, Dec. 25, 1973, Plank Papers.

40. Plank, "Report," PRSA Membership Newsletter, 1973, 3–6, Plank Papers.

41. Smith to Plank, Dec. 25, 1973, Plank Papers.

42. "President of PR Society Resigns," *New York Times (1923–Current file)*, June 29, 1973, 66, ProQuest Historical Newspapers.

43. In his letter nominating Plank for PRSA's 1977 Gold Anvil, James F. Fox said, as president, Plank "gave the Society the first loyalty of her life, putting it above personal comfort, her job, her husband and even her personal health. She probably did more travelling and speaking and thus more to bring chapters, districts and student chapters alive than any other president before or since." He was including himself in that since he served as PRSA president in 1975. Fox to Plank, Aug. 12, 1977; Smith to Plank, Dec. 25, 1973, Plank Papers.

44. Smith to Plank, Dec. 25, 1973, Plank Papers. The following year, Plank was awarded the PRSA Chicago Chapter's Distinguished Service Award "in recognition of her exceptional contributions which she has made to the improvement of the professional competence of her associates." Flier announcing the Distinguished Service Award luncheon, Nov. 19, 1974. In 1973 when she was PRSA Chair, some people wrote to her as Ms. Plank. PRSA still referred to her as chairman. Two women commented on how behind the times PRSA was.

45. Past Presidents' Council Charter, 1959; W. Howard Chase to Mrs. Tulloch, Oct. 14, 1987; Barbara Hunter to W. Howard Chase, Oct. 27, 1987; Plank to PRSA Past Presidents, n.d., ca. 1978, Plank Papers.

46. Plank, "1973 Past Presidents Dinner: Recollections of the Initiate," Plank Papers. Plank made some changes to the "initiation" process after she became a member of the Past Presidents Club, bringing in some of the touches from the Publicity Club of Chicago's annual dinner such as the song parodies. For example, one year her advance instructions to the group sound very similar to her Publicity Club comrades: "Past Presidents: When you come up to perform, you'll be given 'skimmers' [straw boater hats] as headgear to help ham it up. It's a familiar tune, of course, and the pianist will help. Sign or speak out LOUD AND CLEAR—raise your hats to applause!"

47. Fox, Gold Anvil nomination, Aug. 12, 1977, Plank Papers. The International Public Relations Association holds its World Congress, which brings together public relations practitioners from around the world for a meeting, every three years. In 1980, Plank served as the chair of the U.S. section of IPRA.

48. Denny Griswold to Plank, Nov. 9, 1976, Plank Papers. Harold Burson had de-livered the New Year's message the year before. Harold Burson, *Public Relations News*, 31, no. 52, Dec. 29, 1975. "Public Relations, 1977: Communications Need Actions, Integrity, Accountability to Help Solve Nation's Problems," News Release, Dec. 24, 1976. J. Carroll Bateman, to Plank, Dec. 27, 1976; Louis B. Raffel, executive vice president, American Egg Board, to Plank, Dec. 30, 1976; Plank to Raffel, Jan. 4, 1977, Plank Papers.

49. Invitation to First Public Relations News Seminar in combination with the 17th Annual Awards Luncheon. See, Acceptance Speech, Oct. 24, 1978, Plank Papers. Plank was also named one of the World's 40 outstanding PR Leaders by *PR News* in 1984. Fox, Gold Anvil Nomination, Plank Papers.

CHAPTER 5 / A SEASONED LEADER

Epigraph. Plank, "Staff Meeting, Community Affairs and Employee Information, Illinois Bell Corporate Communications," Apr. 25, 1980, Plank Papers.

1. Plank, interview by McNamara. At the time, AT&T's headquarters was locat-ed at 195 Broadway in New York City. Peter Temin, "Fateful Choices: AT&T in the 1970s," 61–77. See, Edward M. Block, "The Legacy of Public Relations Excellence Behind the Name," The Arthur W. Page Society. http://www.awpagesociety.com/site/historical-perspective. Mary Ardito and C. Anne Prescott, "The Road Ahead—Part 2," *Bell Telephone Magazine* 1 (1982).

2. "News Release," AT&T, Sept. 20, 1973, Plank Papers. Cummings wrote to Plank to thank her for her "superb" work as chair of the public relations committee of the Crusade of Mercy in 1973. "You showed all those qualities of leadership which are vital to success, including a dedication of your time beyond the call of duty," he wrote. Cummings to Plank, Mar. 6, 1973; Cummings to John DeButts, Oct. 1, 1973, Plank Papers. Note the use of the term "gal" to describe Plank, who was at this point forty-nine years old.

3. George Lazarus, "Fuller Brush Knocks on Grocery Doors," *Chicago Tribune (1963–1996)*, Apr. 23, 1974, C10, ProQuest Historical Newspapers. According to the U.S. Dept. of Labor, only 11,000 women managers in the United States made more than $25,000 annually in 1972. U.S. Dept. of Labor, Employment Standards Admin-istration, Women's Bureau: Women Managers, Feb. 1972.

4. Plank to G. Patterson Little, Sept. 28, 1973, Plank Papers.

5. Although she had twenty-five years of public relations experience when she joined AT&T, her agency experience with corporate clients began in 1958 with the Ron-ald Goodman Public Relations agency and continued until she left Edelman in 1973. Handwritten notes of speech, Business Panel, PRSA 2006 International Conference, Plank Papers. "Profile," *Today's Chicago Woman*.

6. Littel, "Case Study Project," Dec. 6, 1991, 4.

7. Littel, "Case Study Project," 8.

8. Littel, "Case Study Project," 8–9.

9. Eric N. Berg, "John D. deButts, Ex-chairman of AT&T, is dead," *New York Times (1923–Current file)*, Dec. 18, 1986, B30, accessed May 24, 2020, ProQuest Historical Newspapers.

10. Berg, "John D. deButts"; J. Y. Smith, "John deButts dies; Ex-chairman Who Fought Breakup of AT&T," *Washington Post (1974–Current file)*, Dec. 19, 1986, B4, ProQuest Historical Newspapers.

11. Smith, "John deButts Dies."

12. Edward M. Block, "Planning Division Meeting Comments," Dec. 13, 1971, Plank Papers.

13. Temin, "Fateful Choices." "AT&T Names Choices to Run Restructured Marketing Operation," *Wall Street Journal (1923–Current file)*, July 31, 1978, 16, ProQuest Historical Newspapers. Plank, "Public Relations Fore and Aft," Plank Papers. See also, Plank, interview by Walker.

14. Littel, "Case Study Project."

15. Plank, "Staff Meeting," Apr. 25, 1980, Plank Papers.

16. The report was leaked to the *New York Times*, which said the report had apparently been written by the Planning Division of Illinois Bell. Plank was with Illinois Bell at the time the report was leaked. David Burnham, "Bell Report Offers Strategy on Rulings," *New York Times (1923–Current file)*, June 19, 1974, 90, ProQuest Historical Newspapers.

17. Plank, "Staff Meeting," Apr. 25, 1980, Plank Papers; Littel, "Case Study Project," 6.

18. deButts to Plank, May 22, 1974, Plank Papers.

19. "Richard Plank," Birmingham News, news clipping, Plank Papers. Marion M. Woods, "What Does It Take for a Woman to Make It in Management?" 41. Hennig and Jardim, *The Managerial Woman*, 118.

20. Plank to Paul Lund, Jan. 3, 1974, Plank Papers.

21. When Plank joined the company in 1974, it had approximately thirty-six thousand Chicago-area employees. "Illinois Bell Telephone Co.," Dictionary of Leading Chicago Businesses (1820–2000), *Encyclopedia of Chicago*. (2005). Chicago Historical Society. http://www.encyclopedia.chicagohistory.org/pages/2715.html. Joe Cappo, "Column," *Chicago Daily News*, Apr. 22, 1974, 74, news clipping; George Lazarus, "Fuller Brush Knocks on Grocery Doors," *Chicago Tribune (1963-1996)*, Apr. 23, 1974, C2, ProQuest Historical Newspapers.

22. Harold A. Bergen to Plank, May 6, 1974; Edelman to Plank, April 24, 1974; deButts to Plank, May 22, 1974, Plank Papers. During the few months in the fall of 1973 that Plank was at AT&T in New York and becoming "invaluable" to deButts, he was seeking buy-in from the operating companies on a major reorganization of the entire Bell System. Presumably, Plank assisted him with the logistics surrounding the Bell System Operating Company presidents' semi-annual conference held Nov. 1, 1973, and at which deButts presented his reorganization plan. For a discussion of the plan and the conference, see Temin, "Fateful Choices."

23. James Strong, "Bell, Labor Set National Talks," *Chicago Tribune (1963–1996)*, Jan. 17, 1974, 2, ProQuest Historical Newspapers; Georgette Jasen, "Ma Bell's Daughters: Women Got Big Gains in '73 AT&T Job Pact, But Sexism Cry Persists," *Wall Street Journal (1923–Curent file)*, Feb. 28, 1978, 1, ProQuest Historical Newspapers.

24. Plank, Speech, Advertising Federation, Plank Papers; Jasen, "Ma Bell's Daughters." Plank, Speech, Business Panel, Plank Papers.

25. Office Planning Questionnaire, May 22, 1978, Plank Papers.

26. Edward M. Block to Illinois Bell Headquarters Public Relations Dept., Sept. 27, 1974, Plank Papers. Plank, Speech, Business Panel. As of Nov. 1, 1974, Plank was given a raise. Her new annual salary was $52,500. Block to Plank, n.d., Plank Papers.

27. Employee to Plank, Mar. 10, 1980, Plank Papers.

28. Plank, Speech, Business Panel, Plank Papers.

29. Plank, "How Scientists Can More Effectively Communicate with the General Public" (presentation, International Conference on Energy Use Management, Tucson, AZ, Oct. 25, 1977), Plank Papers.

30. Plank, "Staff Meeting," Apr. 25, 1980, Plank Papers.

31. Plank, "Staff Meeting," Apr. 25, 1980, Plank Papers.

32. Plank, "Staff Meeting," Apr. 25, 1980, Plank Papers.

33. Plank, "Staff Meeting," Apr. 25, 1980, Plank Papers.

34. Plank, "Staff Meeting," Apr. 25, 1980, Plank Papers.

35. Plank, "Personnel Meeting," June 2, 1981, Plank Papers.

36. Plank, "Staff Meeting," Apr. 25, 1980, Plank Papers.

37. Kit Hughes, *Television at Work: Industrial Media and American Labor*, 109, 112. Block's quote, 117.

38. Plank, "The Next Revolution in Public Relations" (presentation, Communication Seminar, Apr. 20, 1983), Plank Papers.

39. Illinois Bell, *Phil Donahue, Meet the Bell System*, Apr. 4, 1981, Plank Papers.

40. Illinois Bell, *Phil Donahue*, Plank Papers.

41. For a discussion about the effects of the rebuttal video on the credibility of *60 Minutes*, see David E. Clavier and Frank B. Kalupa, "Corporate Rebuttals to 'Trial by Television,'" 24–36.

42. Illinois Bell, *Phil Donahue*, Plank Papers.

43. Illinois Bell, *Phil Donahue*, Plank Papers.

44. Carolyn Garrett Cline and Lynne Masel-Waters, "Backlash: The Impact of a Video Case Study on Opinions of AT&T," 39–46.

45. Cline and Masel-Waters, "Backlash," 45.

46. Plank, "IBT Forum 5–81," May 1981, transcript, Plank Papers.

47. Plank, "IBT Forum 5–81," Plank Papers.

48. Plank, "IBT Forum 5–81," Plank Papers.

49. Plank, Speech, Rockford IABC, Mar. 20, 1984, Plank Papers.

50. Plank, Speech, Rockford IABC, Plank Papers. Illinois Bell became part of Ameritech under the agreement. "Illinois Bell Telephone Company History," Funding Universe. http://www.fundinguniverse.com/company-histories/illinois-bell-telephone-company-history/. John T. Soma, et al., "The Communications Regulatory Environment in the 1980's," 1–55.

51. "AT&T Names Choices to Run Restructured Marketing Operation," *Wall Street Journal (1923–Current file)*, July 31, 1978, 16, ProQuest Historical Newspapers; "Effective Feb. 1: AT&T's deButts Will Retire Early," *Chicago Tribune (1963–1996)*, Oct. 19, 1978, C9, ProQuest Historical Newspapers; Trudy E. Bell, "The Decision to Divest: Incredible or Inevitable?" IEEE Spectrum Online. June 2000, 37(6). Reprinted at http://www.beatriceco.com/bti/porticus/bell/decisiontodivest.html.

52. "Ma Bell Dies at 107," Traffic Topics IBEW Local 1944, Reprinted at: http://www.beatriceco.com/bti/porticus/bell/bellsystemdied.html.

53. Bob Greene, "Anger ringing out over Bell's demise," *Chicago Tribune (1963–1996)*, Aug. 14, 1983, O1, ProQuest Historical Newspapers.

54. Barry G. Cole, ed, *After the Breakup: Assessing the New Post-AT&T Divestiture Era*, 3. See also, Melvin D. Barger, "AT&T Divestiture: 'What Killed Ma Bell?'" Apr. 1984. http://www.beatriceco.com/bti/porticus/bell/whatkilledmabell.html.

55. Plank, Speech, Rockford IABC, Mar. 20, 1984, Plank Papers.

56. Cole, *After the Breakup*, 3; C. Anne Prescott, "The Road Ahead," 3; Plank, Speech, Rockford IABC, Plank Papers.

57. "The Illinois Bell Telephone Study: How Hardiness Began," The Hardiness Institute, Inc., https://www.hardinessinstitute.com/?p=776.

58. "The Illinois Bell Telephone Study: How Hardiness Began," The Hardiness Institute, Inc., https://www.hardinessinstitute.com/?p=776. See also, Maddi and Khoshaba, *Resilience at Work,* 17. There is no evidence that Plank was one of the 430 participants in the study, which ran from 1975 to 1987.

59. Ameritech was originally made up of the following Bell operating companies: Illinois Bell, Indiana Bell, Michigan Bell, Ohio Bell, and Wisconsin Telephone Company. http://www.beatriceco.com/bti/porticus/bell/bellopercomp.html. Jack Glascock, "The Role of AT&T's Public Relations Campaign in Press Coverage of the 1982 Breakup," 69. The reference to two-thirds of its operating revenues comes from MacAvoy and Robinson, "Winning by Losing," 21. The reference to five-sixths of its assets comes from the AT&T Annual Report, 1981, 1. "Ma Bell Unbound," *Wall Street Journal (1923–Current file)*, Jan. 9, 1982, 32, ProQuest Historical Newspapers.

60. Len Ackland, "Public is the Real Loser in IBM, AT&T Settlements," *Chicago Tribune (1963–1996)*, Jan. 17, 1982, A1, ProQuest Historical Newspapers; James Worsham, "Soaring Phone Bills Expected to Cause Battle in Congress," *Chicago Tribune (1963–1996)*, Sept. 18, 1983, F8, ProQuest Historical Newspapers; Lydia Chavez, "Rise in local rates may come rapidly," *New York Times (1923–Current file)*, Jan. 9, 1982, 1, ProQuest Historical Newspapers; "Outcry Over Possible Rise in Rates Prompts AT&T Defense of Decree," *The Wall Street Journal*, January 11, 1982, 5, ProQuest Historical Newspapers.

61. Plank, Speech, Rockford IABC, Plank Papers.

62. Plank, Speech, Rockford IABC, Plank Papers. For his part, Wirth contended that his bill was meant to deal with what he saw as deficiencies in the AT&T settlement agreement. AT&T claimed that the bill would have disrupted the country's phone system "by placing undue burdens on long distance lines." Wirth ultimately withdrew his bill, claiming that "AT&T had waged a campaign of 'fear and distortion,' and that '[t]he only way to pass legislation [in the time remaining] would be to accept an agreement dictated by AT&T.'" Soma, et al., "The Communications Regulatory Environment," 46.

63. Plank, Speech, Rockford IABC, Plank Papers. Terrence E. Deal and Allan A. Kennedy, *Corporate Cultures: The Rites and Rituals of Corporate Life*.

64. Christine Winter, "Bell Families as Broken Up as Bell System," *Chicago Tribune (1963–1996)*, Feb. 20, 1984, C1, ProQuest Historical Newspapers.

65. Plank, Speech, Rockford IABC, Plank Papers.

66. Littel, "Case Study Project," 7.

67. Jeff Lyon, "Confusion is the major hang-up at new AT&T," *Chicago Tribune (1923–1996)*, Apr. 24, 1984, E1, ProQuest Historical Newspapers; Littel, "Case Study Project," 7.

68. Jack Koten to Plank, Apr. 9, 1984, Plank Papers.

69. Koten to Plank; Plank to Community Affairs People, Nov. 5, 1986, Plank Papers.

70. Plank to Community Affairs People, Nov. 5, 1986, Plank Papers.

71. Illinois Bell, "Case Study: The Hinsdale Fire," 1989, Plank Papers.

72. "Case Study: The Hinsdale Fire," Plank Papers.

73. "Case Study: The Hinsdale Fire," Plank Papers.

74. "Case Study: The Hinsdale Fire," Plank Papers.

75. "Case Study: The Hinsdale Fire," Plank Papers.

76. Cathy to Plank, May 3, 1974; Nancy Stuckey to Plank, May 3, 1974; John T. Trutter to Plank, May 6, 1985, Plank Papers.

CHAPTER 6 / SHAPING THE FUTURE

Epigraph. "Goal for the '70's: Credible Communications," *Los Angeles Times (1923–1995)*, Mar. 28, 1973, A7, ProQuest Historical Newspapers.

1. Plank, Speech, Rockford IABC, Plank Papers; *Today's Chicago Woman*, May 1984.

2. Peter F. Drucker, *Management*, 319; Plank, "Playing Corporate Hardball: Skills Needed by the Future Public Relations Executive," 11.

3. Plank, "Playing Corporate Hardball," 11–12.

4. Plank, "Playing Corporate Hardball," 13.

5. Plank, interview by Walker, 3.

6. Plank, interview by Walker; James F. Tirone, "Measuring the Bell Systems Public Relations," 23.

7. Plank, Speech, Measurement Coordinators Conference, Chicago, May 16–17, 1978, Plank Papers.

8. Plank, "The Next Revolution in Public Relations," (speech, New Uses of Electronic Communications Seminar, Washington, D.C., Apr. 20, 1983), Plank Papers.

9. Plank, "The New Technology and Its Implications for the Public Relations Profession," 38. Of the articles on technology and public relations published in the *IPRA Review* between 1981 to 1996, Plank's was one of the first to recognize the benefits of technology. Tom Watson, "PR's Early Response to the 'information superhighway': The IPRA Narrative," 1–12.

10. Plank, "The Next Revolution," Plank Papers.

11. Plank, "The Next Revolution": Plank, "The Revolution in Communications Technology: Implications for the Public Relations Profession," (speech, 21st Annual Foundation Lecture, Foundation for Public Relations Research and Education, San Francisco, CA, Nov. 7, 1982, 6), Plank Papers.

12. Watson, "PR's Early Response," 10. In fact, when Plank retired in 1990, the fax machine was the preferred method of communicating with others in business, and

she continued to send faxes until her death. She attempted email but never became comfortable with its use. Plank, Speech, Carbondale PRSSA Chapter, 1983, Plank Papers.

13. Plank was the president of the Chicago Chapter of PRSA at the time. The PRSSA Chapter at Northern Illinois is named in honor of Plank. Walker and Plank developed a lasting friendship.

14. During WWII, drafted men who could write were often put to use writing reports, statements, articles, etc. After the war, many of these men looked for a career in writing, usually journalism or public relations. Jacquie L'Etang, *Public Relations in Britain: A History of Professional Practice in the 20ᵗʰ Century.*

15. When the first board of directors of PRSA met, they established an Education Committee, one of the few standing committees. *PRSSA Reminiscence*, 1986, transcript of audio recording of conversation among Plank, John Riffle, and Frederick H. Teahan, Plank Papers; Raymond Simon, "Six Students to be Honored," 36; Raymond Simon, "Pilot Project Highly Successful," 35.

16. Raymond Simon, "Fourth Student Group Formed at West Virginia," 41. The group at West Virginia was a fraternal organization, Pi Rho Sigma. Two others were also honorary fraternities: Tau Mu Epsilon (Boston University, Utica College, and the University of Maryland) and Pi Alpha Nu (San Jose State University). The fourth group was the Student Public Relations Society at the University of Texas. In September 1966, public relations students from Texas colleges met to discuss the possibility of establishing a national body of public relations students that would not require a pre-established grade point average as Tau Mu Epsilon did. Raymond Simon, "New Student Group Being Formed," 21–22. Seifert made his recommendation in March 1967. That August a group of public relations educators and PRSA representatives reached tentative agreement on the need to establish a nationwide student organization. Raymond Simon, "Agreement Reached on Student Group," 47; F.H. Teahan, Susan Gonders, and Barbara DeSanto, *Public Relations Student Society of America: A Brief History*, 3.

17. Friends of PRSSA, "Newsletter," Sept. 1992, Plank Papers. The first nine PRSSA chapters were chartered by the PRSA Board of Directors on Apr. 4, 1968. Teahan, Gonders, and DeSanto, *Public Relations Student Society of America*, 4.

18. PRSA News Release, Apr. 26, 1971, Plank Papers. The others on the Council were Vice-Chair Howard F. Harris, chair of PRSA's Education Committee; J. Carroll Bateman, former PRSA president and liaison representative to the American Council for Education in Journalism; Herbert B. Bain, member of the board and chairman of the PRSA Institute Committee; William W. Cook, president of the Foundation for Public Relations Research and Education; Kerryn King, chair of the Accreditation Board; William W. Marsh, chair of the Public Relations Student Society Committee; John Moynihan, liaison representative to the American Association of Collegiate Schools of Business; Kenneth O. Smith, chair of the Education Advisory Council; Walter J. Walsh, chair of the Research Committee; Frank W. Wylie, chair of the Subcommittee of the Board on Standards of Professional Practice; and Donald B. McCammond, 1970 president and chair (member-at-large).

19. Plank, "Our Crisis of Identity," Plank Papers. She did the same with the Plank Center Advisory Board, adding the PRSSA National President as an ex officio member to provide a voice for students on the Board.

20. In a letter to the editor of the *PR Journal* in December 1972, Frederick H. Teahan, PRSA Education Director, said that PRSSA membership was at 1,200 with 43 percent of those being female. F.H. Teahan, "'Making It in the Seventies'—Misinterpreted," 40. Teahan, Gonders, and DeSanto, *Public Relations Student Society of America*, 6. "A Visit with Betsy Ann," *PRSSA Forum* (Spring 1973), Plank Papers.

21. Teahan, Gonders, and DeSanto, *Public Relations Student Society of America*, 6.

22. Plank's comments at Jon Riffel's memorial service, Sept. 10, 2005, Plank Papers.

23. In approximately 2000, the Friends changed its name to the Champions of PRSSA. "For the Record: The Champions, Nee Friends, for PRSSA," 2003, Plank Papers.

24. Commission on Public Relations Education, *The Design for Undergraduate Public Relations Education* (New York: Commission on Public Relations Education, 1987), 1, Plank Papers. AEJ is now the Association for Education in Journalism and Mass Communication (AEJMC). It is an academic association for educators.

25. Teahan, Gonders, and DeSanto, *Public Relations Student Society of America*, 8.

26. *Design for Undergraduate Public Relations Education*, Plank Papers.

27. Frank Kalupa and J. Carroll Bateman, "Accrediting Public Relations Education," 20–21.

28. Kalupa and Bateman, "Accrediting Public Relations Educators," 22. PRSA established the APR (Accredited in Public Relations) designation for individual practitioners in 1965.

29. Kalupa and Bateman, "Accrediting Public Relations Educators," 21-22.

30. Kalupa and Bateman, "Accrediting Public Relations Educators," 22-23.

31. Kalupa and Bateman, "Accrediting Public Relations Education," 25.

32. J. Carroll Bateman and Scott Cutlip, "A Design for Public Relations Education: The Report of the Commission on Public Relations Education," (Association for Education in Journalism and Public Relations Society of America, 1975), 5, Plank Papers. See also, Kalupa and Bateman, "Accrediting Public Relations Education.," 19.

33. Raymond Simon, "Practitioners-Educators Exchange Ideas," 29–30.

34. It should be noted that PRSA opted to "certify" programs rather than "accredit" them because of the difficulty in winning the approval of the Council on Post-Secondary Accreditation and the U.S. Department of Health and Welfare as an accrediting agency. Kalupa and Bateman, "Accrediting Public Relations Education," 30.

35. Karlene Lukovitz, "Women Practitioners: How Far, How Fast?"

36. *EEOC, Hodgson, and US* v. *AT&T* (EE-PA-0227) https://www.clearinghouse.net/detail.php?id=11146.

37. "Wanted: 100 Girls," Standard Executive Speech, Women in Illinois Bell, Nov. 1980, Plank Papers.

38. Betsy Plank, "Bell Management Women," July 19, 1984, Plank Papers.

39. Plank, "Bell Management Women," Plank Papers.

40. Marney Keenan, "Forging Ahead: The Chicagoans Who Helped Change the Way Women Do Business," *Chicago Tribune (1963–Current file)*, Oct. 9, 1988, F1, ProQuest Historical Newspapers.

41. Keenan, "Forging Ahead."

42. Littel, "Case Study Project," 6–7; Ron Culp, "Celebrating the Life and Legacy of Jack Koten," *Culpwrit* (blog), April 14, 2014, https://www.culpwrit.com/2014/04/14/celebrating-the-life-and-legacy-of-jack-koten/.

43. Dick Martin, *Marilyn: A Woman in Charge.*

44. William B. Crawford, Jr., "Bell plans to cut 1,000 management jobs," *Chicago Tribune (1923–1996)*, Jan. 27, 1990, 1, ProQuest Historical Newspapers.

45. Plank, "Zanahoria," Brochure, n.d., Plank Papers.

46. Plank, "Zanahoria," Plank Papers.

CHAPTER 7 / LEAVING A LEGACY

Epigraph. Littel, "Case Study Project," 11.

1. Plank, "Searching for a very special man: Sherm's Betsy," n.d., ca. Nov. 1990, Plank Papers.

2. Bruce Berger, interview by Karla K. Gower, July 18, 2016; "Searching for a very special man"; "List of Things to Do," n.d., ca. Nov. 1990, Plank Papers.

3. Plank, "Personal notes to God and Sherm," Mar. 11, 1991, Plank Papers.

4. Plank, "Personal notes to God and Sherm," Nov. 20, 1991, Plank Papers.

5. Plank, "Personal notes to God and Sherm," Dec. 26, 1991, Plank Papers.

6. Plank, "Personal notes to God and Sherm," Dec. 26, 1991, Plank Papers.

7. Clarke Caywood to Plank, Feb. 6, 1992, Plank Papers.

8. Background and Agenda for Integrated Communication Task Force Teleconference, February 1992; Caywood to Plank, Feb. 6, 1992, Plank Papers.

9. Caywood to Plank, Feb. 6, 1992; Plank to Dave Ferguson, Colleen McDonough, Judy VanSlyke Turk, Oct. 14, 1992; Background and Agenda, Feb. 1992, Plank Papers.

10. Minutes of the Integrated Communication Task Force, Mar. 13, 1992, Plank Papers.

11. Minutes of the Integrated Communication Task Force, Mar. 13, 1992, Plank Papers.

12. Caywood to Plank, Mar. 10, 1992; Plank to Ferguson, McDonough, VanSlyke Turk, Oct. 14, 1992, Plank Papers

13. Plank to Ferguson, McDonough, VanSlyke Turk, Oct. 14, 1992, Plank Papers.

14. Plank to Ferguson, McDonough, VanSlyke Turk, Oct. 14, 1992, Plank Papers.

15. Pat Jackson to Jerry Dalton, Dave Ferguson, Lauri Grunig, Colleen McDonough, Doug Newsom, Judy VanSlyke Turk, Dennis Wilcox, Oct. 16, 1992; Plank, Speech, PR Commission, Speech Communication Association, Nov. 18, 1993, Plank Papers.

16. Unfortunately, that assurance was not ultimately honored although the report did contain a dissenting statement from PRSA's Educational Affairs Committee (EAC), which the Society's Educator's Academy endorsed. PRSA Educational Affairs Committee, *Position Statement: Preparing Advertising and Public Relations Students for the Communications Industry in the 21ˢᵗ Century*, July 1993, Plank Papers. See also, PRSA Educators' Academy, *PR Educator Newsletter*, Winter 1993, Plank Papers.

17. Plank to Ferguson and VanSlyke Turk, July 19, 1993, Plank Papers.

18. Plank, "How to Say No to a Marriage of Convenience and Stay Friends" (presentation, Professional Development Workshop: Integrated Marketing Communications—the Great Communication Debate, Nov. 14, 1994), Plank Papers; Plank to Ferguson and VanSlyke Turk, July 19, 1993, Plank Papers.

19. PRSA Educational Affairs Committee, *Position Statement*, Plank Papers.

20. Plank, "The Unpublished View: One Member's Dissent to the Integrated Marketing Communications Task Force Report and Position" (presentation, Speech Communication Association Conference, Miami Beach, Nov. 18, 1993), Plank Papers. As late as 2005, Plank was still expressing her "disdain" for the push toward IMC. Plank to Cully Clark, Apr. 26, 2005, Plank Papers.

21. West to Gower, Oct. 1, 2020. Carl Botan, comment on "In Memoriam: Betsy Plank," https://apps.prsa.org/Intelligence/Tactics/Articles/view/8474/101/In_memoriam _Betsy_Plank_APR_Fellow_PRSA_86.

22. Plank, Speech, PRSA Suburban Chicago Chapter, Sept. 30, 1992, Plank Papers. The definition of public relations Plank used in her speech is part of a widely used definition from Denny Griswold, editor of *PR News*, which was the first newsletter dedicated to public relations. James G. Hutton, "The Definition, Dimensions, and Domain of Public Relations," 201.

23. Bernays had supported the licensing of public relations practitioners since at least the early 1950s. Edward L. Bernays, "Should Public Relations Counsel be Licensed?" 52–54. See also, Edward L. Bernays, "Public Relations Council: A Response," 8–9; Edward L. Bernays, "The Outlook for Public Relations," 34–38; Paul S. Forbes, "Why Licensing is an Opportunity for Public Relations," 9–11; Philip Lesly, "Why Licensing Won't Work for Public Relations," 3–7. See also, Melvin L. Sharpe, "Recognition Comes from Consistently High Standards," 17–25; Bill L. Baxter, "Lawmakers' Views on Licensing in Public Relations," 12–15.

24. Frank A. Tennant, "Survey on Licensing Public Relations Practitioners," 37–42. Interestingly, most of the educators responded that licensing would be an infringement on the First Amendment and therefore unconstitutional. The practitioners did not mention that reason, which probably reflects the journalistic background of the educators. A 1977 survey of public relations educators revealed that "journalism or communication training seems to remain the most significant single force in the academic backgrounds of PR instructors as a group." Thomas B. Johnson and Kenneth Rabin, "PR Faculty: What Are Their Qualifications?" 41.

25. Tennant, "Survey on Licensing," 41.

26. Rea Smith, "Accreditation—A Decade Later," 29. Accreditation was initially developed over the course of two years by and for the PRSA Counselors Section. At its 1963 annual meeting, the PRSA Assembly extended the program to the entire membership. Plank, Speech, PRSA Chicago Chapter, Young Professionals Group, Mar. 2008, Plank Papers.

27. Smith, "Accreditation," 23. For its first ten years, the passing rate for the APR examination was 78.5 percent. The inaugural class of the College of Fellows in 1989 consisted of the Gold Anvil winners to that point. Plank was one of four women in that inaugural class of twenty-six.

28. For the first two years of the program, members with eighteen or more years of experience in an executive capacity could apply for the APR without taking the exam. The purpose was to ensure a sufficient pool of qualified examiners for the oral portion of the process. Plank was one of those "grandmothered" in. In February 1967, the

"grandfather clause" was ended, with 896 members being accredited under its provisions. Smith, "Accreditation."

29. Plank to Patrick Jackson, June 11, 1997, Plank Papers.

30. Plank, Speech, PRSA Suburban Chicago Chapter, Plank Papers.

31. Plank, "Playing Corporate Hardball," 13.

32. The CEPR process involves a site visit from a public relations educator and a practitioner who then write a report with recommendations for the review of PRSA's Educational Affairs Committee. The Committee votes to approve or deny certification based on the report. The report is then forwarded to the PRSA Board of Directors for final adjudication. Plank served on the site review team for Florida State University, Radford University, and Seneca College. Correspondence with the Educational Affairs Committee in May 1990 indicates she served on two other teams as well. See Report of Florida State Site Team Visit, 1991, Plank Papers.

33. Plank to Jackson, Aug. 4, 2000, Plank Papers.

34. Plank to Ray Gaulke, June 11, 2000, Plank Papers.

35. Every three years the International Public Relations Association holds a World Public Relations Congress. In 2000, the World Congress was held in conjunction with PRSA's international conference. IPRA's Story, https://www.ipra.org/history/ipras-story/. Plank to Gaulke, Aug. 2, 2000, Plank Papers.

36. Plank to Chris Teahan, May 29, 1997, Plank Papers.

37. Plank to Jim Grunig, May 24, 1991, Plank Papers.

38. Chapters were also required to have a faculty and a professional advisor, both of whom were to be PRSA members. PRSSA Chapter Requirements. http://prssa.prsa.org/chapters/start/PRSSA_Charter_Application.pdf.

39. Plank to The 50-Plus Concerned Colleagues of PRSA, Sept. 27, 2002; Plank to Jeneen Garcia, Nov. 8, 2002, Plank Papers. See "PRSSA Affiliate Program." Accessed at https://www.prsa.org/prssa/join-prssa/prssa-affiliate-program

40. Plank was the Elmo I. Ellis Visiting Professional-In-Residence in January 2000.

41. Plank to Cully Clark, Feb. 7, 2000, Plank Papers.

42. Plank to Clark, Feb. 7, 2000; Melvin Sharpe to Bill Gonzenbach, Mar. 28, 2000, Plank Papers.

43. Plank to Richard Meltzer, cc'd to Jim Zartman, May 3, 2004, Plank Papers.

44. Jack Koten to Plank, Nov. 22, 2004, Plank Papers.

45. Plank to Bonnie LaBresh, Dec. 16, 2004; Clark to Plank, June 8, 2004, Plank Papers.

46. UA's Board of Trustees officially established the Center on Feb. 4, 2005. The inaugural board consisted of Plank, Cully Clark, Koten, Felton, Culp, Russell, Andre Taylor, Maria Shriver, Bill Heyman of Heyman Associates in New York, and Dr. Linda Hon of the University of Florida. Since several of them would be attending the PRSA conference in Miami that September, Plank seized the opportunity for an informal meeting in advance of the official board meeting to begin discussions concerning the Center's mission; its primary focus, which at the time was ethics; and what the Center might accomplish. Plank to Clark, April 26, 2005; Plank to University of Alabama Plank Center Colleagues, Sept. 30, 2005, Plank Papers.

47. Minutes of the Plank Center Board of Advisors, Jan. 23, 2006, Plank Papers.

48. Minutes of the Board of Advisors, Jan. 23, 2006, Plank Papers.

49. "About the Center," http://comm.psu.edu/page-center/about/about-the-center.

50. Plank, Speech, PRSA Chicago Chapter, Young Professionals Group, Plank Papers.

51. Plank Planner, Dec. 31, 2003; Plank Planner, Dec. 31, 2007, Plank Papers.

52. Susan Gonders to Gower, Sept. 17, 2020.

CONCLUSION

Epigraph. Leo Rosten, *Passions and Prejudices: Or, Some of My Best Friends Are People* (New York: McGraw Hill, 1978). Plank had this quote taped to her bathroom mirror. Plank to Donna Jonas, n.d., Plank Papers.

1. Plank, Acceptance Speech, Public Relations Professional of the Year Award, *PR News*, Oct. 24, 1978, Plank Papers.

2. Plank, "Our Crisis of Identity," Plank Papers.

3. "More Students Studying for Public Relations Careers," *Atlanta Daily World (1932–2003)*, July 10, 1973, 5, ProQuest Historical Newspapers.

4. Alanna Vagianos, "Ruth Bader Ginsburg Tells Young Women: 'Fight for Things You Care About,'" *Huffington Post*, June 2, 2015. https://www.radcliffe.harvard.edu/news/in-news/ruth-bader-ginsburg-tells-young-women-fight-things-you-care-about; the sentiment was on a pen set in Plank's office.

5. Meng and Berger, "An Integrated Model of Excellent Leadership," 143; Loza, Lund Award Nomination, Plank Papers.

6. Robert K. Greenleaf, *The Servant as Leader*, 7.

7. West to Gower, Oct. 1, 2020; Debra Mason, comment on "In Memoriam: Betsy Plank"; Gonders to Gower, Sept. 17, 2020.

8. Charmayne Kreuz to Edelman, Jan. 7, 1969, Plank Papers. Kreuz drafted the letter for Edelman, but he reviewed, approved, and signed it.

9. Greenleaf, *The Servant as Leader*; Margot Opdycke Lamme, *Public Relations and Religion in American History*.

10. Marvin N. Olasky, "Retrospective: Bernays' Doctrine of Public Opinion," 5, 9.

11. Olasky, "Retrospective," 10.

12. Philip Lesly, *The People Factor: Managing the Human Climate*, 8, 197, 221.

13. John W. Hill, *The Making of a Public Relations Man*, 2, 260.

14. Karen S. Miller, *The Voice of Business: Hill & Knowlton and Postwar Public Relations*. Miller argues that Hill attempted to manipulate public opinion in support of his clients' interests.

15. "Goal for the '70s: Credible Communications," *Los Angeles Times (1923–1995)*, Mar. 28, 1973, ProQuest Historical Newspapers.

16. Aneel Chima and Ron Gutman, "What It Takes to Lead Through an Era of Exponential Change," 3, 4.

17. Chima and Gutman, "What It Takes," 9.

18. Reynolds, "Gender-Integrative Leadership." 159.

19. Reynolds, "Gender-Integrative Leadership," 162.

20. Reynolds, "Gender-Integrative Leadership," 164.

21. Laurie Wilson, comment on "In Memoriam: Betsy Plank"; Plank, interview by McNamara, 16.

22. Maria Russell, "Celebration of the Life of Betsy Ann Plank" (presentation at Memoriam Service, Chicago, IL, July 26, 2010), emphasis in original, Plank Papers.

23. Dhliwayo, "20 Qualities that Will Help You Stand Out as a Leader."

SELECT BIBLIOGRAPHY

ARCHIVES

Betsy Ann Plank Papers, 1890–2010, The Plank Center for Leadership in Public Relations, University of Alabama

Betsy Plank interview by Albert Walker, n.d., ca. Nov./Dec. 1978, transcript, Northern Illinois University, DeKalb, Illinois

Betsy Plank interview by Gigi McNamara, The Arthur W. Page Center for Integrity in Public Communication, University Park, Pennsylvania, www.bellisario.psu.edu/page-center/oral-histories/betsy-plank/

BOOKS AND ARTICLES

"A Visit with Betsy Ann." *PRSSA Forum* (Spring 1973): 1.

Baxter, Bill L. "Lawmakers' Views on Licensing in Public Relations." *Public Relations Review* 12, no. 4 (Winter 1986): 12–15.

Bernays, Edward L. "The Outlook for Public Relations," *Public Relations Quarterly* 10, no. 3/4 (Winter 1966): 34–38.

———. "Public Relations Council: A Response," *Public Relations Quarterly* 20, no. 2 (Summer 1975): 8–9.

———. "Should Public Relations Counsel be Licensed?" *Printers' Ink* 245 (Dec. 25, 1953): 52–54.

Bowerman, Charles E. *Unwed Motherhood: Personal and Social Consequences.* Chapel Hill: Institute for Research on Social Science, University of North Carolina, 1966.

Brown, John Crosby. "Public Relations in the Philanthropic Field." *Public Opinion Quarterly* 1, no. 2 (1937): 138–143.

Carney, Brent. *Bethany College: The Campus History Series.* Charleston, SC: Arcadia Publishing, 2004.

Chima, Aneel, and Ron Gutman. "What It Takes to Lead Through an Era of Exponential Change." *Harvard Business Review Email Newsletter* (Oct. 29, 2020). https://hbr.org/2020/10/what-it-takes-to-lead-through-an-era-of-exponential-change.

Clavier, David E., and Frank B. Kalupa. "Corporate Rebuttals to 'Trial by Television.'" *Public Relations Review* 9, no. 1 (Spring 1983): 24–36.

Cline, Carolyn Garrett, and Lynne Masel-Waters. "Backlash: The Impact of a Video Case Study on Opinions of AT&T." *Public Relations Review* 10, no. 3 (Autumn 1984): 39–46.

Cohen, Nancy L. *Delirium: How the Sexual Counterrevolution Is Polarizing America.* Berkeley, CA: Counterpoint Press, 2012.

Cole, Barry G., ed. *After the Breakup: Assessing the New Post-AT&T Divestiture Era*. New York: Columbia University Press, 1991.

Covert, Tawnya J. Adkins. *Manipulating Images: World War II Mobilization of Women through Magazine Advertising*. Lanham, MD: Lexington Books, 2011.

Cummins, D. D. *Bethany College: A Liberal Arts Odyssey*. St. Louis: Chalice Press, 2013.

Cutlip, Scott. *Fund Raising in the United States: Its Role in America's Philanthropy*. New Brunswick: Rutgers University Press, 1965.

Daniel, Robert L. *American Women in the 20ᵗʰ Century: The Festival of Life*. San Diego: Harcourt Brace Jovanovich, 1987.

de Leon, Pat Lawson. "Some of My Best Friends are Chauvinists." *Public Relations Quarterly* 18, no. 2 (1973): 25–26.

Deal, Terrence E., and Allan A. Kennedy. *Corporate Cultures: The Rites and Rituals of Corporate Life*. New York: Perseus Books, 1982.

Dierendonck, Dirk van. "Servant Leadership: A Review and Synthesis." *Journal of Management* 37, no. 4 (2011): 1228–1261.

Drucker, Peter F. *Management*. New York: Harper & Row, 1972.

Edelman, Daniel J. "Managing the Public Relations Firm in the 21ˢᵗ Century." *Public Relations Review* 9, no. 3 (Fall 1983): 3–10.

Falbo, Toni. "Only Children: An Updated Review." *Journal of Individual Psychology* 68, no. 1 (2012): 38–49.

Fierro, Robert D. "'You PR Men Are All Alike'—A Survey of PR People under the Age of 30." *Public Relations Quarterly* 18, no. 2 (Fall 1973): 9–12, 24.

Fitzpatrick, Kathy R. "Evolving Standards in Public Relations: A Historical Examination of PRSA's Codes of Ethics," *Journal of Mass Media Ethics* 17, no. 2 (2002): 89–110.

Foertsch, Jacqueline. *American Culture in the 1940s*. Edinburgh: Edinburgh University Press, 2008.

Forbes, Paul S. "Why Licensing is an Opportunity for Public Relations," *Public Relations Review* 12, no. 4 (1986): 9–11.

Fox, Frank W. *Madison Avenue Goes to War: The Strange Military Career of American Advertising, 1941–1945*. Provo: Brigham Young University Press, 1975.

Fry, John R. *Fire and Blackstone*. Philadelphia, PA: J. B. Lippincott Company, 1969.

Glascock, Jack. "The Role of AT&T's Public Relations Campaign in Press Coverage of the 1982 Breakup," *Public Relations Review* 26, no. 1 (Spring 2000): 67–83.

Goldin, Claudia. "The Meaning of College in the Lives of American Women: The Past One-Hundred Years," Working Paper #4099, NBER Working Papers Series, National Bureau of Economic Research, June 1992.

Goleman, Daniel. *Emotional Intelligence: Why It Can Matter More Than IQ*. New York: Bantam Books, 1995.

Gower, Karla K. *Public Relations and the Press: The Troubled Embrace*. Evanston, IL: Northwestern University Press, 2007.

———. "Rediscovering Women in Public Relations: Women in the Public Relations Journal, 1945–1972." *Journalism History* 27, no. 1 (Spring 2001): 14–21.

Greenleaf, Robert K. *The Servant as Leader*. Westfield, IN: Greenleaf Center for Servant Leadership, 2008, originally published in 1970.

Guth, David W., and Charles Marsh. *Public Relations: A Values-Driven Approach*. Boston: Allyn & Bacon, 2000.

Halberstam, David. *The Fifties*. New York: Ballantine Books, 1993.

Harmon, Richard L. "Job Responsibilities in Public Relations," *Public Relations Quarterly* 10, no. 2 (Summer 1965): 22–24.

Heinrich, Thomas, and Bob Batchelor. *Kotex, Kleenex, Huggies: Kimberly-Clark and the Consumer Revolution in American Business*. Columbus: The Ohio State University Press, 2004.

Hennig, Margaret, and Anne Jardim. *The Managerial Woman*. Garden City, NJ: Anchor Press/Doubleday, 1977.

Hill, John W. *The Making of a Public Relations Man*. New York: David McKay Company, 1963.

Hinds, Lynn B. *Broadcasting the Local News: The Early Years of Pittsburgh's KDKA-TV*. University Park: Penn State University Press, 1995.

Huber, Valerie. "A Historical Analysis of Public School Sex Education in America Since 1900." Master's thesis. Cedarville University, 2009.

Hughes, Howard Penn. "How Corporate Chief Executives View Public Relations. Another Shocker," *Public Relations Quarterly* 18, no. 1 (1973): 5.

Hughes, Kit. *Television at Work: Industrial Media and American Labor*. New York: Oxford University Press, 2020.

Hutton, James G. "The Definition, Dimensions, and Domain of Public Relations." *Public Relations Review* 25, no. 2 (Summer 1999): 199-214.

Johnson, Thomas B., and Kenneth Rabin. "PR Faculty: What Are Their Qualifications?" *Public Relations Review* 3, no. 1 (1977): 38–48.

Kalupa, Frank, and J. Carroll Bateman. "Accrediting Public Relations Education." *Public Relations Review* 6, no. 1 (1980): 18-39.

Lamme, Margot Opdycke. *Public Relations and Religion in American History: Evangelism, Temperance, and Business*. New York: Routledge, 2014.

Lennon, Mary Louise. "The Role of Industry in Consumer Health Education." *Health Education Monographs* no. 31 (1972): 131–135.

Lesly, Philip. *The People Factor: Managing the Human Climate*. Homewood, IL: Dow Jones-Irwin, 1974.

———. "Why Licensing Won't Work for Public Relations." *Public Relations Review* 12, no. 4 (Winter 1986): 3–7.

L'Etang, Jacquie. *Public Relations in Britain: A History of Professional Practice in the 20th Century*. Mahwah, NJ: Lawrence Erlbaum, 2004.

Liden, Robert C., Sandy J. Wayne, Hao Zhao, and David Henderson. "Servant Leadership: Development of a Multidimensional and Multi-level Assessment." *The Leadership Quarterly* 19, no. 2 (April 2008): 161–177.

Lukovitz, Karlene. "Women Practitioners: How Far, How Fast?" *Public Relations Journal* 45, no. 5 (1989): 15-34.

MacAvoy, Paul W., and Kenneth Robinson. "Winning by Losing: The AT&T Settlement and Its Impact on Telecommunications." *Yale Journal on Regulation* 1, no. 1 (1983): 1–43.

Maddi, Salvatore R., and Deborah M. Khoshaba. *Resilience at Work: How to Succeed No Matter What Life Throws at You.* New York: AMACOM, 2005.

Magee, Joe C., and Carrie A. Langner. "How Personalized and Socialized Power Motivation Facilitate Antisocial and Prosocial Decision-making." *Journal of Research in Personality* 42, no. 6 (2008): 1547–1599.

Martin, Dick. *Marilyn: A Woman in Charge.* New York: PRMuseum Press, 2020.

McEnaney, L. "Nightmares on Elm Street: Demobilizing in Chicago, 1945–1953." *Journal of American History* 92, no. 4 (Mar. 2006): 1265–1291.

Meng, Juan, and Bruce Berger. "An Integrated Model of Excellent Leadership in Public Relations: Dimensions, Measurement, and Validation. *Journal of Public Relations Research* 25, no. 2 (2013): 141–167.

Miller, Karen S. *The Voice of Business: Hill & Knowlton and Postwar Public Relations.* Chapel Hill: University of North Carolina Press, 1999.

Olasky, Marvin N. "Retrospective: Bernays' Doctrine of Public Opinion." *Public Relations Review* 10, no. 3 (Autumn 1984): 3–12.

Pimlott, J. A. R. "Public Service Advertising: The Advertising Council." *Public Opinion Quarterly* 12, no. 2 (Summer 1948): 209–219.

Plank, Betsy Ann. "The New Technology and Its Implications for the Public Relations Profession." *IPRA Review* 7, no. 2 (1983): 35–38.

———. "Playing Corporate Hardball: Skills Needed by the Future Public Relations Executive." *Public Relations Quarterly* 21, no. 2 (1976): 11–13.

Pollard, Thomas D. "Ray Rappaport Chronology: Twenty-five Years of Seminal Articles on Cytokinesis in the *Journal of Experimental Zoology.*" *Journal of Experimental Zoology* 301, no. 1(2004): 9–14.

Porter, William E. *Assault on the Media: The Nixon Years.* Ann Arbor: University of Michigan Press, 1976.

Posert, Harvey, and Paul Franson. *Spinning the Bottle.* San Francisco, CA: Board and Bench Publishing, 2004.

Prescott, C. Anne. "The Road Ahead: Beyond the Opening Doors: The Prospective Regions Ready Themselves to Seize New Opportunities." *Bell Telephone Magazine* 62, no. 2 (1983): 2–9.

Reynolds, Kae. "Servant-Leadership as Gender-Integrative Leadership: Paving a Path for More Gender-Integrative Organizations through Leadership Education." *Journal of Leadership Education* 10, no. 2 (Summer 2011): 155–171.

Russell, Karen M. "Public Relations, 1900 to Present." In *The Media in America: A History,* 8th ed., edited by William David Sloan and James D. Startt, 433–450. Northport, AL: Vision Press, 2011.

Ryder, Norman B., and Charles F. Westoff. *Reproduction in the United States, 1965.* Princeton, NJ: Princeton University Press, 1971.

Sharpe, Melvin L. "Recognition Comes from Consistently High Standards." *Public Relations Review* 12, no. 4 (1986): 17–25.

Simon, Raymond. "Agreement Reached on Student Group." *Public Relations Quarterly* 12, no. 3 (Fall 1967): 47-48.

———. "Fourth Student Group Formed at West Virginia." *Public Relations Quarterly* 12, no. 2 (Summer 1967): 41.

———. "New Student Group Being Formed." *Public Relations Quarterly* 11, no. 3 (Fall 1966): 21–22.

———. "Pilot Project Highly Successful." *Public Relations Quarterly* 10, no. 2 (Summer 1965): 35.

———. "Practitioners-Educators Exchange Ideas." *Public Relations Quarterly* 12, no. 1 (Spring 1967): 29–30.

———. "Six Students to Be Honored." *Public Relations Quarterly* 10, no. 1 (1965): 36.

Smith, Brien N., Ray V. Montagno, and Tatiana N. Kuzmenko. "Transformational and Servant Leadership: Content and Contextual Comparisons." *Journal of Leadership and Organizational Studies* 10, no. 4 (Spring 2004): 80–91.

Smith, Rea. "Accreditation—A Decade Later." *Public Relations Journal* (Dec. 1973): 22–23, 29.

Soma, John T., Rodney D. Peterson, Gary Alexander, and Curt W. Petty. "The Communications Regulatory Environment in the 1980's." *Computer Law/Journal* 4, no. 1 (Summer, 1983): 1–55.

Stevens, Art. "PRQ Poll: PR Field Ranks Itself Low on Professional Totem Pole." *Public Relations Quarterly* 17, no. 1 (Spring 1972): 3, 26.

Tamblyn, George O., and John Crosby Brown. *Raising Money.* New York: Tamblyn and Brown, 1921.

Tarr, Joel A., and Bill C. Lamperes. "Changing Fuel-Use Behavior and Energy Transitions: The Pittsburgh Smoke Control Movement, 1940–1950." *Journal of Social History* 14, no. 4 (Summer 1981): 561–588.

Teahan, Frederick H. "'Making It in the Seventies'—Misinterpreted." *Public Relations Journal* 28, no. 12 (Dec. 1972): 40.

Teahan, Frederick H., Susan Gonders, and Barbara DeSanto. *Public Relations Student Society of America: A Brief History.* New York: Champions of PRSSA, 2007.

Temin, Peter. "Fateful Choices: AT&T in the 1970s." *Business and Economic History* 27, no. 1 (1998): 61–77.

Tennant, Frank A. "Survey on Licensing Public Relations Practitioners." *Public Relations Review* 4, no. 1 (1978): 37–42.

Tirone, James F. "Measuring the Bell Systems Public Relations." *Public Relations Review* 3, no. 4 (Winter 1977): 21-38.

Verguawe, Jasmine, Bart Wille, Joeri Hofmans, Robert B. Kaiser, and Filip De Fruyt. "The Double-Edged Sword of Leader Charisma: Understanding the Curvilinear Relationship Between Charismatic Personality and Leader Effectiveness." *Journal of Personality and Social Psychology* 114, no. 1 (2018): 110–130.

Watson, Tom. "PR's Early Response to the 'Information Superhighway': The IPRA Narrative." *Communication & Society* 28, no. 1 (2015): 1–12.

Williams, Marcille Gray. *The New Executive Woman.* New York: Mentor Books, 1977.

Winkler, Allan M. *The Politics of Propaganda: The Office of War Information, 1942–1945*. New Haven: Yale University Press, 1978.

Wisner, Franz. *Edelman and the Rise of Public Relations*. New York: Daniel J. Edelman, Inc., 2012.

Woods, Marion M. "What Does It Take for a Woman to Make It in Management?" *Personnel Journal* 54, no. 1 (January 1975): 38–41, 66.

Wright, Donald K. "History and Development of Public Relations Education in North America: A Critical Analysis." *Journal of Communication Management* 15, no. 3 (2011): 236–255.

Yukl, Gary A. *Leadership in Organizations*. 8th ed. Upper Saddle River, NJ: Prentice-Hall, 2013.

INDEX